Ulrike Ziemer

ETHNIC BELONGING, GENDER, AND CULTURAL PRACTICES

Youth Identities in Contemporary Russia

With a foreword by Anoop Nayak

ibidem-Verlag
Stuttgart

Bibliografische Information der Deutschen Nationalbibliothek
Die Deutsche Nationalbibliothek verzeichnet diese Publikation in der
Deutschen Nationalbibliografie; detaillierte bibliografische Daten sind im
Internet über http://dnb.d-nb.de abrufbar.

Bibliographic information published by the Deutsche Nationalbibliothek
Die Deutsche Nationalbibliothek lists this publication in the Deutsche Nationalbibliografie;
detailed bibliographic data are available in the Internet at http://dnb.d-nb.de.

Cover Picture: Maria Chenovarian taken by © Ovik Arutiunian, Krasnodar 2010.

∞

Gedruckt auf alterungsbeständigem, säurefreien Papier
Printed on acid-free paper

ISSN: 1614-3515

ISBN-13: 978-3-8382-0152-8

© *ibidem*-Verlag
Stuttgart 2011

Alle Rechte vorbehalten

Das Werk einschließlich aller seiner Teile ist urheberrechtlich geschützt. Jede Verwertung außerhalb der engen Grenzen des Urheberrechtsgesetzes ist ohne Zustimmung des Verlages unzulässig und strafbar. Dies gilt insbesondere für Vervielfältigungen, Übersetzungen, Mikroverfilmungen und elektronische Speicherformen sowie die Einspeicherung und Verarbeitung in elektronischen Systemen.

All rights reserved. No part of this publication may be reproduced, stored in or introduced into a retrieval system, or transmitted, in any form, or by any means (electronical, mechanical, photocopying, recording or otherwise) without the prior written permission of the publisher. Any person who does any unauthorized act in relation to this publication may be liable to criminal prosecution and civil claims for damages.

Printed in Germany

Soviet and Post-Soviet Politics and Society (SPPS) Vol. 103
ISSN 1614-3515

General Editor: Andreas Umland,
Kyiv-Mohyla Academy, umland@stanfordalumni.org

Editorial Assistant: Olena Sivuda, *Drahomanov Pedagogical University of Kyiv*, SLS6255@ku-eichstaett.de

EDITORIAL COMMITTEE*

DOMESTIC & COMPARATIVE POLITICS
Prof. **Ellen Bos**, *Andrássy University of Budapest*
Dr. **Ingmar Bredies**, *University of Regensburg*
Dr. **Andrey Kazantsev**, *MGIMO (U) MID RF, Moscow*
Dr. **Heiko Pleines**, *University of Bremen*
Prof. **Richard Sakwa**, *University of Kent at Canterbury*
Dr. **Sarah Whitmore**, *Oxford Brookes University*
Dr. **Harald Wydra**, *University of Cambridge*
SOCIETY, CLASS & ETHNICITY
Col. **David Glantz**, *"Journal of Slavic Military Studies"*
Dr. **Marlène Laruelle**, *Johns Hopkins University*
Dr. **Stephen Shulman**, *Southern Illinois University*
Prof. **Stefan Troebst**, *University of Leipzig*
POLITICAL ECONOMY & PUBLIC POLICY
Prof. em. **Marshall Goldman**, *Wellesley College, Mass.*
Dr. **Andreas Goldthau**, *Central European University*
Dr. **Robert Kravchuk**, *University of North Carolina*
Dr. **David Lane**, *University of Cambridge*
Dr. **Carol Leonard**, *University of Oxford*
Dr. **Maria Popova**, *McGill University, Montreal*

FOREIGN POLICY & INTERNATIONAL AFFAIRS
Dr. **Peter Duncan**, *University College London*
Dr. **Taras Kuzio**, *Johns Hopkins University*
Prof. **Gerhard Mangott**, *University of Innsbruck*
Dr. **Diana Schmidt-Pfister**, *University of Konstanz*
Dr. **Lisbeth Tarlow**, *Harvard University, Cambridge*
Dr. **Christian Wipperfürth**, *N-Ost Network, Berlin*
Dr. **William Zimmerman**, *University of Michigan*
HISTORY, CULTURE & THOUGHT
Dr. **Catherine Andreyev**, *University of Oxford*
Prof. **Mark Bassin**, *Södertörn University*
Prof. **Karsten Brüggemann**, *Tallinn University*
Dr. **Alexander Etkind**, *University of Cambridge*
Dr. **Gasan Gusejnov**, *Moscow State University*
Prof. em. **Walter Laqueur**, *Georgetown University*
Prof. **Leonid Luks**, *Catholic University of Eichstaett*
Dr. **Olga Malinova**, *Russian Academy of Sciences*
Dr. **Andrei Rogatchevski**, *University of Glasgow*
Dr. **Mark Tauger**, *West Virginia University*
Dr. **Stefan Wiederkehr**, *BBAW, Berlin*

ADVISORY BOARD*

Prof. **Dominique Arel**, *University of Ottawa*
Prof. **Jörg Baberowski**, *Humboldt University of Berlin*
Prof. **Margarita Balmaceda**, *Seton Hall University*
Dr. **John Barber**, *University of Cambridge*
Prof. **Timm Beichelt**, *European University Viadrina*
Dr. **Katrin Boeckh**, *University of Munich*
Prof. em. **Archie Brown**, *University of Oxford*
Dr. **Vyacheslav Bryukhovetsky**, *Kyiv-Mohyla Academy*
Prof. **Timothy Colton**, *Harvard University, Cambridge*
Prof. **Paul D'Anieri**, *University of Florida*
Dr. **Heike Dörrenbächer**, *Naumann Foundation Kyiv*
Dr. **John Dunlop**, *Hoover Institution, Stanford, California*
Dr. **Sabine Fischer**, *EU Institute for Security Studies*
Dr. **Geir Flikke**, *NUPI, Oslo*
Dr. **David Galbreath**, *University of Aberdeen*
Prof. **Alexander Galkin**, *Russian Academy of Sciences*
Prof. **Frank Golczewski**, *University of Hamburg*
Dr. **Nikolas Gvosdev**, *Naval War College, Newport, RI*
Prof. **Mark von Hagen**, *Arizona State University*
Dr. **Guido Hausmann**, *University of Freiburg i.Br.*
Prof. **Dale Herspring**, *Kansas State University*
Dr. **Stefani Hoffman**, *Hebrew University of Jerusalem*
Prof. **Mikhail Ilyin**, *MGIMO (U) MID RF, Moscow*
Prof. **Vladimir Kantor**, *Higher School of Economics*
Dr. **Ivan Katchanovski**, *University of Ottawa*
Prof. em. **Andrzej Korboński**, *University of California*
Dr. **Iris Kempe**, *Heinrich Boell Foundation Tbilisi*
Prof. **Herbert Küpper**, *Institut für Ostrecht Regensburg*
Dr. **Rainer Lindner**, *CEEER, Berlin*
Dr. **Vladimir Malakhov**, *Russian Academy of Sciences*

Dr. **Luke March**, *University of Edinburgh*
Prof. **Michael McFaul**, *US National Security Council*
Prof. **Birgit Menzel**, *University of Mainz-Germersheim*
Prof. **Valery Mikhailenko**, *The Urals State University*
Prof. **Emil Pain**, *Higher School of Economics, Moscow*
Dr. **Oleg Podvintsev**, *Russian Academy of Sciences*
Prof. **Olga Popova**, *St. Petersburg State University*
Dr. **Alex Pravda**, *University of Oxford*
Dr. **Erik van Ree**, *University of Amsterdam*
Dr. **Joachim Rogall**, *Robert Bosch Foundation Stuttgart*
Prof. **Peter Rutland**, *Wesleyan University, Middletown*
Prof. **Marat Salikov**, *The Urals State Law Academy*
Dr. **Gwendolyn Sasse**, *University of Oxford*
Prof. **Jutta Scherrer**, *EHESS, Paris*
Prof. **Robert Service**, *University of Oxford*
Mr. **James Sherr**, *RIIA Chatham House London*
Dr. **Oxana Shevel**, *Tufts University, Medford*
Prof. **Eberhard Schneider**, *University of Siegen*
Prof. **Olexander Shnyrkov**, *Shevchenko University, Kyiv*
Prof. **Hans-Henning Schröder**, *University of Bremen*
Prof. **Yuri Shapoval**, *Ukrainian Academy of Sciences*
Prof. **Viktor Shnirelman**, *Russian Academy of Sciences*
Dr. **Lisa Sundstrom**, *University of British Columbia*
Dr. **Philip Walters**, *"Religion, State and Society," Oxford*
Prof. **Zenon Wasyliw**, *Ithaca College, New York State*
Dr. **Lucan Way**, *University of Toronto*
Dr. **Markus Wehner**, *"Frankfurter Allgemeine Zeitung"*
Dr. **Andrew Wilson**, *University College London*
Prof. **Jan Zielonka**, *University of Oxford*
Prof. **Andrei Zorin**, *University of Oxford*

* While the Editorial Committee and Advisory Board support the General Editor in the choice and improvement of manuscripts for publication, responsibility for remaining errors and misinterpretations in the series' volumes lies with the books' authors.

Soviet and Post-Soviet Politics and Society (SPPS)
ISSN 1614-3515

Founded in 2004 and refereed since 2007, SPPS makes available affordable English-, German- and Russian-language studies on the history of the countries of the former Soviet bloc from the late Tsarist period to today. It publishes approximately 15-20 volumes per year, and focuses on issues in transitions to and from democracy such as economic crisis, identity formation, civil society development, and constitutional reform in CEE and the NIS. SPPS also aims to highlight so far understudied themes in East European studies such as right-wing radicalism, religious life, higher education, or human rights protection. The authors and titles of all previously published manuscripts are listed at the end of this book. For a full description of the series and reviews of its books, see www.ibidem-verlag.de/red/spps.

Note for authors (as of 2009): After successful review, fully formatted and carefully edited electronic master copies of up to 250 pages will be published as b/w A5 paperbacks and marketed in Germany (e.g. vlb.de, buchkatalog.de, amazon.de) and internationally (e.g. amazon. com). For longer books, formatting/editorial assistance, different binding, oversize maps, coloured illustrations and other special arrangements, authors' fees between €100 and €1500 apply. Publication of German doctoral dissertations follows a separate procedure. Authors are asked to provide a high-quality electronic picture for the object of their study for the book's front-cover. Younger authors may add a foreword from an established scholar. Monograph authors and collected volume editors receive two free as well as further copies for a reduced authors' price, and will be asked to contribute to marketing their book as well as finding reviewers and review journals for them. These conditions are subject to yearly review, and to be modified, in the future. Further details at www.ibidem-verlag.de/red/spps-authors.

Editorial correspondence & manuscripts should be sent to: Dr. Andreas Umland, DAAD, German Embassy, vul. Bohdana Khmelnitskoho 25, UA-01901 Kyiv, Ukraine. e-mail: umland@stanfordalumni.org

Business correspondence & review copy requests should be sent to: *ibidem*-Verlag, Julius-Leber-Weg 11, D-10457 Hannover, Germany; tel.: +49(0)511-2622200; fax: +49(0)511-2622201; spps@ibidem-verlag.de.

Book orders & payments should be made via the publisher's electronic book shop at: www.ibidem-verlag.de/red/SPPS_EN/
Authors, reviewers, referees, and editors for (as well as all other persons sympathetic to) SPPS are invited to join its networks at www.facebook.com/group.php?gid=52638198614
www.linkedin.com/groups?about=&gid=103012
www.xing.com/net/spps-ibidem-verlag/

Recent Volumes

95 *Eva Fuchslocher*
Vaterland, Sprache, Glaube
Orthodoxie und Nationenbildung am Beispiel Georgiens
Mit einem Vorwort von Christina von Braun
ISBN 978-3-89821-884-9

96 *Vladimir Kantor*
Das Westlertum und der Weg Russlands
Zur Entwicklung der russischen Literatur und Philosophie
Ediert von Dagmar Herrmann
Mit einem Beitrag von Nikolaus Lobkowicz
ISBN 978-3-8382-0102-3

97 *Kamran Musayev*
Die postsowjetische Transformation im Baltikum und Südkaukasus
Eine vergleichende Untersuchung der politischen Entwicklung Lettlands und Aserbaidschans 1985-2009
Mit einem Vorwort von Leonid Luks
Ediert von Sandro Henschel
ISBN 978-3-8382-0103-0

98 *Tatiana Zhurzhenko*
Borderlands into Bordered Lands
Geopolitics of Identity in Post-Soviet Ukraine
With a foreword by Dieter Segert
ISBN 978-3-8382-0042-2

99 *Кирилл Галушко, Лидия Смола (ред.)*
Пределы падения – варианты украинского будущего
Аналитико-прогностические исследования
ISBN 978-3-8382-0148-1

100 *Michael Minkenberg (ed.)*
Historical Legacies and the Radical Right in Post-Cold War Central and Eastern Europe
With an afterword by Sabrina P. Ramet
ISBN 978-3-8382-0124-5

101 *David-Emil Wickström*
"Okna otkroi!" – "Open the Windows!"
Transcultural Flows and Identity Politics in the St. Petersburg Popular Music Scene
With a foreword by Yngvar B. Steinholt
ISBN 978-3-8382-0100-9

102 *Eva Zabka*
Eine neue „Zeit der Wirren"?
Der spät- und postsowjetische Systemwandel 1985-2000 im Spiegel russischer gesellschaftspolitischer Diskurse
Mit einem Vorwort von Margareta Mommsen
ISBN 978-3-8382-0161-0

Contents

List of Figures and Tables	8
Glossary of Abbreviations and Terms	9
Foreword by Anoop Nayak	11
INTRODUCTION	15

1 FRAMING YOUTH IDENTITIES IN RUSSIA: THE STATE, ETHNICITY AND BELONGING — 21

THE SOVIET STATE AND ITS NATIONALITIES POLICIES	21
THE SECURITIZATION OF MIGRATION IN POST-SOVIET RUSSIA	27
THEORIZING YOUTH IDENTITIES: ACCOUNTING FOR ETHNIC BELONGING IN CULTURALLY DIVERSE SOCIETIES	34
Identity	34
Gender identity: performing femininity and masculinity	37
Here and there: synthesizing sameness and difference	40
The concept of diaspora and cosmopolitanism	43
THE EMPIRICAL PROJECT: ETHNOGRAPHY AND REFLEXIVITY	47
CONCLUSIONS	52

2 ETHNOCENTRIC POLITICS IN THE (POST-)SOVIET CONTEXT: A REGIONAL PERSPECTIVE — 55

THE AMBIVALENCE OF THE POLITICS OF MIGRATION AND CULTURAL DIVERSITY IN KUBAN	55
Migration and demography	56
Migration politics in post-Soviet Krasnodar krai	62
'Krasnodar - edinaia sem'ia': the politics of cultural diversity	67

THE ARMENIAN DIASPORA IN KRASNODAR KRAI: FROM PAST TO PRESENT	71
The Armenian history of migration	71
Russian policy towards Armenians	74
The role of Armenian voluntary associations	75
THE REPUBLIC OF ADYGHEA	82
People and migration	82
Adyghea and its people: a historical background	84
Islam - the religion of Adyghea	86
Adyghea's current political situation	89
CONCLUSIONS	94

3	**NARRATIVES OF TRANSLOCATION, DISLOCATION AND LOCATION**	**97**
	DIASPORA AND BELONGING: CONSTRUCTING A PAN-ARMENIAN IDENTITY	97
	Historical dimensions of Armenian diasporic belonging	98
	Armenia's independence and Karabakh: narratives of translocation and disclocation	102
	WHERE IS HOME? PERCEPTIONS OF HOME	109
	'Home is where you are born'	110
	'Home is where you live'	115
	Multifarious identities: between sameness and otherness	118
	HOMEGENEITY AND LOCATION: AN ETHNIC MINORITY AT HOME	123
	The Caucasus: a geographical - cultural location of belonging	125
	Adygh identity: feeling and being Adygh	128
	CONCLUSIONS	131
4	**GENDERED ARMENIAN AND ADYGH IDENTITIES**	**133**
	ARMENIAN TRADITIONS AT THE CROSSROADS	133
	'Ia pokorna': patriarchy and traditional Armenian gender roles	135
	The gender order of the Armenian community in Krasnodar	137

Young Armenian women positioning themselves	141
Maintaining cultural continuity: the question of endogamy	147
ENACTING AND TRANSGRESSING THE 'IDEAL' ARMENIAN	152
A symbol of diasporic identity: Armenian women's sexuality	152
Gossip as a means of social control	155
Young men asserting symbolic Armenianness	158
ADYGH GENDER RELATIONS AND TRADITION	162
Culture as morality: a legacy of gender relations	163
Marriage and endogamy: choosing their calling	168
CONCLUSIONS	171

5 SITUATING YOUTH CULTURAL PRACTICES AND EXPERIENCES IN THE LOCAL CONTEXT — 173

YOUTH AT LEISURE	174
The politics of friendship patterns	175
Gendered leisure practices: the different meanings of guliat'	179
The vernacular culture as a medium to reach the 'global'	185
Leisure and public spaces	191
ROUTINIZING DIFFERENCE	198
Everyday xenophobia and prejudice in contemporary Russian society	199
Encountering everyday prejudice and racism	202
Dealing with racist attacks	210
CONCLUSIONS	213

6 CONCLUSION: YOUTH CULTURAL IDENTITIES REVISITED — 215

Appendix 1	223
Appendix 2	223
Appendix 3	226
Bibliography	229

Figures and Tables

Figures

2.1	Natural population growth and migration growth in Krasnodar krai, 1989-2000	59
2.2	St. Mesrop and St. Saak Armenian Apostolic Church in Krasnodar	79
2.3	St. Hovannes Armenian Apostolic Church in Krasnodar	80
2.4	The premises of the APO in Krasnodar	81
2.5	The mosque in Adygheisk	89
3.1	*Arin Berd* - Armenian dance group	105
3.2	Children performing traditional Armenian dance	106
3.3	Armenian Identity Web	119
3.4	Adygh Identity Web	124
5.1	Young men hanging out on the benches near the fountain in the centre of Adygheisk	181
5.2	Young men hanging out in their cars in the centre of Adygheisk	182
5.3	The main street in Adygheisk	183
5.4	*Ploshad' Revoliutsii* (Revolution Square) at *Krasnaia ulitsa* in the centre of Krasnodar	189
5.5	*Krasnaia ulitsa* in the centre of Krasnodar	190
5.6	Teenagers dancing during a celebration	196
5.7	Dance group, *Arin Berd*, practicing for their next dance performance	197

Tables

2.1	Demographic change according to nationality in Krasnodar krai between 1939 and 1989	58
2.2	Population and proportion of individual nationalities in Krasnodar krai in 1989, 2000 and 2002	60
5.1	Survey on xenophobic attitudes in Russia in 2007	202
5.2	Survey on the reasons for nationalism in Russia in 2007	206

Glossary of Abbreviations and Terms

Russian words cited in this book are transliterated according to the Library of Congress system, except for place names, where the most common transliteration in academic literature is used (i.e. Adyghea, not Adygeya). Those Russian words that could not be adequately translated, are used in the text transliterated rather than translated (i.e. Krasnodar krai).

Adyghage	Adygheanness
Adygh Khabze or *Adygh Nemys*	Adyghean Etiquette
Apsuara	Ethical system, a code of norms of traditional Abkhazian culture.
Cherkesogai	Circassian Armenians
Dukhovnoe upravlenie musulman Adygei i Krasnodarskogo kraia	Council for Muslims of the Republic of Adyghea and Krasnodar krai
khase	Council
korennoi	Indigenous
kul'tura styda	Culture of shame
litso kavkazskoi natsional'nosti	A person of Caucasian nationality
natsiia	Nation
natsmeny (natsional'nye menshinstva)	National minorities in Russia
pereselentsy	Resettlers
rodina	Homeland, home
rossiiskoe grazhdanstvo	Russian citizenship
rossiiskoe obshchestvo	Russian society
rossiiskii	A civic term referring to Russian culture
russkii	Russian in ethnic terms
sovetskii narod	Soviet people
Tsentr meznatsional'nykh kul'tur	Centre for National Cultures
zemliachestvo	Place of origin
zemliaki	Fellow-country men

Foreword

On returning from a sustained period of international fieldwork it was once commonplace for ethnographers to write unreflexively about the people and places they had encountered. Hair-raising tales of strange customs, peculiar mannerisms and taboo practices frequently peppered the prose of the academic voyeur. Youth scholars fared little better and were often drawn to 'spectacular' youth cultures that were quickly marked out as 'deviant', 'delinquent' and source of sustained 'moral panic'. It is then no easy task to write an authoritative but sensitive account of contemporary youth relations as Ulrike Ziemer has done in her thoroughly engaging book exploring gender, ethnicity and identity in Russia's diverse and newly-contoured post-socialist landscape.

Another problem facing the contemporary ethnographer is that where anthropologists, sociologists and those working as area specialists could once locate their findings within a fixed geography of the local – the village, community or 'tribe' – processes of globalization have rendered such 'bounded' understandings of local relations anachronistic. As Ziemer's meticulous account of Russia's youth relations demonstrates processes of migration, cosmopolitanism and transnationalism are as much features of modern Russia as rubbles, vodka and caviar.

However, as the respondents from this book lucidly testify these postnationalist transformations are not complete nor do they go uncontested. For Adygh youth indigenous to the Republic of Adyghea, and Armenian young people who are the product of diasporic movement to Krasnodar krai, ethnicity is something that is struggled over and contingently worked upon in the spaces and territories they inhabit. Above all what Ziemer's fascinating account reveals is that racism and nationalism continues to cast a long shadow in the lives of Russia's ethnic minority youth even as they stretch towards the mercurial possibilities of a shiny, ambivalent cosmopolitanism.

This timely book reveals how new generations grapple with and respond to large-scale social transformations.This includes a shift towards a post-socialist society, a negotiation of difference aligned to new patterns of multi-culturalism, as well as the experience of living in an increasingly interconnected world where the flow of capital, media images, fashion, music and consumer goods has ushered in new cultural practices and ways of being. While the scale of these transformations cannot be underestimated, for the erstwhile ethnographer concerned with the micro-worlds of young people, theorizing social change writ large can appear a herculean task. This throws up a series of questions regarding how social change is made manifest in young lives, how we might theorize youth transitions with the withdrawal of the iron curtain, and the types of conceptual tools and theoretical apparatus appropriate to the study of contemporary youth in Russia.

Amongst his rich and voluminous work the scholar Edward Said (1983) has long reminded us of the value and limits of what he calls 'travelling theory'. By this he refers to the ways in which ideas, like people or commodities, can circulate across nation-states and influence the spaces in which they cluster and take root. In many ways Ziemer's book exemplifies the mobility and proliferation of ideas that have invariably spread out from the Western 'core' to non-Western 'peripheries'. Ziemer skilfully mobilizes the theoretically rich insights derived from youth Cultural Studies, Sociology and Russian Area Studies, packs them into her knapsack and allows them to travel with her on the journey to research sites in the Southern districts of Russia. Using this framework it can be productive to see how Soviet legacies might be 'symbolically erased' in young people's everyday lives, even as such past histories silently inscribe who they are seeking to become in the present. By allowing theory to travel in all directions – here, there and everywhere – we are beginning to move towards a new global understanding of youth. Importantly these understandings are not simply the product of academic dialogue but as in the case of Ziemer's accomplished account are the outcome of a committed and dedicated appreciation that the starting point of any ethnography is surely the respondents whose lives we can only hope to lightly trace and archive with diligence, dedication and no little affection.

While a reflexive and theoretically attuned study of this kind cannot undo the ethnographic failings of the past overnight, the new global scholarship on young people may in the future help provincialize Western conceptual understandings of youth. In doing so we might begin again to 'make the familiar strange' by reflecting upon the parochial qualities of youth cultural studies which has been predominantly Anglo-American in its structure and focus. It is here that the original aspects of Ziemer's monograph can be found. For if there is one thing that this book teaches us it is that in a globalized world the study of youth culture is always a matter of time and place.

Anoop Nayak
Newcastle, UK, June 2011

Introduction

The demise of the Soviet Union in 1991 resulted in substantial changes throughout Europe. Old frontiers were redrawn and whole nations disappeared and (re-)emerged. At the same time, these changes have not left research on young people unaffected, but have inspired a diverse body of empirical and theoretical literature which appreciates the complex and distinct positions of young people in a wide range of local contexts within and outside the new borders of Europe (cf. Ali 2003; Pilkington *et al.* 2002; Roberts and Pollock 2009; Walker 2009). At the beginning of the twenty-first century, there is recognition of the need for in-depth accounts of the new and challenging forms of youth cultural practice and youth identities which have emerged as a result of globalizing cultural processes and multiple identity politics (cf. Back 1996; Nayak 2004; Shildrick *et al.* 2009). Thus, the aim of this book is twofold. First, this book explores the complex processes of identity formation and cultural experiences amongst young people from ethnic minorities in Russia. Second, the material presented in the chapters which follow contribute empirically grounded research on the lived experience of interacting identities both to the wider debates on youth, ethnicity and cultural practice and to the existing literature on Russian society.

A central aspect of this book is an examination of how ethnic belonging and living in an ethnically diverse society impact on young people's lives. Accordingly, the empirical analysis of this book is set within wider debates on youth cultural identities and ethnicity. In these debates, ethnic belonging is often considered a key element of youth identities (cf. Mørck 2000; O'Donnell and Sharpe 2000), reflecting the fact that ethnicity has been a fundamental source of meaning and recognition throughout human history and is a founding structure of social differentiation (Castells 1997). Many studies, however, illustrate that youth identities cannot only be viewed in terms of their ethnic markers, but are formed by a web of power relations from within and outside their ethnic communities (cf. Alexander 2004; Ali 1992; Dwyer 2000; Gunter and Watt 2009; Hopkins 2007). Social categories, such as gender and class, influence the ways in which young people construct their identities in a way commensurate with the influence of locality and the politics of the country in question. As Nayak (2004: 4) notes 'alongside "historical" and "structural" transformations', there is also 'a dazzling array of new "cultural" processes, practices and ways of being' for young people. As such, to sufficiently explore the formation of youth cultural identities one must consider the ways that ethnicity/ethnic identity interact with other markers of difference. These markers include gender, social class, age and nationality, which interact with ethnicity/ethnic identity and create diverse experiences.

This study considers young people to be active agents who exercise reflexivity in their daily lives and form their identities by drawing on resources available to them in their particular environment. Although the particular geographical area of investigation in this book – Southern Russia – is ethnically and culturally diverse, framing this study as an investigation of youth identity formation in a 'multicultural' society is considered too restrictive. Multiculturalism as a theoretical framework does not provide enough scope to account for the ways in which young people position themselves in society. As Back (1996) asserts, conducting an analysis of youth cultural practices and identity formation within the framework of multiculturalism tends to reify the 'minority' and 'host culture'. In recent years, multiculturalism has been subject to attack for its tendency to generate, rather than prevent various forms of racism (Anthias 2006; Back 1996). As Gidley (2007: 155) notes, multiculturalism, as a body of theory and policy, cannot account for the diversity of youth identities, 'as it assumes a mosaic of authentic, definitive "cultures"'.

Multiculturalism assumes a society comprised of an ethnic majority and various ethnic minorities. While the concept of 'ethnic minority' may maintain its use in describing the ethnic composition of society, it is problematic in that it assumes the marginality of 'minorities' while perpetuating the myth of white homogeneity (Parekh 2000a). The concept of 'ethnic minority', as an analytical category, also has its limitations owing its narrow conceptualizations in public and political discourses in contemporary Russia, largely a result of the legacy of the Soviet model of multiculturalism. The Soviet government and its administration was organized according to what may be called the principle of ethno-territoriality; allocating territory in accordance with the ethnic groups living in these territories (Pilkington and Popov 2008). In this way, ethnic self-identification of Soviet citizens became institutionalized and has not lost its significance to date.

This book presents a picture of youth cultural identities and experiences in an ethnically diverse society, prioritizing their individual perspectives. At the same time, it is accepted that these youth cultural identities must be understood within both the national as well as regional political regimes. Hence, this book is comprised of different levels of analysis – the state level, the regional level and the level of the individual. Chapter One begins with the discussion of key developments of Soviet nationalities policies that have transformed the nationality/ethnicity category into an important identity marker for contemporary Russia. It then proceeds with an exploration of the changes in post-Soviet Russia's migration policy. It also establishes the different notions of identity on which this book is premised. Identities are not fixed, but are constantly changing and exist at the intersection of multiple identity resources. Social categories like 'woman' or 'man', 'diasporic' or 'indigenous', are only partial signifiers. It is necessary to combine these categories and place them in context in order to arrive at a complete description of a person. Throughout the book, it is shown that identities are discursively constructed through difference and sameness, whereby they are established by a symbolic marking of representation in relation to others. Somers and Gibson (1994: 39) maintain that 'identities are constituted through our daily narratives, which constitute the ways we experience social life'. Young people's personal sense of identity depends on their internal references and on the views of other people.

Young people draw upon a wide range of resources to construct their youth cultural identities. The interacting of gender and ethnic identities at various moments, leads young people to draw on performative identity resources. In this book, gender and ethnic identities are considered to be constructed through performative acts. In addition, another potentially important identity resource is cosmopolitanism. Cosmopolitanism is understood as the result of the long history and tradition of migration and cultural mixing that exists in this part of Russia. In this book, cosmopolitanism as an identity resource is employed to challenge conventional sociological, as well as popular and political, conceptions of diasporic and indigenous identities. In the context of this research, cosmopolitanism as a strategy for managing cultural diversity is considered an identity resource that is still in its infancy in the post-Soviet cultural space. However, this resource has the potential to become more widely used in the future. As this book uses an ethnographic approach, Chapter One concludes with a note on the empirical project and the ways the dialogue between researcher and researched took place.

Chapter Two introduces readers, who are not familiar with the two ethnic communities in question, to the history of both communities in this part of Russia. The empirical focus of this research is young Armenians and Adyghs in Southern Russia. This part of Russia is a multi-ethnic region with more than 120 different ethnic groups, depending on definition. Thus, young Armenians and Adyghs, living in two different sites of the same region, were selected to examine a small part of this ethnic diversity. In the first site, located in Krasnodar, the main city in Krasnodar krai, the focus is on young Armenians. Here, Armenians are one of the largest ethnic minorities with more than 250,000 people. In the second site, located in Adygheisk, a small town in the Republic of Adyghea, formerly part of Krasnodar krai, the focus is on young Adyghs. Adyghs are a minority in their own republic numbering only 108,115, with Russians (288,280) constituting the majority. Both ethnic groups, Armenians and Adyghs, have a minority status in Russia, yet Adyghs are indigenous to the region while Armenians are a diaspora people.

Together with introducing the reader to the two ethnic groups of this research project, Chapter Two also examines how post-Soviet identities are shaped and constructed at the regional level within public and political discourses. It scrutinizes the media discourse on ethnic migration in the region, together with the administrative and policing practices of the regional authorities. This is vital, since the media and legislative discourses create the basis for discrimination against ethnic minorities and 'non-Russian' migrants in this region. The main aim of this chapter is to situate the experience of young people in its regional and political context; a prerequisite for subsequent empirical chapters in the book.

Chapter Three, as the opening empirical chapter, addresses the substantive question of this book – that of subjective definitions of ethnic belonging among diasporic Armenians and indigenous Adyghs. This chapter shows that while Armenian ethnic identities are entwined within a complex web of diverse cultural attachments, Adygh ethnic belonging is marked by rootedness and location. Both Armenians and Adyghs have a strong sense of their own ethnic belonging. While young Armenians and Adyghs emphasize their 'fixed' origins, young Armenians have begun to draw upon cosmopolitanism as an identity resource in their identity constructions, in order to deal with cultural diversity within and outside their ethnic community.

Chapter Four focuses on the gendered identities of young Armenians and Adyghs. In this chapter, the social construction of gender and the idea of 'performed' gender identities provide a theoretical framework that consists of notions of multiple femininities and masculinities. This chapter argues that gender mediates ethnic identification and is a medium for diasporic as well as indigenous ethnic identification. The lives of young Armenian and Adygh women are marked by patriarchal gender relations and class structures. For both young Armenians and Adyghs, it is suggested that ethnicity becomes essentialized through its intersection with gender systems of differentiation.

Chapter Five explores the complex relationship between youth cultural identities and place, together with the contradictory experiences that result. For both Armenians and Adyghs, the notion of place embodies a dual experience of interethnic dialogue and cultural pluralism, as well as racism and xenophobia. Although their leisure spaces are ethnically structured, they are not ethnically exclusive, but are characterized by inclusive notions of ethnic plurality and tolerance. It is at leisure that young adults are most likely to draw on cosmopolitanism as an identity resource. At the same time, gender has a significant impact on youth at leisure. The picture changes when these young people pass through public spaces, where they are sometimes racialized/ethnicized. In these public spaces, difference is acknowledged and routinized. While some have begun to draw on cosmopolitanism as an identity resource, they do not actively transcend ethnic boundaries, but rather relive and reproduce these boundaries.

Chapter Six concludes by answering the question posed at the beginning of this book: How are youth cultural identities constructed? This is a book about young people from ethnic minorities and their everyday experiences in contemporary Russia. It seeks to provide a detailed case study of how local-global relations are experienced outside the West. In doing so, this book suggests that ideas of place, ethnicity and gender relations are necessary components for understanding young people's everyday lives in this part of Russia. To provide an appropriate multifaceted analysis, this book draws on a wide range of theoretical concepts, including cosmopolitanism and Bourdieu's cultural capital. In this way, it draws upon interdisciplinary research, including youth cultural studies, human geography and sociology, but also Russian area studies. By engaging with theory and debates from various disciplines, this study emphasizes and speaks for the complex processes of youth cultural identities.

1 Framing Youth Identities in Russia: The State, Ethnicity and Belonging

This chapter establishes the focus of research and the main theoretical framework for the book. Questions of ethnicity and ethnic relations have been part of the political landscape in imperial Russia, the former Soviet Union and have not lost their significance in Russia today. As a multi-ethnic state, Russia has always faced the problem of how to imbue its citizens with a sense of identity which strengthens the state without causing dissent among the majority ethnic Russians or the many different minorities living on its territory. A vast amount of literature already exists tracing the history and the consequences of the Soviet nationalities policies and modernization processes (cf. Slezkine 1994; Suny 1993; Tishkov 1997). Hence, this chapter begins by briefly discussing key developments of Soviet nationalities policies which have transformed the nationality/ethnicity category into an ample identity marker for contemporary Russia. In this context, the emerging constructions of nationality/ethnicity are juxtaposed with Western conceptions of race, so as to clarify the differences between these categories. Second, this chapter explores the changes in the migration policy of post-Soviet Russia. Such an exploration is a productive lens through which to frame wider questions of youth identities, ethnicity and belonging in contemporary Russia. Third, the chapter establishes the conceptual framework – identity and cosmopolitanism – which shape the empirical analysis in subsequent chapters. The last part of this chapter introduces the empirical project.

The Soviet state and its nationalities policies

Not only was the collapse of the Soviet Union in 1991 partly seen as a result of the Soviet model of multiculturalism (Brubaker 1996; Suny 1993; Tishkov 1997), but it also led to a growth of national self-awareness during the subsequent democratic reforms (Ryzhova 2005; Stepanenko 1997; Yemelianova 2005). Some scholars refer to such developments as one of the 'unexpected outcomes' of liberal transformations after the fall of communism (Burawoy and Verdery 1999). Indeed, the impact of the Soviet legacy on ethnic relations plays a critical part in the formation of post-Soviet cultural identities in Russia. As Verdery (1993: 174) argues, 'ethnonational tensions had persisted and perhaps even intensified under socialism' since 'ethnonationalism was in certain ways "built into" the organization of socialism, manifesting itself differently in different countries but fully absent from none'.

Notions of 'indigenous' and 'native' are often criticized for imposing a hierarchy on different peoples, as these terms were obtained from the vocabulary of missionaries, explorers and colonial administrators, confining 'native' people to certain places (Appadurai 1988). The concept of 'indigenous people' becomes even more problematic in regions which have not undergone 'classical' colonialism (Popov and Kuznetsov 2008; Stammler-Grossman 2009). Russian ethnography and the concepts of 'ethnicity' and 'indigenous' date back to the seventeenth century - a time of territorial expansion in the form of military conquests and colonization by the Russian Empire. At that time, ethnic differences and distinctions between 'indigenous' and 'non-indigenous' people were made according to fiscal status, land (or region), and faith, but not according to culture or ethnicity as such (Sokolovskii [not dated]).[1] In 1845, the Russian Geographical Society with its Ethnographic Division was founded in St Petersburg and began to publish materials on different regions and languages in Central Asia, Siberia and the Far East, which later contributed to the territorialization of ethnicity in the Soviet Union. In other words, during Tsarist colonization, the first basic link between ethnicity and territory was established. In this way, ethnic groups were not distinguished according to 'racial' categorizations, as it was the case for Western colonization.[2]

After the 1917 Revolution, the established conceptual linkage between ethnic groups and territories were used to organize the USSR. Soviet ethno-

---

1   During colonization, the local (Russian language) terms for non-Russian groups were *iazachnye* (paying special tribute in furs), *tuzemtsy* (literally 'living in another land'), *inorodtsy* (meaning, 'being born into an alien, foreign or non-Russian group'), or *inovertsy* and *iazychniki* (meaning pagans, non-Orthodox, non-Christian, or belonging to another faith) (Sokolovskii [not dated]: 3).

2   In the United States, for example, before the end of the eighteenth century, it was customary to refer to the three main groups of people, distinguished by their visual characteristics - whites, 'Indians,' and blacks or Negroes (Banton 2005).

territorialism was based on a 'naturalistic' conception of ethnicity rooted in territory, rather than on the conception of race as lineage, like it was the case in early Western understandings of different peoples (Banton 1987). Towards the end of the twentieth century, in Western sociological thinking the concept of race has been predominantly viewed as a sociological construct, often with no biological basis (Banton 1987; Richardson and Lambert 1985). In contrast, the foundation of a primordial understanding of ethnicity in Soviet academic debates can be found in Iulian Bromley's (1973) so-called 'theory of ethnos'. According to this theory, an ethnos is an 'ethno-social organism', that is an 'historically stable entity of people developed in a certain territory and possessing common, relatively stable cultural features' (Tishkov 1997: 3).[3] Thus, in Russia today, the concept of 'indigenous' (*korennoi*) ethnicity is used to signify people who belong to a certain territory and have a homogenous culture and identity.

The Bolsheviks' early nationalities policies and later the official policy of *korenizatsiia* (indigenization) in the 1920s and 1930s in particular were developed in accordance with a 'naturalist' understanding of ethnicity. Ethnic minority groups were often seen as 'backward' in terms of their traditional cultures and the main task of the Soviet State was to ensure that these groups would be modernized, emancipated and educated. By the time of the second All-Russia Congress of Soviets on 25 October 1917, it was already declared that the Soviet power 'shall provide all the nations that inhabit Russia with the genuine right to self-determination' (Lenin 1962 cited in Tishkov 1997: 29). While Lenin was the founder of the Soviet nationalities policy, it was Stalin who became the true 'father of nations', although not of all nations and not at all times (Slezkine 1996: 203). For example, under Stalin and during the time of the 'Great Transformation' between 1928 and 1932, ethnic diversity was celebrated.

---

3   In Soviet literature, the term ethnos or ethnic community predominantly described a human community referred to in Russian as 'a people' (*narod*). The substitution of the term ethnos for the word 'people' was necessary, since (in Russian and many other languages) the word 'people' has a number of different connotations, and the Russian *narod* is used to describe not only ethnic communities but also large groups of people (Bromley and Kozlov 1989).

Nevertheless, the early nationalities policies and the policy of *korenizatsiia* also served as a tool for the system of indirect governance and for imposing Communist indoctrination under strict control of the Centre. Thus, through this dual use of repressions and privileges the regime was able to exercise control over the peripheries. Such indoctrination led also to the construction of new ethnic- or nationality-based borders, together with changes in and the (re)-creation of ethnic groups and borders.[4] By the end of the 1930s, the nationality category had become a fundamental marker of Soviet identity and was embedded in Soviet administrative structures. While other control mechanisms, like the allocation of a living place and a work place, could be changed or subverted in some way or other, nationality had become a marker of belonging which was presented and perceived in everyday Soviet life as inherited from parents and a biologically essential category (Oswald 2000).

In contrast to the time of the 'Great Transformation', from the mid-1930s onwards, Stalin reversed his political approach of celebrating ethnic diversity and began to reduce the field of ethnic diversity in the USSR (Slezkine 1996). Stalin's politics of *russifikatsiia* (Russification) deprived many diaspora nationalities of their national institutions. The Russian people were promoted as manifestations of primordial being and the model nationality for all other nationalities living on the territory of the USSR. This notable policy shift from *korenizatsiia* to *russifikatsiia* not only transformed Russians into an essentialized, virtually racialized nation, but also led to substantial ethnic and national purges (Weitz 2002: 13). A quota system at universities and in the army was introduced to ensure an 'ethnic balance' and even one's employee cards documented ethnic belonging. Additionally, in 1932 the practice of

---

4   A good example of these processes of changing ethnic borders can be found in Abkhazia. Abkhazia and the Shervashidze dynasty lost autonomy and was subjugated by the Russian Empire in 1864. After the 1917 Revolution, the Abkhaz people again regained autonomy, this time in the form of a union republic within the new Soviet Union. In 1931, however, Abkhazia found itself demoted to the status of an autonomous republic and incorporated in the Georgian Union Republic, a status it was to retain until the break-up of the Soviet Union (Kolstø and Blakkisrud 2008: 485). Furthermore, Soviet officials faced difficulties in applying 'ethnic' categorizations in view of the Kazakh, Kirgiz and Turkmen steppe nomads, whose 'tribal self-identity' was so strong that Soviet categorizations, such as those based upon linguistic, cultural and religious differences, were almost useless for creating 'new' ethnic borders (Slezkine 1996: 214).

nationality registration was introduced in inland passports (Oswald 2000). It became an administrative unit marked in the passport as the fifth paragraph (*piatyi punkt* or *piataia grafa*). This 'fifth paragraph' in the passport was legally abolished only in 1997 in the hope that in future it would reduce the importance of one's nationality in present-day Russia.

Alongside the construction of nationality as an administrative and political category, the *propiska* system was also revived in 1932 as another control mechanism in Soviet life.[5] Like in imperial Russia, Soviet authorities used *propiska*, or permission, as a means of limiting people's movement from rural and impoverished areas into the cities. When changing residence, individuals had to petition the authorities for *propiska*, to move; without *propiska* they would be unable to register for housing, find work, or even register a marriage in the new place of residency (Rubins 1998: 1). Essentially, *propiska* embodied a bureaucratic method of arranging and maintaining zones of privilege and disempowerment, of confining unwanted 'others' to their place on the periphery (Gupta and Ferguson 1992: 17). This Soviet institution of *propiska* as a mechanism of control over population movement was officially abolished in June 1993, when a new Law on the Rights of Russian Nationals for Freedom of Movement and for Choice of Residence within the Russian Federation was adopted. Nonetheless, legislative acts accompanying the law virtually restored the old system and regional governments could continue to officially restrict registration for representatives from an ethnic minority on a regular basis (Voronina 2006).

It is now widely accepted that Stalin and his successors – Khrushchev, Brezhnev, Andropov, and Chernenko – generally promoted the policy of Russification of the non-Russian nationalities and often manipulated the symbols of Russian nationhood (Szporluk 1990: 12; Tishkov 1997). At the same time, the Soviet leaders did not allow the Russian nation to thrive independently of the party and the state. In 1972, Brezhnev publicly announced that a 'united Soviet people' had been successfully created, ignoring the fact that the Russian people together with many other nations had been forcefully dissolved in the Stalinist state.

---

5 Registration first appeared in the Tsarist period, when it was intended to keep peasants tethered to their villages.

At the beginning of the 1980s, however, the contradictions within the nationalities policies became clear. While Mikhail Gorbachev, the new leader of the Soviet Union, concentrated on overcoming the country's economic and social crisis, the solving of the 'national question' and the seething nationalisms within the Soviet Union was essentially deferred, only to be addressed after the economic and social crises were taken care of (Shanin 1989: 422). However, Gorbachev had underestimated the possibility that, when the Soviet Union collapsed, most citizens would turn to their nearest and most obvious identity – that of their ethnic group, since Soviet federalism had employed ethnicity as an organizing principle (Flenley 1996). In this way, the break-up itself was shaped by the territorial-political crystallization of nationhood (Brubaker 1996). The policies of federalism and *korenizatsiia* served as a foothold for nationalities in the non-Russian republics to create ethnically distinct political elites within their respective republics. The use of the national idea and ethnic consciousness became widespread in the non-Russian republics as well as Russia itself.

To conclude this discussion, it can be said that many studies on ethnic relations in post-Soviet Russia stress the significance of the Soviet nationalities policies for the formation of social identities in contemporary Russia (cf. Brubaker 1996; Popov and Kuznetsov 2008; Tishkov 1997). After the disintegration of the Soviet Union, it was ethno-territoriality and the nationality discourse that began to occupy state and regional political discourses (Kuznetsov 2007a; Popov and Kuznetsov 2008). On the level of the individual, personal ethno-identifications provided 'a collection of boundaries and legitimate forms of collective and individual identity' (Brubaker 1996: 24). Hence, the category 'nation' (*natsiia*) in post-Soviet Russia is not so much defined by citizenship of a given state, but in ethno-cultural terms (Popov and Kuznetsov 2008: 227). It appears that ethnic identities in contemporary Russia and in Krasnodar krai as well as the Republic of Adyghea are indeed characterized by an ethnic consciousness that is based on primordial 'loyalties' (Appadurai 2003). In Russia, these primordial 'loyalties' are frequently articulated in public discourse and have become part of an everyday reality that is significant for the construction of individual social identities.

The securitization of migration in post-Soviet Russia

In the space of the past two decades Russia has gone from being almost entirely insulated against international migration flows to being the second biggest receiving country in the world after the United States (Mansoor and Quillin 2006: 1). The political, economic and social transformations which led to the collapse of the Soviet Empire, also instigated sweeping migration flows of approximately 25 million people after the ethnic conflicts began (Korobkov 2008: 69). Already, by the fall of 1991, there were 710,000 forced migrants in the USSR territory, mostly coming from Azerbaijan, Armenia, and some ethnic regions of Russia (ibid.: 70). Moreover, 1,191,900 refugees from ethnic conflicts were recorded in Russia in 1998, a total which is approximately 0.7 per cent of the whole of Russia's population (ibid.: 70). Given the largely ethnic Russian migration, the 1990s saw a '"securitizing" of migration not so much around the image of the cultural "otherness" of the immigrant but around a rather more physical securing of Russia's post-Soviet borders' (Pilkington 1998: 89).

The start of the first Chechen War (1994-1996), with its consequent extensive waves of migration, was a significant event for the move to a more restrictive migration policy toward refugees and forced migrants. In 1994, the Federal Migration Service (FMS) declared that 'uncontrollable migration is acquiring a threatening character, aggravating the epidemiological, criminal and social situation in major cities and causing harm to the security of the country' (Robarts 2006: 103). While the FMS in the early 1990s was primarily concerned with protecting the rights of migrants and refugees, in the mid-1990s its priorities shifted to controlling immigration flows (Voronina 2006). Hence, under Russia's migration regime, those who were being securitized as migrants in Russia's political and social discourse were increasingly viewed as threats to Russia's national security (Robarts 2008: 103). Whereas the early stages of Russia's migration laws largely revealed no ethnic trace in their securitization, perceptions of migration were shifting and preparing the ground for more individualized, even racialized hostility. Such a shift can also be interpreted as a response to a series of bomb attacks claiming almost 300 lives on Russian cities after 1999 (Laryš and Mareš 2011).[6] These terrorist attacks had an impact on the sense of security in Russian society and have led to an increase of hostilities against representatives of ethnic minorities from the Caucasus.

Under the Putin administration (2000-2008), once again the focus shifted to combating illegal migration and regulating labour migration (Gavrilova 2001, Molodikova 2007). The output of this securitized approach consisted of two new laws and various administrative innovations (cf. Zhukava 2006). The first law to be passed was the federal law 'On Citizenship of the Russian Federation' in May 2002. While previously, the relatively liberal law on citizenship, ratified in November 1991, had allowed former Soviet citizens, regardless of their ethnicity, to apply for Russian citizenship, this new law was extremely restrictive. It gave no special status to former citizens of the USSR; eligibility now, amongst other things, required at least five years' legal residency (Robarts 2008: 103). Various stipulations in the law transformed three million former citizens of the USSR virtually overnight into stateless illegal aliens (ibid.). While before 2002 approximately 300,000-400,000 people a year obtained Russian citizenship, in the first half of 2003 only 213 people managed to do so (Molodikova 2007: 63).

Noteworthy here is that the new law 'On Citizenship of the Russian Federation' broke away from its Soviet past, because Russian citizenship was no longer an entitlement; it was now a privilege. It does, however, share a commitment to a civic conception of citizenship which the Soviet law on citizenship also entailed (Duncan 2005: 294). Moreover, Putin's strive for a strong state and a modern great power was reflected in the strictness of this law (Tsygankov 2006: 129). Whilst the political context might seem peculiar to Russia, this shift in policy may also be interpreted as generic. Discussing the securitization of migration within the EU, Huysmans (2000: 762) maintains that 'social and political agencies use the theme of immigration, foreigners, asylum-seekers and refugees to interrelate a range of disparate political issues in their struggle over power, resources and knowledge.'

---

6   Nonetheless, the perpetrators of these attacks remain unknown. The Russian government accused Chechen rebels.

The second law passed in 2002 was the law 'On the Legal Status of Foreign Citizens in the Russian Federation', replacing the 1981 law of the USSR which had been in force hitherto. Broadly speaking, the new law created a three-level hierarchy of statuses which in a slightly altered form prevails to this day. The first step for all foreigners was to register their place of stay within three days. Bureaucratic structures and the requirement for the host party (usually a landlord) to go in person to officially register the migrant made merely a first step up a huge and insurmountable obstacle. In short, a contradictory situation emerged, because the basic legal acts embodied in these two laws intended to regulate migration in Russia were inconsistent with each other (Molodikova 2007). The rules surrounding work permits even further complicated the picture. Employers had to observe quotas on jobs and to secure work permits, via a costly process. The permits could then be used for the legal employment of foreign citizens. Although the purpose of these measures was to eliminate illegal migration, they proved to be ineffective and the complicated legal nexus was clearly constructed to impede rather than facilitate flows of migrants. In 2003, 45,000 foreigners and stateless persons were expelled from Russia and 1.5 million people were reported for violating the migration regulations (ibid.: 65).

Nonetheless, since 2002 this new system of registration has remained very similar to the *propiska* (permit of residence) system of Soviet Russia. The main differences between them are first, that in Soviet times there was no such institution as registration; and second, that the *propiska* did not necessarily imply proof of accommodation, so it was possible to get a *propiska* without having a permanent place of residence (Osipov 2004: 35). Because of this new policy, former Soviet citizens who do not have a *propiska* are now considered 'illegal migrants'. As a result, it may be said that this new passport system has contributed ominously to the appearance in public discourse of 'legal and illegal residents'.

This marginalization of migrants by overly complicated bureaucratic structures clearly has an impact on the politics of belonging. Examining Mexican migration in the United States, for example, De Genova (2006: 433) argues that 'the socio-political category "illegal alien"... has come to be saturated with racialized difference'. It is argued that such an observation has occurred in Russia as well, where one's skin has become an index of illegality (Dubas 2008; Laruelle 2010; Roman 2002). This association between 'illegality' and ethnicity is well illustrated in President Dmitry Medvedev's address to the Ministry of Internal Affairs in February 2009:

> There is one more problem – illegal labour migration. We all know that crime rates amongst the citizens from the near abroad illegally working in Russia is gradually growing.[7]

Illegality, then, and conversely legality, takes on an ethnic colouring. As a result, 'illegals' becomes a catch-all for the various titular nationals of the post-Soviet republics migrating to Russia (Dubas 2008). As subsequent empirical chapters show, such a racializing also applies to both members of the Armenian diaspora and to the indigenous Adyghs in Krasnodar krai.

Despite this negative portrayal of migration in terms of a security threat, the severity of Russia's demographic crisis means that the country cannot afford to lose its supply of migrant labour. It is estimated that between 2007 and 2025 the Russian population will see the loss of 16.2 million able-bodied persons, equivalent to one-third of today's employed workforce (Mukomel 2008: 2). In his annual speech to the Federal Assembly on 26 April 2007, former President Vladimir Putin was already addressing Russia's demographic crisis and need for an inflow of migrants:

> ...our priority remains to attract our compatriots from abroad. In this regard, we need to encourage skilled migration to our country, encourage educated and law-abiding people to come to Russia. People coming to our country must treat our culture and national traditions with respect.[8]

As this excerpt indicates, in line with the general public discourse on migration, he refers to the Russian population and thus makes 'ethnic' distinctions between those who are wanted and those who are not wanted in

---

7 Lenta.ru (2009) *Medvedev potreboval u MVD derzhat' na kontrole trudovykh migrantov*, Online. Available HTTP: <http://lenta.ru.news/2009/02//06/crimes> (accessed 03 February 2011).
8 Putin, V. (2007) *Poslanie federal'nomu sobraniiu Rossiiskoi Federatsii, Prezident Rossii*, Online. Available HTTP: <http://archive.kremlin.ru/text/appears/ 2007/04/125339. shtml> (accessed 23 March 2011).

Russia. In this context, he also points out that the migration regime is failing and there is a need for reform (Voronina 2006: 78). Thus, he continues:

> ...an increase in our population should be accompanied by a carefully planned immigration policy. It is in our interest to receive a flow of legal and qualified workers. But there are still a lot of companies in Russia making use of the advantages of illegal immigration. Without any rights, after all, illegal immigrants are convenient in that they can be exploited endlessly. They are also a potential danger from the point of view of breaking the law.

In short, these migration laws were clearly conceptualized to enhance control. Even when officials speak of the importance of improving the legal status of migrants, it often seems instrumental, because a migrant without rights 'is dangerous in terms of criminal offences'.[9] To sum up, the political discourse on migration depicts migration as a problem which needs to be controlled as otherwise it imposes a threat to national security.

In response to such calls, new laws and initiatives were introduced in the summer of 2006, coming into force the following January. The new amendments to Russian migration policy initially had three key components: a programme for the resettlement of compatriots, which foresaw various forms of support for them according to the level of priority assigned to the region in which they resettled (Molodikova 2007: 701). Naturalization was envisioned as the endpoint of the programme, which was aimed at the largely ethnic Russian community of Russian speakers in the former Union Republics. Second, these new amendments targeted labour migrants from CIS countries with visa-free regimes. An amended law 'On the Legal Status of Foreign Citizens' and a new law 'On Recording the Migration of Foreign Nationals and Stateless Persons' instituted a number of hugely significant changes: registration procedures were simplified so that migrants could now register through a wide range of entities, such as employers, employment agencies or by post. Third, in these major changes, an expansion of the

---

9   See Konstantin Romanovsky, Head of the FMS, cited in Itar Tass Daily (22 December 2006) *If Russia Shuts Door to Migrants, Some Industries May Stop – FMS*, Online. Available HTTP: <http://dlib.eastview.com/sources/article.jsp?id=11245423> (accessed 25 June 2009).

quota system for work permits was implied.[10] The expansion of quotas and simplification of procedures offered the possibility of not only of legal stay but also the possibility of naturalization for migrants from all the titular nationalities of the CIS (Zhukava 2006: 27). It thus radically reaffirmed the civic conception of citizenship noted in the 2002 Law on Citizenship of the Russian Federation, now liberalized out of demographic pragmatism.

Although the 2007 amendments to migration policy, seem to present a new 'open doors' policy which reverses the strict migration policy to reduce the flow of immigrants (Molodikova 2007: 60), these changes in migration policy were also self-contradictory. In 2006, Putin called on the Duma to introduce new rules 'to regulate immigration flows so that our citizens do not feel infringed upon in certain sectors of the economy'.[11] In due course, together with the above-mentioned new measures, in November of the same year a decree was passed banning migrants from selling alcohol and pharmaceuticals and setting an immediate limit 40 per cent of total staff on the number of migrants employed in markets and kiosks, which was set to reduce this number to zero per cent by April 2007.[12] The decree on establishing quotas for migrants in markets, however, could be interpreted as superficial, since it concerns mainly the visibility of migrants to the public rather than their actual presence at the markets.[13] Migrants were forbidden to work only where they would be in direct contact with the public.[14] This ban, although it impacted on migrants' livelihoods, seems to have embodied a

---

10　Human Rights Watch (2009) *'Are You Happy to Cheat us?' Exploitation of Migrant Construction Workers in Russia,* Online. Available HTTP: http://www.hrw.org/sites/default/files/reports/russia0209web_0.pdf> (accessed 18 February 2010).
11　The Current Digest of the Post-Soviet Press (2006), 58 (40): 6.
12　See The CDPSP (2006), 58 (52): 2.
13　In December 2010, in response to the Russian government sending a zero-tolerance message to the migrant workers, Renat Karimov, a spokesman for the Labour Union of Migrant Workers, said that 'there is really nothing new in all this because the government has been issuing the same law every year since 2007', (Adelaja 2010: 1).
14　Itar Tass Daily (1 April 2007) *Migrants Banned to Sell at Russia's Markets,* Online. Available HTTP <http://dlib.eastview.com.sources/article.jsp?id=11770322> (accessed 10 March 2010). In addition, those with temporary residence permits could continue to work in any capacity.

shallow populism designed to reassure a xenophobic majority while leaving the more substantial aspects of the new migration regime untouched.

Although some of these measures introduced in 2007 seem to constitute a harsh approach to solving the problem of illegal migration, a closer look at some of the major control measures listed above reveals that they served merely to symbolically emphasize the monopoly of state bureaucracy. In practice, these measures were far more flexible than stated at their introduction. Whilst the work permit quota for visa-free migrants in 2008 was set at 1.15 million compared to six million in 2007, when this reduced quota ran out towards the middle of the year, the government increased it to 2.24 million (Human Rights Watch 2009: 25). In 2009, a dramatic decision to halve the initial quota of four million turned out to be meaningless in practice, for the government maintained a 'reserve' stock which left the true figure of available permits unchanged.[15]

To conclude, it is wise to put these changes in migration policy into an everyday Russian context, for it would be tempting to interpret some of these contradictory amendments to the migration policy in 2007 as a response to noticeable tensions within Russian society. Xenophobia, negative attitudes towards migrants and sometimes even racist attacks typify the everyday normality in Russia. For instance, according to a survey conducted by the Levada Center in July 2005, 57 per cent of survey respondents were in favour of barring people from the Caucasus from residence in their city or district, while 53 per cent would support a similar ban for Central Asian migrants (Mukomel 2006: 4). The statistics of race assault in Russia also highlight this ongoing problem. In 2008, there were 526 recorded racist attacks in the Russian Federation. No less than 95 victims were reportedly of Caucasian origin with an additional 157 victims representative of Central Asian Republics (Kozhevnikova and Verkhovskii 2009 cited in Laryš and Mareš 2011: 142).

Furthermore, the events of the town of Kondopoga in September 2006 present an excellent example of tensions originating in an ethno-cultural understanding of Russianness. A clash between Russian and Chechen men began in a Chechen-owned restaurant in Kondopoga and sparked a wave of ethnically charged rioting and violence. This incident ignited calls from

---

15 For the original quota announcement see The CDPSP (2008), 69 (49): 10.

nationalist groups for a crackdown on immigration (Bigg 2006; Shlapentokh 2010). Such a confusion of internal minorities and migrants from outside clearly springs from an ethno-cultural understanding of Russianness and the capacity for mobilization which these nationalist organizations demonstrated after Kondopoga showed the extent to which their outlook struck a chord with the wider population (Verkhovsky 2009). Thus, the analysis in the subsequent empirical chapters of the present work seeks to shed light on these contradictions which affect the lives of young people from ethnic minorities and the ways in which these young people live with these new, yet old, divisions in Russian society.

Theorizing youth identities: accounting for ethnic belonging in culturally diverse societies

Exploring the complex processes of identity formation amongst young Armenians and Adyghs in Russia provides a challenge not only to existing conceptualizations of youth cultural identities outside the West, but also to debates on diaspora. A detailed study of these processes and everyday experiences needs to investigate both the state and the individual level. In order to negotiate these complexities of the theoretical and empirical field, youth identities are here explored within two major interrelated conceptual frameworks: those of identity and cosmopolitanism. In this context, it is assumed that young people draw upon a wide range of resources to construct their youth cultural identities, one of which is cosmopolitanism. Cosmopolitanism is understood as the result of the long history and tradition of migration and cultural mixing which permeates this part of Russia. Cosmopolitanism as an identity resource is employed to challenge conventional sociological, as well as popular and political, conceptions of diasporic and indigenous identities.

Identity

The notion of identity itself is based on four theoretical assumptions in this study. First, following (Hall 1996a), it is presumed that identities are not fixed, but rather processual and constantly changing in the process of making sense of experience. Second, identities are discursively constructed through difference, whereby they are established by a symbolic marking of representation in relation to others. Third, identities are constructed through our daily narratives, which constitute the ways we experience social life (Somers and Gibson 1994). Finally, identities are performances that vary in different contexts. Following Butler (1993, 1999 [1990]), this postulation presupposes that narratives are more than informative; they are also performative.

Identity formation is part of a meaning-making process, where meanings are the symbolic identification by social actors of the purpose of their actions (Castells 1997: 7). In this way, identities involve a process of self-construction that takes place 'within' and 'not outside discourse' (Hall 1996a). In some academic literature, the concept of 'identification' is used, although it is implied that the use of this concept could be 'as tricky as' the concept of identity (Hall 1996a: 2). Nonetheless, Hall (1996a) maintains that identification is the discursive construction of meanings of the 'self'; at times consciously, at other times unconsciously. As for the concept of identification, Brubaker and Cooper (2000: 14) argue that the use of this concept stresses the importance of 'agents doing the identifying'. In addition, they contend that the process of identification takes place within wider historical, political and cultural contexts, where 'actors' are affected by practices and discourse external to them and that change over time.

Like other social identities, ethnic identities are generally viewed as social constructions, even though ethnicity is still a highly contested term.[16] There has been a tendency to treat ethnic groups as primordial – rooted in ancient histories and bound together by blood ties, customs, language, memories and symbols. This approach in particular continues to prevail in the social sciences in Russia. Nevertheless, Smith (1981) argues that ethnic groups cannot be seen as primordial, since any identity is constructed through shared culture. Anthias (2005: 526) maintains that ethnic identity is a

---

16   For example, in both Western and Russian social science debates on ethnicity there is the long-standing tradition of treating ethnicity as an instrument for political mobilization (Tishkov 1997) and in terms of conflict (Arutiunian and Drobizheva 2000; Drobizheva and Gotte Moelier 1996).

'relational category that denotes the ontological space of collectivity'.[17] Following Anthias (2005), the empirical analysis in subsequent chapters treats ethnic identity as a social construction that comes into being through social interactions both with those from within and outside the boundaries of an ethnic group. Ethnic identity is a symbolic entity that can be reshaped and transformed in response to varying situational contexts. In other words, ethnic communities are seen to be collectivities which are articulated as ethnic by their group members for purposes of belonging.

Defining ethnic identities in terms of social interaction within and outside group boundaries rests on the logic of difference and belonging – who belongs to the group and who does not. It is a process in which one's own group is distinguished from others, whereby the distinction between 'us' and 'them' is constructed. Difference is organized hierarchically and can be a mode of contestation against oppression and exploitation or a vehicle for the legitimation of dominance (Brah 1996). It is also necessary to make a distinction between 'difference' as a process of differentiation, referring to the particularities of the social experience of a group, and 'difference' as a modality, in which domination is articulated (Brah 1996: 91).

Theorizations of 'othering' processes have been heavily influenced by two major schools of thought: psychoanalytic conceptions of identity; and identity as an ideological construct. As for psychoanalytic conceptions of identity, Lacan's formulation of 'self' in terms of a 'mirror image' are considered most influential. Lacan describes the process of identity construction as a process by which the 'infant, still sunk in his motor incapacity and nursling dependence, misrecognizes itself in its mirror image' (Lacan 2000 [1949]: 45). Most relevant for this discussion is that Lacan's account describes a process in which the subject is constituted 'from the outside'. The mirror-image 'situates the agency of the ego, before its social determination, in a fictional direction' (Lacan 2000 [1949]: 45). Hence, according to Lacan's account, identity is not immediately present at birth, but comes into being through language and social interactions with the 'other'.

---

17   Instead of using the term 'ethnicity', Anthias (1992, 2005) refers to the construction of ethnos or collectivity. For her 'the category of ethnos denotes populations attributing and attributed a commonality derived from some point of "origin", essential and distinctive trajectory or experience' (Anthias 2005: 524).

In his 'germinal ideological state apparatus' essay, Althusser elaborated further on Lacan's account. Althusser (2000 [1969]: 31) argues that 'the subject is only constitutive of all ideology insofar as all ideology has the function (which defines it) of "constituting" concrete individuals as subjects'. He develops an account of 'interpellation' as the means by which individuals are 'recruited' to certain subject positions, which are made available by 'ideology'. 'All ideology hails or interpellates concrete individuals as concrete subjects' (Althusser 2000 [1969]: 33). In other words, an individual comes into being when recognized by other individuals. In this sense, Rutherford (1990) maintains that identification is an ever-changing process, which is constituted by exchanges between self and structure.

This book also assumes that all identities are constituted by narratives. Such an approach stresses identity as a relational and situational category. The initial preoccupation with narratives took place on an abstract level, as modes representing knowledge or explaining social life. In recent times, however, claims about narratives propose that 'social life is itself storied and that narrative is an ontological condition of social life' (Somers and Gibson 1994: 38). It is 'through narrativity that we come to know, understand and make sense of the social world' and can form our social identities (Somers and Gibson 1994: 59). Somers and Gibson (1994: 38) further argue that the stories we tell each other guide our actions and are 'a repertoire of emplotted stories' which people employ 'to make sense of what has happened and is happening to them'.

Gender identity: performing femininity and masculinity
Any identity is the site of interplay between structure and agency, discourse and practices, ideology and subjectivity. Accordingly, gender identity is defined as a product of social relations constituted through interaction within discourses of power, rather than an innate and stable attribute. For Oakley (1972) gender is manufactured through social structure and cultural specificities, either actual or normative. It is not a category that is only based on biological difference. Although individuals are born male or female, they acquire gender identity – that is, they acquire an understanding of what it means to be a man or a woman. It must be recognized, however, that social

relations between genders are historically and locally dependent. Gender relations become established at particular periods of time, and in particular contexts, reflecting the dominance of specific ways of being masculine or feminine (Connell 1998 [1987]). Each society prescribes different activities and characteristics for males and females, which may be perceived as 'natural', while at the same time they are produced according to societal discourses.

Following this understanding of gender, the question arises of how gender might be exhibited or portrayed through interaction in order to produce appropriate discourses of femininity and masculinity in society. To explore how the gendered identities of young people from these two ethnic communities are socially constituted, this study employs Goffman's (1959, 1976) concepts of 'performance' and 'gender display'.[18] Goffman (1976: 69) formulates 'gender display' as follows: 'If gender be defined as the culturally established correlates of sex (whether in consequence of biology or learning), then gender display refers to conventionalized portrayals of these correlates'. The conventionalized portrayals are culturally established sets of behaviours, appearances, mannerisms, and other markers which individuals have learnt to associate with members of a particular gender (Goffman 1976). Although these gendered expressions might reveal manifestations of the underlying, fundamental dimensions of the female and male, in Goffman's view, they are optional and embody a particular striving as expressions of masculinity and femininity.

For Goffman, gender is an act of performance according to the culture's idealization of feminine and masculine natures which is always staged for an audience with certain expectations or conventions. Performing gender means that the presentation of self 'will tend to incorporate and exemplify accredited values of society' (Goffman 1959: 45). Individuals express themselves in order to affirm and reproduce societal values with their social performance.[19] Gender is, therefore, constituted in 'acts, gestures, and desire which produce

---

18 The approach to gender identity as a 'performance' is discussed thoroughly in Butler (1999 [1990]) and West and Zimmerman (1987) and is also applied in other published literature on ethnicities and gender (cf. Qureshi 2004; Harris 2004) and youth and gender (Nayak and Kehily 2008).
19 In this way, it is not gender identity only that is performed, but also ethnic identity.

the effect of an "internal core" or substance, but produce this on the surface of the body, through the play of signifying absences that suggest, but never reveal, the organizing principle of identity as a cause' (Butler 1999 [1990]: 173). In other words, the effect of acts, practices, behaviour and mannerisms bring gender performatively into embodied being. For Butler, gender attributes are not expressive but performative and thus constitute the identity they are said to express or reveal. Accordingly, gendered behaviour is produced by gender identity which is 'tenuously constituted in time, instituted in an exterior space through a stylized repetition of acts' (Butler 1999 [1990]: 174).

Identities as narratives, or stories we tell, are performative, as well as informative. Butler (1993: 12) contends that 'performativity is not a singular "act"', but a 'reiteration of a norm or set of norms' and 'acquires status' by disguising and dissimulating 'the conventions of which it is a repetition'. In this sense, repeated performances become normalized by their own repeated assertions. According to Butler (1993), it is crucial to distinguish between performance as a singular act and performativity as a routine. The performative subject is both subject and object in a process where norms and values have become normalized and routine.

Discursive/performative constructions of masculinities and femininities also involve processes of 'othering', where masculinity is defined in opposition to femininity and vice versa (Kimmel 2000). The discursive/performative production of gendered identities is also closely linked with the construction of ethnic identities and at the same time influenced by other categories, such as class (Skeggs 1997). Dwyer (2000) in her study on young South-Asian Muslim women in Britain demonstrates that the way in which participants positioned themselves varied considerably depending on their social and class position. This means that they drew upon diasporic identifications in different ways and in different circumstances. Gender performances, thus, can be conceptualized from different perspectives, either in terms of a particular social situation, or social, gendered, ethnic or other personal or collective 'identities',

For young people from ethnic groups in a culturally diverse society, another aspect is significant for the discursive/performative construction of gendered identities. Their performances are not only played for one audience, using Goffman's words, but for two different audiences. On the one hand, it is the ethnic community to which they belong together with certain cultural expectations; on the other, it is the society in which they live and the conventions that influence gendered behaviour. Often the two societies have contradictory expectations and constraints, but they also give them complex opportunities to express their multifarious identities and senses of 'belonging'. In order to explore the complexity of gendered identities of young 'Edinburgh Pakistanis', Qureshi (2004) employs Goffman's (1959) 'audience segregation', which she argues helps young 'Edinburgh Pakistanis' to manage their multiple identities. According to Goffman (1959: 57), 'audience segregation' – keeping observers of different presentations of 'self' separate – 'is a device for protecting impressions', With the help of this concept, Qureshi (2004) shows how young 'Edinburgh Pakistanis' are able to negotiate between different cultural contexts. In other words, 'audience segregation' is a device for expressing different identifications, as well as engaging with and negotiating particular cultural values in different environments.

Here and there: synthesizing sameness and difference
While performed gender identities are a crucial resource from which young people construct their cultural identities, diasporic and indigenous identities are also resources on which young people draw at particular moments and in particular situations. To premise assumptions about identity formations on classical notions of diaspora and indigenous identity, however, neglects the complex nature of the formation processes of youth identity. Instead, in view of the debates on globalization and the complex relationships between local and global, structure and agency; cultural cosmopolitanism can provide an alternative to diasporic and indigenous identity constructions. In this book, cultural cosmopolitanism is understood as an identity resource which young people have begun to draw upon for managing cultural diversity.

In recent years, debates on cosmopolitanism have been criticized for neglecting cultural and sociological perspectives, which consider everyday practices and identifications, in particular the category of gender (Stivens 2008) and the general structural realities of cosmopolitanism (Skrbis *et al.*

2004).[20] Nava (2007), for example, criticizes Hannerz's (1990,1992) view of cosmopolitans for always implying a 'he' in his depictions of real cosmopolitans.[21] Others, like Werbner (1999: 18), criticize cosmopolitanism on the basis that it is 'the claimed prerogative of elites' within the newly expanding global economy, while ignoring common-sense connections. Nonetheless, increasingly in scholarly literature, cosmopolitanism is discussed as a form of practice used by 'ordinary people to bridge boundaries with people who are different from them' (Lamont and Arksartova 2002: 1, Werbner 1999, 2008). Appiah (2005), in his discussion of 'rooted' cosmopolitanism, proposes that cosmopolitans are people who construct their lives from whatever cultural resources to which they find themselves attached (cited in Delanty 2006: 30). Accordingly, culture is understood as a reality that is constantly being constructed and reconstructed, instead of being anchored in a particular way of life. The notion of cosmopolitanism augments 'a mode of cultural framing which is not reducible to rights or particular identities, but concerns cultural models by which the social world is constituted' (Delanty 2006: 31).

Many of the issues raised in these debates on cosmopolitanism are echoed in Beck's work on cosmopolitanism and its implications for sociology. Beck stresses a process of cosmopolitanization that counteracts globalization, identifying it as a methodological concept which has the power to provide an alternative image of social life, one which seeks to comprehend the otherness of nature, other civilizations and other modernities. Cosmopolitan sensibilities are not merely something taking place 'out there', generated through greater global mobility and interconnectedness; rather, cosmopolitanism has to be viewed 'from within' (Beck 2002). This is

---

20 Some recent academic literature on cosmopolitanism places emphasis on the importance of structural realities. Appiah (1998: 96), for example, stresses that the state cannot be dismissed, since 'the cultural variability that cosmopolitanism celebrates has come to depend on the existence of a plurality of states'. Appiah's postulation, however, should not be seen as a glorification of the state, but rather as 'recognition of one of the structural elements of the contemporary social landscape' (Skrbis *et al.* 2004: 125).

21 According to Hannerz (1992), the cosmopolitan has reflexive cultural competencies, which enable 'him' to move around skilfully within new meaning systems. Besides this desire for experiencing cultural diversity, the cosmopolitan is also willing to become involved with the Other, although 'he' does not become committed to it.

especially true when it comes to sociological debates on 'new identities', which include the demonstrative reassertion of national, ethnic and local identities all over the world (Smith 1995). Ang (2001: 14), for example, identifies an irresistible appeal of the homeland myth among transnational communities, which intensifies anti-cosmopolitan feelings of ethnic absolutism and exclusionism. Thus, as Beck (2006) suggests that in view of 'new' identities, it is essential to examine their peculiarities.

To understand the peculiarities of 'new' identities, Beck employs the idea of a cosmopolitan outlook, which is exemplified by a reflexive engagement with both sameness and difference, and opens up useful ways to investigate personal and cultural levels of cosmopolitanism. A cosmopolitan outlook is characterized 'by reflexive awareness of ambivalences in a milieu of blurring differentiations and cultural contradictions' and contains 'the possibility of shaping one's life and social relations under the conditions of cultural mixture' (Beck 2006: 4). At the same time, Beck (2006: 8) contends that it is:

> a sceptical disillusioned, self-critical outlook ... The world of the cosmopolitan outlook is in a certain sense a glass world. Differences, contrasts and boundaries must be fixed and defined in an awareness of the sameness in principle of others. The boundaries separating us from others are no longer blocked and obscured by ontological difference but have become transparent.

The notion of cosmopolitanism is not applied to generalize youth cultural experiences and identity constructions in Krasnodar krai, but to explicate the interwoven complexities of difference and sameness that influence identity formation processes. In this book, cosmopolitanism is seen as an identity resource on which young people sometimes draw to manage cultural diversity. It is understood as an identity resource that rests on an engagement with the other, acknowledging both similarities and differences (Silverstone 2006). Being locally rooted in a culturally diverse society can create cosmopolitan experiences, since it compels individuals to constantly manoeuvre within different cultural systems. In view of the specificities of this region, however, cultural cosmopolitanism as a resource for identity construction is still in its infancy as subsequent empirical chapters show.

Since young people demonstrate reflexive cultural competencies in their everyday practices, it could be considered an alternative resource by which to transcend ethnic and racial boundaries.

The concept of diaspora and cosmopolitanism
The concept of diaspora has been used to write about displaced people, migrants and transnational peoples.[22] Yet, in recent years the concept of diaspora has been criticized for being antiquated and out of touch with contemporary diasporic social life. The concept of diaspora in its traditional usage has also been criticized for neglecting internal markers of difference, such as class and gender (cf. Anthias 1998). Notions of 'homeland' and 'ethnic community' as the main pillars for diasporic being have been deconstructed in many studies (cf. Brah 1996; Hall 1990). There is no doubt that homeland and diaspora are tightly intertwined and that the notion of homeland has been accorded a particular primacy in the diasporic imagination. Nonetheless, a substantial amount of literature on diasporas (cf. Ali 2003; Falzon 2003) suggests that the meanings of 'home/homeland' have changed for diasporic people; often the ancestral home is no longer considered to be the true or ideal home.

Closely linked to the notion of diaspora and home is the idea of diasporas maintaining a collective historical memory which constitutes a dimension of subjective definitions of ethnic belonging. Appadurai and Breckenridge (1989: i) argue that 'diasporas always leave a trail of collective memory about

---

[22] Safran's (1991) definition of diaspora, mainly applied to the Jewish diaspora, was the most influential definition that marked the beginning of diaspora studies (Cohen 2007). His definition goes as follows: 1) diasporic people, or their ancestors, have been dispersed from a specific original 'centre' to two or more 'peripheral'; or foreign regions; 2) they retain a collective memory, vision or myth about their original homeland – its physical location, history and achievements; 3) they believe that they are not – and cannot be – fully accepted by their society and therefore feel partly alienated and insulated from it; 4) they regard their ancestral homeland as their true, ideal home and as the place to which they or their descendants would (or should) eventually return – when conditions are appropriate; 5) they believe that they should, collectively, be committed to the maintenance or restoration of their original homeland and to its safety and prosperity; and 6) they continue to relate, personally or vicariously, to that homeland in one way or another, and their ethnocommunal consciousness and solidarity are importantly defined by the existence of such relationship (Safran 1991: 83-84).

another place and time and create new maps of desire of attachment'. In general, a diaspora can, to some degree, be held or recreated through the mind, through cultural artefacts and through a shared imagination. In this way, Cohen (1996: 516) stresses that 'identification with a diaspora serves to bridge the gap between the local and the global'. The complexity of cultural identification and the consequent awareness of multi-locality amongst diasporic peoples stimulate a constant process of formulating and reformulating diasporic representations. Hence, for Hall (1990) diaspora is comprised of ever-changing representations which provide an 'imaginary coherence' for a net of flexible identities. It is these diasporic representations that are not fixed any longer in the age of globalization.

Despite the relevance of collective memory for the formation of diasporic belonging, the concept of diaspora does not allow enough flexibility to properly describe young Armenian people's sense(s) of belonging sufficiently. It has been pointed out in previous studies that diasporas think globally as a result of cultural and territorial movement (Clifford 1997a). Cohen (1997: 176) in his study on global diasporas argues that 'globalization has enhanced the practical, economic and effective roles of diasporas, showing them to be particularly adaptive forms of social organization'. In other words, diaspora in a global world is defined by interconnectivity and adaptability, allegiances to community, locality and nation. Hence, the notion of cosmopolitanism could provide an alternative means of accessing and theorizing diasporic experiences.

The traditional concept of diaspora has been criticized for conveying essentialism that does not exist under global conditions. Diasporic forms flourish and ethnicity is replaced by hybridity (Clifford 1997a) or a 'third space' (Bhabha 1990) only known to diasporic people. Critics stress a cross-fertilization between different cultures as they interact, leading to creolization (Cohen 2007) or 'new (hybrid) ethnicities' (Hall 1996b). In recent studies on cosmopolitanism, it is shown that diasporic people familiarize themselves with other cultures and know how to move easily between them (Falzon 2005, 2009). Nonetheless, in the debates on cosmopolitanism and diaspora it is emphasized that this might not always be the case. Cultural diversity can also lead to a mythologizing of traditions (Shukla 1997) or what Beck (2006) terms 'as if' nationalisms that oppose any cosmopolitanization of one's diasporic culture. It is argued here that although most young people strongly identify with Armenian culture, this does not mean that they cannot develop a positive relationship with other cultures. The historical tradition of migration and mixing in this part of Russia, passed on from generation to generation, contributes significantly to such attitudes.

In view of the shrinking time and space distances under global processes, individuals from diasporic communities are often understood as having dual attachments or more recently a multitude of cultural attachments (Bhabha 1990; Ali 2003; Nilan and Feixa 2006). Gilroy (1987), for example, alluding to Du Bois's notion of 'double consciousness', describes a kind of duality of consciousness amongst individuals from diasporas. For him, diasporic individuals are decentred in their attachments – they are simultaneously 'home away from home' or 'here and there', or British and something else. Similarly, Clifford (1994: 322) proposes that 'the empowering paradox of diaspora is that dwelling *here* assumes a solidarity and connection *there* ... [it is] the connection (elsewhere) that makes a difference (here). But *there* is not necessarily a single place or an exclusivist nation'. In other words, if young Armenians draw on cosmopolitanism as an identity resource, this does not imply an absence of belonging, but rather the possibility of belonging to more than one ethnic and cultural locality simultaneously (Werbner 1999). It is argued that young Armenians are not decentred in their attachments, but have a clear sense of belonging. Both, the *here* and *there* are constituted by Armenian belonging. Whereas the *here* implies a stance toward diversity, mainly invoked by growing up in a culturally diverse society, the *there* is constituted by individual narratives of translocation or dislocation.

In this book, narratives of translocation or dislocation are explored in relation to research participants' associations with 'home' in Chapter Three. Perceptions about home are about location, which is not always confined to a single place. Location recognizes the importance of context (cf. Appadurai 1995, Anthias 2006); it can be about the lived experience in one particular place, but it can also be about a mythic place of desire in the diasporic imagination (Brah 1996). In view of the latter, narratives of translocation and dislocation are explored. Translocation describes the feeling of belonging to more than one place (Clifford 1997a). An individual can feel at home in the country where he or she was born, but also where he or she is living. Dislocation, however, assumes that the place for which someone feels attachment is lost, in the sense that one cannot go back there and thus one has become dislodged; in extreme cases the place may no longer exist, as it will be shown in Chapter Three.

Before concluding this discussion, it is necessary to note that the post-socialist context is a vital aspect for understanding youth cultural experiences in this part of Russia and is also almost absent from the debates on cosmopolitanism.[23] Studies emerging in the first decade after the collapse of communism employed post-socialism as a merely descriptive category, restricting analysis to the state-level of political and economic change (cf. Malia 1994; Stiglitz 1994). Such an approach portrays 'transitions' in post-socialist regions as case studies of the way in which 'the micro' is determined by or an expression of macro structures (Burawoy and Verdery 1999). However, as has been demonstrated in a number of sociological and anthropological studies, everyday experiences are rather characterized by innovative responses that reveal the influence of the socialist legacy in some or another way (cf. Kay and Kostenko 2008; Mandel 2002; Popov 2008).

Although most of this body of literature has stressed the specificities and peculiarities of the post-socialist context, it has also been shown in these studies that everyday experiences cannot be viewed as completely different from the West. Instead, many of the issues discussed in these studies transcend national boundaries and artificial 'East-West' divisions (Kay and Kostenko 2008). This, however, does not mean that people's everyday experiences in post-socialist regions and their responses to societal and political changes can be generalized, but rather have to be situated within the particularities of place, specific histories, cultural and socio-economic conditions. Considering the socialist past in an analysis of the post-socialist present can highlight the tensions and ambiguity that influence people's present experiences.

---

23 Only Richardson (2006) employs the concept of cosmopolitanism in her analysis of the interplay of diverse religions and local identity in Odessa.

In view of the above, the perception of cosmopolitanism as an identity resource for managing cultural diversity has its limitations, especially when it comes to cultural practices of young people from non-Russian groups in the post-Soviet space. Yet, this does not mean that cosmopolitanism has to be abandoned completely. Instead, in such cases cosmopolitanism can highlight the different ways in which young people form their cultural identities and sense(s) of belonging by a selective and diversified engagement with the Soviet past.

The empirical project: ethnography and reflexivity
The fieldwork was conducted in the Southern Federal District of the Russian Federation. Two sites were selected for this fieldwork: first, Krasnodar, which is the main city in Krasnodar krai. Here the focus was on the Armenian community. Second, Adygheisk, a small town in the Republic of Adyghea in Russia, which was formerly part of Krasnodar krai. Here the focus was on young Adyghs. Features of the two sites, including detailed descriptions of migration, history and culture in these two localities, are discussed at length in the next chapter. This eight month ethnographic study involved speaking to, observing and interacting with young people from these two ethnic communities, over time and within particular spatial contexts. The ethnography incorporates participant observation of young people in multiple settings, 'thick' description of people and places, and taped in-depth interviews with groups and individuals. A fieldwork diary was also used to record events as they happened and provide biographical information, as well as personal reflections on my impressions.

It has been noted elsewhere that 'ethnography is all about encounters and throughout the ethnographic process from fieldwork to text there are a myriad of small, interlinked acts of translation' (Jordan 2002: 96). Ethnographic research cannot be seen as a separate space, it rather consists of complex 'spatial practices' (Katz 1994; Clifford 1997b). Therefore, ethnographic researchers have to weave their text through their selves when talking about their research. Overall, 'telling stories about the unfolding of the field experience is a useful way to explicate processes of how one's own consciousness as an ethnographer is shaped and transformed' (Murphy 1999: 481). The question of the researcher's identity and intellectual autobiography was an important one in the context of the research dialogue and needs to be discussed here in more detail. Therefore, the subsequent discussion will be written in the first person so as to scrutinize the impact of the researcher on the ethnographic process and the gathering of empirical data.

During my fieldwork, I simply could not fit into a neutral research role and therefore different parts of my identity were strategically involved in the research process and continually (re-)negotiated, the deeper I became immersed in the field and built relationships with my research subjects. In the first place, my accent made it undoubtedly evident to everyone that I was not Russian, and from my physical appearance that I was not Armenian or Adygh. My national identity had certain advantages and disadvantages. On the one hand, I often found that relationships of trust and confidentiality were formed reasonably easily between myself and most young people, as I was not categorized as one of 'them' in the 'them and us' relationship (that is, Russians and 'us'). It was an advantage that a foreigner with no predefined connections wanted to study Armenian and Adygh youth. Often it made young people very keen to talk to me. On the other hand, sometimes my contacts were disturbed by what could be called spy-mania, which is an attitude formed during Stalinist repression. This conclusion was mainly inspired by my ambiguous ethnic status – why would a German living in England be interested in Adyghs or Armenians in Russia. In some cases, after an interview or a first encounter, I would hear, though jokingly, but with an underlying seriousness, that I was a spy working for the Federal Security Service (FSB).[24]

Gender is one of a researcher's subjectivities that cannot be disguised and has been a major concern for feminists in the process of research. My research was conducted in what can be described as a patriarchal society, in which women have a relatively subordinate status. In the field setting, I was 'naturally' located closer to girls. However, it is not my intention here to see

---

24   I am not the only researcher in Russia to encounter this problem (cf. Popov 2005: 95).

YOUTH IDENTITIES IN RUSSIA 49

my gender as a source of difficulty in the conduct of my fieldwork. Rather, following Back's (1993: 218) reasoning, 'gender difference is a source of knowledge within the field and the exploration of gender identity is tightly intertwined with the process of knowing'. According to feminist approaches, subjectivities, such as gender, race and class, for example, have always been perceived as creating unequal relations between researchers and researched. Opposing this argument, Back (1993) shows how his 'whiteness' and his masculinity became an integral part of the process of construction and presentation of self in the context of the multi-ethnic neighbourhood he studied.

In this research, female participants constituted the majority of research subjects, although male participants constituted a third of all the interviews. My field relations with male and female participants were different. Nonetheless, this should not be seen as an obstacle created only by my gender. It is an issue of the degree to which power relations between men and women is mediated in the research process. Back (1993), in response to feminist criticism that challenged the unequal relations between male and female research participants, notes that it is beneficial not to follow this myth of gender differences. Although admitting that his masculinity restricted his ability to speak openly to young women during the course of his participant observation within the youth-club setting, the issue was not his gender, but more that his female participants were placed in a vulnerable position by other male peers. In other words, it was men who stopped him from interacting with young women on a one-to-one basis publicly.

Like Back (1993), I felt that it was not so much my own gender subjectivity that influenced my relations, but rather these relations were influenced by cultural patterns of these two sites. Thus, it is beneficial to elaborate on this issue of vulnerability to say that it was not so much 'male' research participants who were placed in a vulnerable position, but that I was perceived by my female participants to be in a vulnerable position during a one-to-one interview context. This arose from female research participants' cultural understanding and the way inter-gender relations work in both communities. On many occasions, when I had an interview with a young man, his female cousin or sister took part in the interview, as it was unimaginable that I could talk on my own to a young man. In addition, some male research participants perceived a one-to-one interview with a female researcher as an opportunity to 'chat-up a foreigner' and to display their masculinity. Overall, many participants preferred to be interviewed in groups. In short, it was not gender alone that had an impact, but rather the social construction of gender relations in these two communities. It is not that sex inhibits cross-sex social interaction per se, but rather the construction of the appropriateness of such communication within these two communities.

Although the social construction of gender relations in these two communities had an impact on interviews with male research participants, it also affected the construction of knowledge in interviews with female participants, especially interviews with Armenian girls. My female participants' behaviour was often influenced by 'gossiping processes' within the Armenian community. Gossiping is an important part of Armenian life and restricts Armenian girls in many ways.[25] Their whole future depends on this gossiping network. A single rumour about an Armenian girl might influence her whole future negatively; she might have problems finding a suitable husband. This gossiping network meant that some girls were frightened to talk to me because they thought I would gossip about them. Also, some of the girls would only give me some general information, such as '*All Armenians are good*'. This type of information, however, was also spurred by a patriotic attitude.

Class and age have always been perceived as critical in forming equal relationships between researchers and researched. The work of the Centre for Contemporary Cultural Studies (CCCS) at the University of Birmingham, for example, has been criticized as the product of researchers from a middle-class background researching working-class youth. In a broader context, Muggleton (2005) even argues that scholars from the CCCS artificially re-

---

25 Armenian women are not the only women who are affected by gossiping as a means of social control. This type of control is highlighted in other studies on gender relations. Harris (2004), for example, discusses in detail the power of gossiping as a means of controlling gender relations in Tajikistan. For the purposes of Armenian research participants' anonymity, first names are changed in this book. In ensuing discussions, Armenian research participants are only referred to by their pseudonyms and their age. Here the pseudonyms are traditional Armenian first names. The real first names of Armenian research participants were often Russian.

inserted social class at the heart of youth cultural studies by theorizing youth subcultures in terms of working-class resistance to the dominant culture, employing Gramsci's concept of hegemony.

Cultural differences in respect to the significance of class as a category are also expressed by other researchers. Hollands (2003), for example, stresses that his own social background was not really transferable to the English context, reflecting on his ethnographic study of cultural identities and transitional experiences of fifty working-class youths. He describes his social background as rural, upwardly mobile working-class Canadian, which roughly translates that he has experienced both a working-class upbringing (albeit in a different cultural context) as well as the opportunity to study class as a theoretical concept (Hollands 2003: 163). Whereas Hollands (2003) hints at the importance of class in his study as a result of his focus on working-class youth, Wood (1984) argues that class is not always a crucial category in the study of working-class young people. Talking from his own personal experience as a middle-class boy, he shows that boys' sexist sexual practices cut across class and are to some extent dependent on social situations.[26] Crucial for the discussion here is that both Hollands (2003) and Wood (1984) stress the significance of class with respect to the research focus.

This argument becomes obvious when discussing class in the Russian context. In some studies (cf. Connor 1988), communism is considered to have atomized social relationships and disaggregated social classes. Here the assumption is that the operation of egalitarian economic policies and the disaggregation of social resources, such as property, education, status, occupation and wealth, have inhibited the formation of social classes and led to the emergence of social homogenization (Evans and Whitefield 1993: 529).[27] In this respect, one could argue that people living in Russia do not have a political grasp of class relations or think in terms of class, as it is understood in England. Nonetheless, recent scholarly publications on post-communist societies (cf. Roberts and Pollock 2009, Roberts *et al.* 2009,

---

26   He conducted his research on forms of sexism amongst boys in a unit for 'disruptive' kids in a London coeducational secondary school.
27   See Connor (1988) for a discussion on this problem. Additionally, Evans and Whitefield (1993) discuss the problem of an absence of a middle class in East European countries with regard to voting behaviour in these countries.

Walker 2010) and my fieldwork experience showed the opposite and I argue that class remains a significant category for youth cultural research beyond the Western context. First of all, my 'educated' background as a researcher from England in Russia created a certain status for me in the field, although not preventing me from becoming friends with research participants. Second, research participants came from different socio-economic backgrounds and subsequent empirical chapters show how those socio-economic backgrounds shape the identities of research participants.

Age differences can also help to create certain relations between researchers and their subjects. During my fieldwork, I was thirty years old when hanging around with and interviewing young people aged between 16 and 25. It was perhaps the way I looked, that young people at least did not ask me about my age. In fact, both age and class (status) may have worked to change many young people's impressions of me as a researcher. In view of what Hollands (2003: 157) refers to as 'the social relations of fieldwork', I maintain that age and education did not have such an impact on my relationship with research participants because they were only minor differences in comparison to the bigger distinction of a foreign status (being seen as a 'Westerner') in the field (Pilkington 1994: 199, Walker 2010).

To conclude, feminist research demands that a researcher accounts for the subjective experiences of doing research by critically examining and exploring analytically the research process as well as examining the researcher's 'intellectual autobiography'. Throughout this final section of this chapter, I have stressed that this ethnographic study should be seen as an interactive product of negotiating boundaries between the researched and researcher. Hence, what is to follow in subsequent empirical chapters can only be understood in relation to my reflexive positioning in the field.

Conclusions

This chapter has introduced the focus of research and the main theoretical framework that guides the empirical analysis in the subsequent empirical chapters. It began by examining the legacy of the Soviet nationalities policies. In doing so, it stressed the major developments which transformed the nationality/ethnicity category into a vital identity marker for contemporary Russian society. It continued by analysing the changes in migration policies and citizenship laws in post-Soviet Russia. This is considered necessary, since such changes have an impact on the politics of belonging and indeed the analysis has revealed a significant paradox for the politics of belonging in present-day Russia. While in some ways Russia's migration policies imply fairly liberal notions of inclusion, in other ways some amendments have led to discriminatory and racialized distinctions of migrants. It is argued that such changes in migration policies and their consequent impact on the politics of belonging have also affected the everyday lives of the research participants. Although all research participants have Russian citizenship, on many occasions in everyday life they are juxtaposed with migrants and for this reason members of the two groups do not always perceive belonging in the same way. Despite the need to consider the construction of ethnicity in the national and historical discourse, this book still prioritizes young people's individual experiences at the micro-level, as discussed in Chapters Three, Four and Five. It is, however, accepted that to get a full picture of young people's experiences, the politics of belonging have to be placed in the local context; this is therefore the focus of the next chapter.

2 Ethnocentric Politics in the (Post-) Soviet Context: A Regional Perspective

The previous chapter argued that social identity is constituted within discourse and as such is a product of power relations. It follows that young Armenians and Adyghs, like the rest of the population, are subject to the identity politics in Russia as well as their regions. Moreover, young people are not only positioned within political discourses, but reproduce and to some extent routinize them through their everyday cultural practices. Moving the analysis from the national to the regional, this chapter examines how such post-Soviet identities are shaped and constructed by the regional political discourse in Krasnodar krai and the Republic of Adyghea. In both Krasnodar krai and the Republic of Adyghea, regional political discourses are structured around the discourse of 'interethnic relations'. This chapter also scrutinizes the local media discourse on ethnic migration together with the related administrative and policing practices of the regional authorities. This is crucial, since the media and legislative discourses create the basis for discrimination against ethnic minorities and migrants in this region. This chapter is structured in two parts. The first is an examination of the regional political discourse of 'migration' politics and cultural diversity and how this has affected the Armenian diaspora in Krasnodar. The second part focuses on the Republic of Adyghea whose political regime might be best described as rooted in an ethno-nationalist ideology that nonetheless enables ethnic minorities to participate in the republic's political processes.

The ambivalence of the politics of migration and cultural diversity in Kuban

Krasnodar krai is one of Russia's southernmost regions: it borders the Sea of Azov to the west, the Black Sea to the south, and the Caucasus Mountains and Georgia to the southeast. Krasnodar krai shares a border with Abkhazia as well as with the 'national' republics of Karachaevo-Cherkessia and Adyghea. Adyghea had the status of an autonomous region (*oblast'*) within the krai until 1991, but now forms an enclave completely surrounded by

Krasnodar krai. Krasnodar krai, also known as Kuban after the Kuban River flowing through the region, is well-known for its tourist industry and its image of a thriving region in Southern Russia. Aside from its image as a peaceful tourist region, Kuban is also known for its political regime of discrimination against ethnic minorities and migrants (cf. Kuznetsov 2004; Magomedov and Kirichenko 2004; Popov and Kuznetsov 2008). As with the national discourse on migration discussed in the previous chapter, regional migration and the resultant 'nationalities policies' are based on the assumption that so-called 'ethnic migration' disrupts the ethnic balance of the region and creates the potential for ethnic conflict and therefore presents a threat to the 'native' population.[28]

Migration and demography
As a result of large-scale migration flows, Krasnodar krai has become one of Russia's most multi-ethnic regions over the last two centuries. Nonetheless, Krasnodar krai is still considered to be one of the 'Russian' regions in the North Caucasus (the other two are Rostov *oblast'* and Stavropol krai). In fact, almost all ethnic groups living in Krasnodar krai could be defined as resettlers (*pereselentsy*) (Popov 2002: 194). For example, Russians, constituting the ethnic majority in this region, came to this part of Russia at the end of the eighteenth century when the northern part of the Kuban region became part of the Russian Empire (Boeck 1998: 636). Overall, the region's history of migration until the collapse of the Soviet Union can be divided into three distinct periods: the first period from the eighteenth century until the early twentieth century, the second period from the 1920s until the 1940s and the third period from the 1950s until the end of the 1980s (Rakachev and Rakacheva 2003).

After the appearance of the first Russian settlements, Russian- and Ukrainian-speaking Cossacks began to settle in the region. The Caucasian War (1816-1864) is a crucial historical event in this first period of migration

---

28 A substantial amount of literature has been published by the Sociology Department at the Kuban State University that takes a conflict approach to ethnic migration and ethnic relations on the whole. See, for example: Matveev, Rakachev, V. N. and Rakachev, D. N. (2003); Petrov *et al.* (2002) and Savva, M. V. and Savva, E. V. (2003).

that led to substantial changes in the region's 'ethnic' composition. As a result of the Caucasian War, many indigenous (*korennoi*) peoples, the so-called Circassians[29], left the region for the Ottoman Empire and vast swathes of land became uninhabited. In March 1866, a governmental decree, providing various benefits for resettlers, was issued in order to attract people to the region (Rakachev and Rakacheva 2003). Consequently, people from various ethnic groups, including Armenians and Greeks from Turkey, Moldovans, Bulgarians, Czechs, Germans and Estonians, resettled in Krasnodar krai.

The October Revolution of 1917 and the subsequent years of consolidation of the Bolshevik regime gave a new impulse to in-migration into the region. Extensive migration had already begun during the Russian Civil War (1918 - 1922). The introduction of the first Five Year Plan in 1928, which was accompanied by a new distribution of land, led to a migration influx of Cossacks and mountainous peoples, such as Ossetians, Karachais, Ingush, Chechens, Nogais, together with peoples from other ethnic groups (Rakachev and Rakacheva 2003). Poor agricultural output following the first Five Year Plan was followed by the years of collectivization (1929 -1937). These years of collectivization were a tragedy for many people who were deported from Kuban and forced to resettle in Siberia, including Greeks, Moldovans, Bulgarians, Germans and Cossacks. Nevertheless, this out-migration was accompanied by the in-migration of those who resettled into the region as part of Stalin's policy of Russification. The years that followed Stalin's death in 1953, marked a new period of rehabilitation in which formerly deported people began to return. Together with these 'returnees' other people from Transcaucasia (Armenia, Azerbaijan) as well as Russians resettled in Krasnodar krai.

As Table 2.1 shows, there was no major ethnic shift in the population despite migration flows in and out of the region during the Soviet period.

---

29 The term Circassians encompasses people from a number of tribes: Kabardinians, Beslanay, Temirogoi, Bzhedug, Abzakh, Shapsugh and Adyghs (Jaimoukha 2001: 23-25).

Table 2.1: Demographic change according to nationality in Krasnodar krai between 1939 and 1989 (% of the whole population)[30]

NATIONALITY	1939	1959	1970	1979	1989
Russians	88.1	90.9	89.8	89.2	86.7
Ukrainians	4.9	3.9	3.8	3.6	3.9
Belorussians	0.4	0.6	0.7	0.7	0.8
Adyghs	0.3	0.3	0.3	0.4	0.5
Armenians	2.0	2.2	2.3	2.6	3.7
Greeks	1.4	0.3	0.4	0.6	0.6
Germans	1.2	0.1	0.4	0.6	0.7
Georgians	0.1	0.2	0.2	0.2	0.3
Tatars	0.2	0.2	0.3	0.4	0.3
Moldovans	0.3	0.2	0.2	0.2	0.2
Jews	0.2	0.2	0.2	0.1	0.1

It is noteworthy that although the absolute size of the Armenian population remains small, Table 2.1 demonstrates a relatively significant rise in the proportion of ethnic Armenians in the region; their proportion almost doubles between 1939 and 1989. The only other group to grow in this way is Belorussians.

With the start of ethnic conflicts in the Caucasus region in 1988, a new wave of migrants came to Krasnodar krai. These new arrivals were Armenians from Azerbaijan and Nagorno Karabakh (1988-1994), Meskhetian Turks from the Ferghana Valley in Uzbekistan (1989), refugees from the Georgian-Abkhazian conflict (1992-1994) and forced resettlers from

---

30 This table is adopted from Matveev, Rakachev, V. N., and Rakachev, D. N. (2003: 10). The data is derived from the population censuses of 1939, 1959, 1970, 1979 and 1989.

Chechnya (1994-1996 and 1999-2001). After the collapse of the USSR, former Soviet citizens from Kazakhstan, Georgia and Armenia settled in Krasnodar krai, having been forced to leave their homes due to economic difficulties in these new post-Soviet states. It was these in-flows that turned migration into the major political concern noted earlier. In fact, although Krasnodar krai did experience an extensive migration influx during the 1990s, it did not significantly alter the ethnic composition of the region. Overall, this in-migration did not create pressure on jobs or services etc. as it barely exceeded natural population decline, which had affected Krasnodar krai, like other regions in Russia, in the early 1990s. Most importantly, since the 1990s migration numbers have decreased, as Figure 2.1 shows.

Figure 2.1: Natural population growth and migration growth in Krasnodar krai, 1989–2000[31]

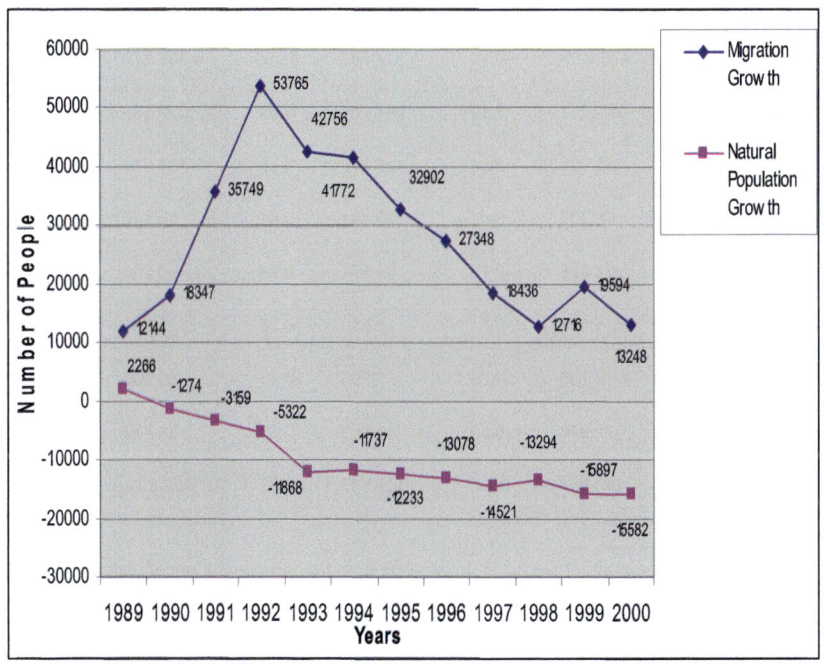

---

31   Matveev, Rakachev, V.N. and Rakachev, D.N. (2003: 130).

According to the last population census, conducted in 2002, Krasnodar krai has a population of around five million, with Russians constituting the majority at 86.56 per cent (4,436,272). Nonetheless, the region is 'multi-national'; it is home to 125 different nationalities.[32] Armenians (274,566) and Ukrainians (131,774) are the most numerous of the ethnic minorities, and comprise 5.36 per cent and 2.57 per cent of the region's population respectively.[33]

Table 2.2: Population and proportion of individual nationalities in Krasnodar krai in 1989, 2000 and 2002[34]

NATIONALITY	1989		2000		2002	
	Persons	%	Persons	%	Persons	%
Total Population	462 076	100.00	5 014 280	100.00	5 125 221	100.00
Russians	400 611	86.71	4 314 783	85.89	4 436 272	86.56
Armenians	171 757	3.72	241 964	4.83	274 566	5.36
Ukrainians	182 128	3.94	198 570	3.96	131 774	2.57
Greeks	28 337	0.61	30 461	0.61	26 540	0.52
Belorussians	34 688	0.75	38 971	0.78	26 260	0.51
Tatars	14 547	0.31	14 240	0.28	25 589	0.5
Georgians	12 105	0.26	17 595	0.35	20 500	0.4
Germans	29 946	0.65	16 359	0.33	18 469	0.36
Others	140 557	3.04	141 337	2.82	165 251	3.22

---

32 The precise number depends on what groups are considered 'nationalities'.
33 Krasnodarskii kraevoi komitet gosudarstvennoi statistiki. *Natsional'nyi sostav i vladenie iazykami, grazhdanstvo*. Itogi vserossiiskoi perepisi naseleniia 2002 goda po Krasnodarskomu Kraiu, Tom 4, Krasnodar, 2005.
34 Source for 1989 and 2000: Rakachev and Rakacheva (2003: 128). Source for 2002: Krasnodarskii kraevoi komitet gosudarstvennoi statistiki, *Natsional'nyi sostav i vladenie iazykami, grazhdanstvo*. Itogi vserossiiskoi perepisi naseleniia 2002 goda po Krasnodarskomu kraiu, Tom 4, Krasnodar, 2005.

As Table 2.2 demonstrates the ethnic composition of Krasnodar krai has not changed significantly since 1989. While according to the 1989 and 2002 censuses the ethnic Russian population has decreased in the Russian Federation as a whole[35], the data in Table 2.2. indicates that the proportion of ethnic Russians in Krasnodar krai has remained stable. This contradicts what is portrayed in Krasnodar krai's public discourse, when, for instance, it is stressed that the number of Russian people is falling and that many Russians have emigrated abroad.[36] Instead, the data confirms Kuznetsov's (2002) suggestion that since the 1989 population census, the ethnic composition of the krai's population has only changed slightly, and that as many Slavic resettlers (*pereselentsy*) have come to the region as other ethnic migrants.[37] Less than 10 per cent of the migrants, who came to Krasnodar krai in 2001, came from outside the Russian Federation. This suggests that approximately 90 per cent of the newcomers were Russian citizens, and 82 per cent were ethnic Russians (Popov 2005: 52-53). A similar opinion was expressed by Zhurbin (2005), that according to statistics on 'ethnic' migration, Russians predominate migration numbers.[38] This opinion is often contradicted by other sources, for example, Matveev, Rakachev, V. N. and Rakachev, D. N. (2003) claim that Armenian migrants are the largest group in statistics based on ethnicity. Following the official anti-migration discourse, experts in the field predominantly discuss migration in terms of illegal migration as a threat to the region's stability and disturbing the region's demographic balance, ignoring the fact that approximately 90 per cent of the migrants are Russian citizens.

The share of Armenians and Georgians, nonetheless, increased and this is often portrayed negatively in the press, for example: '*At present several million Armenians live in Russia, but only about 15,000 Russians live in Armenia...*'(Begletsov 2004: 1-2). Indeed, according to Russian official statistics every fourth Armenian in Russia lives in Krasnodar krai and as

---

35   Between the last two censuses, the proportion of ethnic Russians fell from 81.5 per cent to 79.8 per cent (Dubas 2008: 35).
36   Begletsov (2005) writes that 'in the next 40 years the number of Russians will decrease to 100 million'.
37   Kuznetsov cited in Sokolov-Mitrich (2002:10).
38   Interview with M.S. Zhurbin on 25 August 2005, conducted by R. Kuznetsova, at the Centre for Pontic and Caucasian Studies (Krasnodar), as part of a mini-project on migration conducted for the RIME Project 2004-2006, University of Warwick.

Tkachev, the governor of Krasnodar krai, claims *'there are approximately one million Armenians too many in the krai'*.[39] In addition, in the regional discourse there are different opinions about the exact number of Armenians in Kuban. While Tkachev claims there are one million Armenians in Kuban, Kuznetsov (2002), an expert on Armenians in the region, suggests that there are no more than 350,000 Armenians in Krasnodar krai.[40] According to the population census however, 274,566 Armenians are living in this part of Russia.[41] These differences in opinion on the exact number of Armenians in Krasnodar krai question the reliability of the census data, which is viewed as capturing only a part of the actual population. Thus, there is the widespread assumption that there are many more (unregistered) Armenians than these figures suggest.

The questionable accuracy of the 2002 population census data can be explained by several shortcomings in the data. First, whereas previous Soviet censuses were carried out in a controlled state and compliance with the census was mandatory, the 2002 population census was conducted during unstable times, where the population's distrust had increased, which led to difficulties in conducting the census (Heleniak 2003: 431). Second, there is the problem of ethnic self-identification, especially with regard to people from ethnically mixed origins. As noted by others (cf. Oswald 2000), if one identifies with more than one ethnic group, self-identification may fluctuate according to the external environment. Thus, there is no way of knowing how many people of mixed origins considered themselves Russian in the census due to the perception of possible discrimination.

Migration politics in post-Soviet Krasnodar krai
As a political reaction to the migration waves of the early 1990s, ethnic discrimination and anti-migrant policy became tightly intertwined. The exploitation of regional conditions and the institutionalization of discrimination against migrants and ethnic minorities intensified when Aleksandr Tkachev

---

39   *Armiane Kubani* film by Artem Erkanian (2005).
40   Kuznetsov cited in Sokolov-Mitrich (2002: 10).
41   The 2002 All-Russian Population Census. Online. Available HTTP: <http://www.perepis2002.ru> (accessed 12 December 2006).

was elected to the post of regional governor in December 2000.[42] In a newspaper interview, Aleksandr Tkachev accentuates the importance of the fight with illegal migration, premising his statement on the assumption that there are more non-Russian 'unregistered' migrants in the region than statistics certify:

> Again, I want to stress that we do not oppose migration in general, but we oppose illegal migration. A migrant's nationality, whether Ukrainian, Armenian or Georgian, is not important as long as the person has passed all stages in the legal process [of obtaining a legal residence permit] and according to the law.[43]

In public discourse the emphasis is mainly placed on the fact that every fifth person in the krai is a migrant.[44] Noteworthy here is that in public discourse the term 'migrant' is particularly pliable and subject to different forms of manipulation. In official rhetoric and media discourse the term 'migrant' is frequently used to refer to many, if not all, ethnic minorities, including Armenians, regardless of when they settled in Krasnodar krai and whether or not they possess permanent registration (Popov and Kuznetsov 2008). Thus, juxtaposing the problem of illegal migrants with certain ethnic groups, Tkachev proclaims that regional authorities ' ... *will look ... at the endings of surnames!*' (cited in Petrosian 2002a: 4). Surnames can indicate a person's ethnic belonging; for example, surnames ending with *–ian* are Armenian surnames. Popov and Kuznetsov (2008: 233) maintain that

---

42 Tkachev was not the first governor in Krasnodar krai to implement discriminatory legislation. It is generally believed that Nikolai Kondratenko, who was elected to the post of governor in 1996, was the initiator of stricter territorial politics concerning migration. For example, he introduced the restrictive law 'On Movement and Residence in the Territory of Krasnodar krai', which was implemented as part of a strict anti-migrant policy in Krasnodar krai. However, the ideological roots of the current policies were established earlier, when in 1992-1993, under the leadership of the so-called democratic governor V. Diakonov and the chairman of the Executive Committee in Krasnodar krai, A. Zhdanov, residence registration was gradually tightened to 'prevent' ethnic conflicts (McAuley 1997). For a detailed discussion of legislation introduced by Kondratenko and its consequences, see Magomedov and Kirichenko (2004) or Osipov (1999a, 1999b).
43 Aleksandr Tkachev in an interview with Panchenko (2002).
44 Aleksandr Tkachev in an interview with Panchenko (2002). M.S. Zhurbin also stressed that every fifth person in the krai is a migrant (Interview 25 August 2005).

migrants are categorized according to an 'ethnic coding' that is premised on the assumption that migrants are viewed as representatives of ethnic groups considered to be non-indigenous to the region. As a result, regional authorities apply their restrictive migration policy to ethnic groups that are perceived as 'non-indigenous', even if they have lived in the region for centuries.

Together with this categorization of 'migrants' along ethnic lines, regional authorities have also created the myth that the indigenous inhabitants of the Kuban region are Cossacks.[45] This is reflected in a local regulation introduced in 1997, Article 2, Decree 1, which states that Cossacks have the status of an indigenous people.[46] Thus, the Cossack movement is one weighty part of Krasnodar krai's ideological discourse: *'Kuban is the land of Cossacks and everyone should know this ...'*.[47] Nonetheless, as noted earlier a number of other ethnic groups appeared in the region at the same time as the Cossacks. Armenians, for example, inhabited Kuban territory even before Cossacks came to the region at the end of the eighteenth century; therefore, Cossacks are only as indigenous as many other ethnic groups.

A number of regulations effectively grant Cossacks a privileged status in the region; they are considered to be a distinct part of a greater ethnos, the Russian nation, which itself is part of a meta-ethnos, the Slavs (Boeck 1998: 645). This is also often communicated in the press with headlines, such as *'Russia – that's us! The first Cossack guard'* (Kuromatchenko and Shevchenko 2006). These publications not only report on the Cossacks' 'great' cultural achievements, but also on their political significance for the region, in particular their role in keeping law and order in Krasnodar krai. Thus, Tkachev is quoted frequently expressing his warm attitude towards the Cossacks: *'Cossacks are precisely the force one can always rely on ... they are ready to serve the homeland not out of fear, but out of conscience. Cossack squads ... keep order on the streets'* (Vakulin 2004: 2).

---

45 This goes back as far as the 1970s, when regional authorities started to cultivate a distinct Kuban Cossack identity (Abelsky 2007, Schorkowitz 2008).
46 This regulation states that 'Krasnodar krai is the historical territory of the Kuban Cossacks, the native land of the Russian (*russkii*) population ...This is supported by the state and local authorities' (Kuznetsov 2004: 60).
47 Tkachev cited in Petrosian (2002a: 4).

Returning to the discussion of migration politics in this region, under Tkachev, Krasnodar's regional government also adopted a strict new law on migration and residence in the region in March 2002, which had serious implications for illegal (unregistered) migrants from the Caucasus. Krasnodar authorities began to implement a broad deportation program in April 2002 and an estimated 13,000 Meskhetian Turks without legal resident permits were forced to leave the region (Kuznetsov 2007a). Regional authorities also began to prepare deportation proceedings against Kurds, Abkhazians, Georgians and Armenians living in the region without legal residence permits (Petrosian 2000b). The Krasnodar authorities justified their policy by reference to the need to maintain an 'ethnic balance' in order to secure stability in 'interethnic relations' and to protect the interests of the 'local population'.[48]

Noteworthy here is that in the context of migration reforms conducted in the whole of Russia in 2002, these official attitudes in Krasnodar krai do not come as a surprise. Although it was not the Krasnodar krai's authorities who initiated this mechanism of registration; manipulating the law, however, proved easy (Osipov 2004: 22). The resolution of the authorities to root out the problem of illegal migration has remained visible, even though, from 2005 onwards, it has received less coverage in the printed press. Whereas in 2004 the problem of illegal migration received wide coverage in the press, in 2005 it was portrayed as having been almost solved owing to the hard work of the police[49] and the establishment of a 'deportation' camp – the first of its kind in Russia.[50] Press reporting of this deportation camp suggested it was the only way to overcome the problem of illegal migration:

---

48   The discriminatory regime against migrants and ethnic minorities which has been established within Krasnodar krai has even attracted international comment. For example, an official report by the US Department of State Bureau of Democracy, Human Rights and Labor (25 February 2004) twice notes the unacceptable situation which has formed in Krasnodar krai: in section 2, point D 'Freedom of Movement within the Country, Foreign Travel, Emigration, and Repatriation' (regarding relations with one group of migrants – Meskhetian Turks), and in section 5, under the subheading 'National/ Racial/ Ethnic Minorities' (cited in Popov 2005: 50).

49   Press-sluzhba administratsii Krasnodarskogo kraia, 'Situatsiia v krae stabil'na, militsiia – professional'na', *Kubanskie novosti*, 12 October 2006, p. 1.

50   This deportation camp was opened on 1 January 2005. According to a newspaper article by Pavlova (2004), the deportation camp consists of heated tents with 24

Everything the krai's administration does in relation to illegal migrants, is exclusively done in the interests of the krai's inhabitants irrespective of their ethnic and racial belonging (*prinadlezhnost'*). We all have an interest in Krasnodar krai being economically and politically stable and in laws being observed in Krasnodar krai as laws are observed throughout Russia.[51]

Although in this newspaper excerpt Tkachev attempted to distance himself from any allegation that illegal migrants are viewed in terms of their ethnicity; his attempt appeared superficial. Local newspapers are heavily dependent on funds from the regional budget and are therefore obliged to conform to the anti-immigration political discourse and report on migrants in terms of ethnic belonging.[52] In Krasnodar in 2002, 0.8 per cent of the budget was allocated to mass media outlets in the region, a figure quite high in comparison to other regions. For example, in Saint Petersburg only 0.1 per cent of all expenses were for the financial support of mass media outlets (Savva, M. V. and Savva, E. V. 2002: 15-16). In addition, the Krasnodar Human Rights Centre claims that three local newspapers are directly subsidized by the administration's budget, which is distributed by Tkachev himself.[53] Thus, Tkachev's attempts at distancing himself from any allegation of categorizing migrants according to their ethnic belonging seem insincere.

To conclude this discussion on migration politics in Krasnodar krai, it is crucial to stress that although illegal migration has been a dominant subject in the press, at the end of 2005 and in 2006 this problem received less coverage and there were even some 'neutral/positive' articles, reporting on

---

beds for men and two railway carriages (*vagony*) for women. All together this camp's capacity is between 50 to 80 people.
51 Tkachev quoted in Pavlova (2004).
52 For example: '...a 40 year old citizen of Ukraine, who has illegally resided in the region for more than two years was convicted of drug dealing' in an article by the Press-sluzhba administratsii (2006) in *Kuban' segodnia*. Another example was published by Novokhatskii (2006) in *Kuban' segodnia*. In this article the opening sentence stated that 'drug dealing in Russia clearly has an ethnic character. As a rule the main drug dealers are representatives of national minorities'.
53 Krasnodar Human Rights Centre (2002), 'Monitoring proiavlenie natsionalizma, ksenofobii i neterpimost', Online. Available HTTP: <http://www.hro.org/ngo/krasnodar/dnaci.html> (accessed 24 May 2004). It is worth mentioning here that in 2004 regional authorities ordered the Krasnodar Human Rights Centre to stop its activities.

the multi-ethnic traditions of the region, including reports on 'ethnic' festivities or celebrations (cf. Gvozdetskaia 2004; Pavlova 2005). This slight change in press coverage has several explanations, not least that Tkachev's public hate speeches attracted a great deal of criticism. One could argue that this change in press coverage was inevitable in order to create a positive image for the region that would attract foreign investors. A positive image for the region is also desirable for the Winter Olympics in Sochi in 2014.

In February 2011, Tkachev even admitted his unjustified comments in the TV talk show, *Pozner*, saying that he was far too emotional and further explaining that:

> ...up to the age of 30, I didn't think about how an Armenian can be distinguished from a Georgian, or how an Adygh can be distinguished from a Cherkess. Such distinctions didn't matter to me. I always think that this was positive about my Soviet upbringing.[54]

'Krasnodar – edinaia sem'ia': the politics of cultural diversity

The flipside of the coin of this negative approach concerning migration and consequent discriminatory practices is the public discourse of promoting cultural diversity. Despite ethnocentric political discourses pertaining at regional level, it is support for and promotion of so-called 'ethnic voluntary associations' that is universal in Russia in general and a particular feature of the official politics of Krasnodar krai.[55] In accordance with this political approach of promoting cultural diversity, there is an administrative unit within the regional executive organs that works closely with ethnic voluntary associations on a regular basis. At the same time, this administrative unit provides support, including financial support, to a variety of cultural events, conferences or round tables on the subject of improving interethnic relations.[56]

---

54 Aleksandr Tkachev in a talk with Vladimir Pozner, 26 February 2011, on *Russia 1*, a state-owned Russian television channel. Online. Available HTTP: <http://www.1tv.ru/prj/pozner/vypusk/06.02.2011> (accessed 02 March 2011).
55 Judging by the press coverage, the discourse of cultural diversity has grown significantly over the last two years.
56 For example, from 2001, the krai's budget has included two million roubles every year to support various projects of Shapsughs, a sub-tribe of the Western Adyghs

In line with the discourse of promoting cultural diversity, Krasnodar krai's government officially declares that its politics are directed towards 'the preservation of a civic world and interethnic agreements, supporting the principle of equality for the representatives of different nationalities, religious beliefs of those living in the krai, and the strengthening of mutual respect and understanding between them'.[57] Nevertheless, in 1992, when the local authorities introduced the 'Programme for stabilizing interethnic relations in Krasnodar krai', which included references to the 'rebirth', 'development' and 'cooperation' of ethnic groups, they also adopted a decree on restricting migration into the krai (Osipov 2004: 14). As a result, the political discourse in Krasnodar krai embodies a contradiction in itself. On the one hand, a world of cultural diversity is portrayed, where all ethnic groups living in the region are equal. On the other hand, a political ethnocentric rhetoric is used that publicly distinguishes between indigenous and non-indigenous ethnic groups according to a politically prescribed 'ethnic coding',

In accordance with the discourse of cultural diversity in Krasnodar krai, ethnic voluntary associations represent the interests of their respective members (whether migrants or locals) and are politically, economically and culturally active. The origins of ethnic voluntary associations, however, are closely linked to the Soviet model of multiculturalism, when ethnic associations were effective political and economic institutions that existed alongside official state structures (Suny 1993). As discussed in the previous chapter, Soviet multiculturalism encouraged the cultural production of the ethnically diverse population of Russia. The aim of the Soviet model of multiculturalism was to ensure a peaceful co-existence of diverse ethnic groups, which all belonged to a Soviet people (*sovetskii narod*). With the fall of the Soviet Union and subsequent political transformations, these voluntary ethnic associations more often than not have become modes for citizens' self-organization and political mobilization (Pilkington and Popov 2008).

In 1992, the Centre for National Cultures (*Tsentr mezhnatsional'nykh kul'tur*) was founded in Krasnodar, comprising at that time more than thirty

---

and has provided support in different forms for other indigenous small peoples of Russia also (Osipov 2004: 14).
57 Addendum no 1 to the Decree of the head of the administration of Krasnodar krai, 25 July 2002, no 826 (cited in Osipov 2004: 14).

ethnic voluntary associations. The krai's administration works closely with the Centre and in recent years articles about the Centre and its activities have been published in the press, following the official approach of cultural pluralism.[58] According to official information, the languages of ethnic minorities (including Armenian and Georgian) are taught in 57 comprehensive schools in the krai.[59] Koriakin's (2006: 67) more recent information on teaching Armenian language, however, depicts a different picture. Whereas in Sochi[60] Armenian language is taught in 15 schools, in Krasnodar there are no schools teaching Armenian language. Armenian voluntary ethnic associations help to cover this deficit; opportunities to learn Armenian are provided by the Armenian organization in the Centre for National Cultures and the *Armianskaia Pashkovskaia Obshchina* (APO).[61]

Whilst it might appear that these ethnic voluntary associations serve as mere camouflage for the local authorities' discriminatory practices, in fact their existence fully conforms to Krasnodar krai's officials' ethnocentric understanding of society as a conglomerate of ethnic groups, each with its own collective identity and interests. This is largely the result of Soviet politics, as mentioned earlier, and the understanding of ethnos as a stable 'ethno-social organism', as discussed in Chapter One. The relationship between these ethnic voluntary associations can develop in a positive way, through collaboration, or in a negative confrontational way. In this way, the government sees its role as one of controlling interethnic relations by either

---

58   Such publications include a series on 'Dom sta narodov' [trans. *The house of a hundred peoples*] in *Krasnodarksie izvestiia* starting 11 March 2006, followed by a publication on this Centre at the beginning of each month.
59   In accordance with the 1992 Law on Education of the Russian Federation 'Citizens of the Russian Federation have the right to receive primary education in their native language. They also have the right to select the language instruction.' The Constitution of the Russian Federation of 1992 guarantees cultural self-determination and the right of local organizations to establish educational institutions to promote native language and culture (Osipov 2004: 15).
60   Sochi is a city in Krasnodar krai, situated just north of Russia's border with the de facto independent republic of Abkhazia on the Black Sea coast. Sochi is the largest Russian holiday resort and has a substantial Armenian population.
61   In the APO the teaching of Armenian language and literature is conducted on Saturdays and Sundays in two groups of 8 to 15 years old and 16 to 30 years old (G. Sarkisian, APO Chairman for Culture and Education, 23 March 2006).

providing support for, or opposing, activities that are perceived to be damaging to official political discourse.

To conclude, these ethno-cultural projects and the positive representation of cultural diversity coexist with and complement the local political discourse that sees non-Russian migration as potentially dangerous and a destructive factor for the region. In this way, the two policies do not contradict one another, but are compatible politically and organizationally (Osipov 2004: 18). As a result, this official approach is characterized by discursive strategies that produce ethnic categorizations, in which unwanted or 'problem' groups are excluded and some other ethnic groups are favoured within the framework of the positive representation of cultural diversity. For example, regional politicians in their public rhetoric occasionally praise 'well-assimilated ethnic diasporas' (Tsygankov 2003 cited in Popov 2005: 67), whilst imposing cultural differentiation between so-called 'ours' (*nashi*) and 'not ours' (*ne nashi*).[62]

---

[62] Gromov, ataman of the Kuban Cossacks, makes a distinction between 'Kuban Armenians' (*ours*) and 'Armenian migrants' (*not ours*) in *Armiane Kubani*, a film by Artem Erkanian (2005). Furthermore, in the Cossacks' 'indigenization' discourse, which has been used to present themselves as a part of the 'North Caucasus civilization', they include some native ethnic groups, such as the Adygh, but at the same time distance themselves from other non-Slavic ethnic groups (Popov 2005: 63-67).

The Armenian diaspora in Krasnodar krai: from past to present

Together with the Jewish, Tartar and Greek diasporas, the Armenian diaspora is one of the 'oldest' and largest diasporas in Russia.[63] According to the 2002 population census, there are 1,130,491 Armenians in Russia, constituting 4.1 per cent of Russia's population.[64] The Armenian diaspora was formed as a result of national and religious persecution, of genocide and forced resettlement of Armenians from Armenia in connection with a series of wars, beginning with the Arab conquest in the eighth century and Armenia's invasion by Seljuk Turks in the eleventh century (Ter-Sarkisiants 1995: 5). The formation of the Armenian diaspora in the North Caucasus took place in the eighteenth and nineteenth centuries, although the very first Hamshen Armenians came to this region in the eighth century (Kuznetsov 2008). At present, the Armenian diaspora in the Kuban region is characterized by a sub-ethnic diversity, including sub-ethnoses such as Hamshen Armenians or Circassian Armenians (*Cherkesogai*). Despite the diversity within the Armenian diaspora, all members of the Armenian diaspora have a shared history of migration and are united by a sense of co-ethnicity.[65]

The Armenian history of migration

The history of Armenian migration into the Kuban region can be seen in terms of five waves. The first wave took place in the late 1780s until the 1860s,

---

63 In Chapter One, it was argued that Armenians are as indigenous to this region as other people. For some parts of the Armenian population this is certainly true, since they have been living in Krasnodar krai for more than a century. Nonetheless, all Armenians belong to the Armenian diaspora in the sense that a diaspora is an ethnic community, which is formed on the basis of common cultural and ethnic references (Soysal 2000). Generally speaking, a diaspora is considered to be an ethnic community of people driven away from its homeland to other parts of the world by force or other catastrophic events (Cohen 1997). Armenians were driven away from their primordial homeland Armenia as a result of the 1915 genocide. A diaspora implies not just a part of one nation living among the representatives of another nation, but an ethnic community that has its own national characteristics (language, culture, consciousness), which it preserves and maintains.
64 The 2002 All-Russian Population Census. Online. Available HTTP: <http://www.perepis2002.ru> (accessed 12 December 2006).
65 The only exception is that of Hamshen, who were originally Armenians, but converted to Islam and qualify today as a separate ethnos. For a further discussion on Hamshens, see Kuznetsov (2000, 2008), Shahnazarian (2008).

when approximately three thousand Armenians came to the region from towns such as Astrakhan, Kizliar, Mozdok, as well as approximately 300 Persian Turkish Armenians (Simonian 2003: 160). This period was also characterized by a migration of the Circassian Armenians (*Cherkesogai*) to the region inhabiting some districts (*raiony*) under the control of the Russian Tsarist government.[66] As a result, the first Armenian settlements were founded in the Kuban region of which Armavir, founded in 1839, is considered to be the very first Armenian settlement in the Kuban region (Kuznetsov 2007b). Armenian communities were also established in bigger towns such as Novorossiisk, Anapa and Ekaterinodar.[67]

The second wave of migrants, comprising approximately thirty thousand people, came to the region at the end of the nineteenth century and the beginning of the twentieth century. Most of these migrants came from Turkey, mainly Hamshen Armenians, and only a small part came from Persia and Transcaucasia. During this period two different types of migrants can be identified: those who came for economic reasons and were attracted by the Russian government, and those who were forced to leave as a result of repression and the genocide at the hands of the Ottoman Empire. The peak of migration activity was reached at the end of the 1870s as a consequence of the Russian-Turkish War (1877-1878), in the 1890s when pogroms against Armenians in Turkey and Baku took place, and in 1915 to 1920 when a mass persecution of the Armenian population in Turkey occured (Ter-Sarkisiants 1995).

The third wave of migration took place in the 1950s, when most migrants settled in the *Anapskii raion* (district), mainly in the settlement of Gaikadzor. These were migrants from Georgia, so-called Akhalkalaki Armenians, named after the town of Akhalkalaki in Southern Georgia, and comprised less than 300 people (Simonian 2003). The fourth wave took place in the 1970s mainly

---

66 At present, the term Circassian Armenian has a conditional character, since many original elements of Circassian Armenian culture had been rooted out by the beginning of the twentieth century. Some Circassian Armenians became part of the multi-ethnic environment in the North Caucasus or completely assimilated into Russian culture, while others assimilated and started to identify themselves with Adyghs (Simonian 2003: 138).

67 Ekaterinodar was the official name of Krasnodar before the Bolsheviks came to power.

from two regions: those who came from Azerbaijan, the so-called Karabakh Armenians, and those from Central Asia, such as Kazakhstan, Kirgizia and Uzbekistan, for instance Hamshens. They primarily came to Krasnodar krai for economic reasons and their number ranged from five to seven thousand people (Kuznetsov 2000). From the end of the 1980s to the mid-1990s, additional numbers of Armenian migrants (approximately 300,000) resettled in the Kuban region as a result of the eruption of ethnic conflicts across the former Soviet Union, when they had to leave so-called conflict areas, such as Azerbaijan, Abkhazia, Ferghana Valley (Uzbekistan and Kirgizia) and Chechnya (Simonian 2003). After these conflicts, there were also migrants who came as a result of poor economic conditions in the newly formed republics, from Armenia, Georgia, Kazakhstan and republics of Central Asia.

Since the Armenian diaspora in the North Caucasus has been formed by various migration processes, there is diversity within the Armenian community, evident in different dialects, divisions into various Armenian sub-ethnoses or distinctions made according to place of origin. In particular, a sense of community based on place of origin (*zemliachestvo*) has increased in importance as a result of the migration into the region beginning in the late Soviet era. First, there are Azerbaijani Armenians who came to the region in the 1980s during the Karabakh conflict. They are subdivided into Armenians who came from *Shaumianovskii raion* (district) in Azerbaijan and those from Kirovabad. Second, there are Karabakh Armenians (Artsakh Armenians), who can be subdivided according to the towns in which they used to live, such as Baku, Martuni, Martakert, Hadrut Stepanakert or Shushi. Third, Georgian Armenians are represented by Dzhavakh and Abkhazian local groups, among them Armenians from Tbilisi and Akhalkalaki are in the majority.[68] The Abkhazian group mostly consists of Hamshen Armenians, who are subdivided according to their locality in Abkhazia, such as Sukhumi, Gudauta, Gagra and others (Simonian 2003: 145). For Dzhavakh Armenians, divisions are mainly formed according to the territorial-administrative divisions in Georgia, such as Akhalkalaki, Akhaltsikhe, Ninotsminda *raiony* (districts). Finally, there are Armenians from Armenia, who left Armenia after the

---

68 They primarily came to Krasnodar krai in the 1990s, when socio-economic conditions worsened in Georgia.

earthquake in 1988 and after socio-economic conditions worsened in the 1990s.

Russian policy towards Armenians

The policies of the Russian government as well as local authorities in relation to the Armenian diaspora have changed over the years. Initially, the Russian government had an interest in establishing Armenian settlements in this region. During the period of the first wave of migrants, during the late eighteenth and the beginning of the nineteenth centuries, the Russian government introduced laws that stimulated this migration process and attracted Armenians to the region (Khachaturian 2000). Those who came received many privileges, such as the right to organize their own system of self-government in their ethnic settlements, for example in Armavir (Simonian 2003: 162). At the end of the 1880s, when migration took on an uncontrolled character, the Russian government started to restrict earlier privileges and even introduced forced resettlement for some Armenians (Khachaturian 2000). As a result of these restrictions, in some areas of the North Caucasus the number of Armenians halved, whereas in the Kuban region the number of Armenians increased.

In the context of the changes in the official approach of the Russian government, the role of the Armenian Apostolic Church is worth noting.[69] Simonian (2003) notes that of the different confessions amongst Armenians, only adherents to the Armenian Apostolic Church were able to maintain a strong sense of community. In the history of the Armenian diaspora in the Kuban region, the Armenian Apostolic Church often served as a 'mediator' for the Kuban diaspora with other Armenian diasporas in the colonies and the homeland. This functional role of the Armenian Church was perceived negatively by the Russian/Soviet government; since it was considered the main obstacle to the policy of Russification (Simonian 2003). The Russian

---

69　The Armenian diaspora is not only diverse as a result of in-migration from other regions into the North-West Caucasus over the last centuries, but also in terms of confessional orientations within the Armenian diaspora. Whereas most Armenians are followers of the Armenian Church, some profess Catholicism or Greek-Orthodoxy, and Hamshens Islam. In history, the Church fulfilled a culture-preserving role and even today the Church plays a significant role in the Armenian community life in Krasnodar.

government thus took measures to weaken the influence of the Church, such as removing the Armenian clergy from the education process in national schools in the 1870s until the 1890s and confiscating Church property in 1903.[70]

When in 1915 the number of Armenians in the north-western parts of the Caucasus increased again, the authorities took measures to limit migration. Nonetheless, these measures were unsuccessful and the number of Armenian refugees increased, especially during the crisis period of 1917 to 1920. According to Simonian (2003: 163), ethnic minorities received the right to territorial self-administration, as part of the nationalities policy in the Soviet Union and, thus, twenty Armenian rural councils and one national district (*raion*) were founded in the North-West Caucasus. However, from the end of the 1930s onwards the politics of autonomy were continually restricted in the Soviet Union and in the 1960s all national districts (*raiony*) were liquidated in Krasnodar krai (ibid.). After the fall of the Soviet Union, the local authorities in Russia again received the right to self-administration and additional powers. At the same time, the number of Armenian refugees in the North-West Caucasus increased as a result of ethnic conflicts. Owing to the absence of federal laws regulating migration processes, local authorities introduced stricter territorial politics concerning migration.[71]

The role of Armenian voluntary associations
Armenian voluntary associations have played an important role in the formation of the Armenian diaspora in Kuban. Like other ethnic groups living outside the boundaries of their original homeland, throughout history Armenians in Krasnodar krai have tried to form a sense of community and belonging by preserving traditions and promoting their culture. Initially, this took place through the formation of religious and educational institutions. Nevertheless, the Armenian community's national and cultural evolution was

---

70 Most of the information on the Armenian Apostolic Church in Krasnodar krai was obtained from an interview with Priest Dr. Ter-Daniel Kukuian, 22 May 2006.
71 For example, Nikolai Kondratenko, elected to the post of regional governor in 1996, introduced the restrictive law 'On movement and residence in the territory of Krasnodar krai', which generally made it harder for any new migrants to get permanent residence rights in the krai (McAuley 1997).

spurred by the activities of various Armenian voluntary associations, which substantially contributed to the community's well-being as a whole. Even today, Armenian voluntary associations have not lost their significance and so their past and present role needs to be considered more closely.

Armenian voluntary associations first appeared in Krasnodar krai at the end of the nineteenth century. In 1889, for example, a branch of the 'Armenian Charity in the Caucasus' (ACC) (*Armianskoe blagotvoritel'noe obshchestvo na Kavkaze*), originally founded in 1881 in Tbilisi, was opened in the Kuban region (Simonian 2003: 33). As stated by Simonian (2003: 33-34), the ACC was active in Krasnodar krai by 1882, making short visits to Armavir and Ekaterinodar to collect donations given by members of the organization. Moreover, the political activity of the Armenian diaspora in the North-West Caucasus increased substantially with the help of national parties, such as '*Gnchak*' or '*Dashnaktsutiun*' (Karapetian 2006).[72] The growing political influence of Armenian national political parties and the subsequent rise in ethno-nationalism in the Kuban region resulted in measures taken by the Tsar's administration that restricted the rights of Russian (*rossiiskie*) Armenians. According to Simonian (2003: 37), this led to the closure of Armenian schools in the Caucasus in 1896, as well as Armenian voluntary associations in 1898 and, finally, the introduction of a law on the confiscation of Armenian Church property in 1903.[73]

From 1907 onwards, however, various Armenian voluntary associations were reopened or established anew in Krasnodar krai, including the first two ethnic voluntary womens' associations, the 'Armenian Charity for Women' in Maikop (*Armianskoe zhenskoe blagotvoritel'noe obshchestvo*) and the 'Armenian Charity for Ladies' in Ekaterinodar (*Armianskoe damskoe blagotvoritel'noe obshchestvo g. Ekaterinodara*) (Simonian 2003:34). The activities of these voluntary associations were primarily aimed at education as well as helping orphans and children from poor families. Membership fees

---

72 The very first political participation of Armenians in the region dates back to the mid-1890s, when the first editions of the newspaper '*Mshak*' were printed in Armavir and Ekaterinodar (Simonian 2003: 36).
73 In 1900, for example, former members of the Armavir branch of the ACC attempted to organize their own independent voluntary association, but permission for this was refused by the regional administration in the same year (Simonian 2003: 34).

and cultural events, such as concerts, paid for these activities. Armenian voluntary associations' activities not only focused on the well-being of the Armenian community, but also generally served the improvement of education in the region and the well-being of the region as a whole.

During the Soviet period, the Armenian Church as a structural organization was liquidated, together with Armenian political parties and other voluntary associations.[74] For thirty-two years there was no Armenian Church in Krasnodar and only two Armenian Churches functioned in the whole of the North-West Caucasus. Furthermore, the influence of the government affected all aspects of Armenian diasporic life, although Armenians were granted the right to develop their culture to some extent, for example, printing Armenian newspapers and establishing Armenian educational institutions. Nonetheless, between the 1950s and the 1980s Armenian schools, voluntary organizations and newspapers were closed again, as part of the new nationalities policy in the Soviet Union.

From the end of the 1980s onwards, as a result of the process of national-cultural renaissance and the presence of a strong Armenian diaspora, numerous Armenian voluntary associations were established anew.[75] At present, Armenians are actively engaged in developing and maintaining a strong community life in the region and Armenian voluntary associations are active in all main towns of the region. Nevertheless, Koriakin (2006: 69) argues that the majority of these organizations are unable to play a significant role in the Armenian community life and society as a whole. As a result of the political climate in the region, they can respond only to the needs of a small group of people. Although this might be true to some extent, especially in smaller towns of the region, personal contacts with the *Armianskaia*

---

74 In Ekaterinodar the first Armenian Church was founded in 1801 and in 1922 there were three Armenian Churches in the city, of which two were closed in the same year (Priest Dr. Ter-Daniel Kukuian, 22 May 2006).

75 For example, the *Armianskaia Pashkovskaia Obshchina* (APO) was first founded by local Armenians in Krasnodar in 1992 and was active until 1997. However, in 2003 the APO re-emerged again owing to the initiative of local Armenians, who provided substantial financial support to refurbish its premises in order to conduct cultural events, Armenian language lessons etc. At present, the APO has 200 members. This information was obtained from an interview conducted with the head of this organization (G. Serobian, 12 April 2006).

Pashkovskaia Obshchina (APO) in Krasnodar suggest that the APO contributes significantly to Armenian community life and is able to reach those people who choose to get involved.[76]

These Armenian voluntary associations represent the interests of Armenian migrants as well as local Armenians (Koriakin 2006: 69). This stands in contrast to suggestions by the regional authorities that there are tensions between the two:

> Those who live legally here, Armenians, Georgians and other nationalities - these are our people, our fellow-countrymen (*zemliaki*), these are Kuban people and we don't make any distinctions. What I am talking about is illegal migrants, those who came to Kuban in the last two, three or five years, and I know that there are already tensions with those who came from Armenia' (Tkachev 2004).[77]

Such official discourse artificially divides Armenian into new and old - 'us' and 'them', to justify discriminatory practices. This line is also maintained by Gromov, the ataman of the Kuban Cossacks, who suggests:

> When speaking about Armenians, we clearly distinguish between those who are our local Armenians, they are 'ours,' and those new ones, who have come in the last 10 to 15 years to the region and whom even local Armenians don't accept as such.[78]

The question of internal divisions within the Armenian diaspora, therefore, is more complex than suggested by the local authorities and is examined in more detail in Chapter Three.

---

76 The main aim of the APO is to preserve Armenian culture and traditions amongst young people living in Krasnodar. Therefore, apart from organizing cultural events, such as a historic discussion club and also conferences, Armenian language and traditional Armenian dance are taught. Furthermore, in 2005 the APO actively participated in solving social and legal questions and continually worked with the Armenian Consul in Sochi and, for example, enabled Armenian citizens, living in Krasnodar krai to participate in the referendum on changing the Constitution of the Republic of Armenia. The organization is also active in maintaining close contacts with other Armenian communities in Krasnodar krai (Head of the APO, G. Serobian, 12 April 2006).
77 Tkachev cited in *Armiane Kubani* film by Artem Erkanian (2005).
78 *Armiane Kubani* film by Artem Erkanian (2005).

Figure 2.2 St. Mesrop and St. Saak Armenian Apostolic Church in Krasnodar (built in 2011)

Figure 2.3 St. Hovannes Armenian Apostolic Church in Krasnodar

YOUTH IDENTITIES IN RUSSIA 81

Figure 2.4 The premises of the APO in Krasnodar

The Republic of Adyghea

The autonomous Republic of Adyghea is a federal subject of Russia located within Krasnodar krai. It is situated in the foothills of the Caucasus Mountains and geographically divided between plains in the north and mountains in the south. Both in Krasnodar krai and the Republic of Adyghea, regional politics are structured around the discourse of 'interethnic relations'. However, while the political discourse in Krasnodar krai is characterized by the coexistence of a politics of cultural diversity alongside discriminatory practices with regard to non-Russian migration, the political discourse in Adyghea is defined by an ethno-nationalist ideology that reflects the interests of Adygh people. Such rhetoric is mainly spurred by the fact that Adyghs, although the titular nationality in the Republic of Adyghea, remain a minority group.[79] The political discourse in Adyghea, however, leaves room for the participation of ethnic minorities in the political processes in the republic.

People and migration

In 2002, 445,000 people were living on the territory of Adyghea which covers 7800 square km.[80] Of these, 240,000 are urban (52.6 per cent) and 205,300 (47.4 per cent) rural inhabitants (Smirnov 2006: 2). The urban population is concentrated in the two main cities of the Republic, Maikop, the capital, and Adygheisk with 190,000 and 13,000 respectively. As in Krasnodar, and across Russia, the Republic is affected by population decline: in 1996 this decline totalled -1.9 per cent, in 1997 -1.63 per cent, and in 1998 -1.61 per cent. Moreover, in 1998 population decline was 1.2 times higher than migration growth.[81] Over 80 different ethnic groups live in Adyghea, where Russians constitute 64.4 per cent (288,280) of the population, Adyghs 24.1 per cent (108,115), Armenians 3.4 per cent and Ukrainians 3.2 per cent.[82]

Like Krasnodar krai, Adyghea's history is characterized by large-scale migration. The Caucasian War (1816-1846) was a crucial event for Adyghs,

---

79 In numerical terms, they are a minority group, but politically, they are the dominant ethnic group in the republic.
80 'Spravka Izvestii: Respublika Adygeia', *Izvestiia*, 20 March 2007, p. 6.
81 The 2002 All-Russian Population Census. Online. Available HTTP: <http://www.perepis2002.ru> (accessed 12 December 2006).
82 'Spravka Izvestii: Respublika Adygeia', *Izvestiia*, 20 March 2007, p 6.

as a result of which many Circassians left the region for the Ottoman Empire. After the 1917 revolution, the Soviet government pursued a similar nationalities policy in Adyghea as in other regions populated with non-Russian minorities. During the period of industrialization, the Soviet government established large industrial enterprises and brought Russian speakers from other parts of the country to work in Adyghea. As a result, the proportion of ethnic Russians was artificially increased. In 1922, when Adyghea was established as an autonomous province (*oblast'*), Adyghs comprised the majority of the population, yet by the start of World War Two, there were far more Russians than Adyghs in the republic (Smirnov 2006: 3). This process radically changed the ethnic composition of the region and even today, Adyghea's population is overwhelmingly Russian; the titular group comprises only slightly over 20 per cent of the total population.

The collapse of the USSR gave a second impetus to migration into Adyghea; people from conflict areas in the former Soviet Union, such as Abkhazia, Azerbaijan and Chechnya, but also from Armenia, came to the republic. However, Armenians came to this region long before the demise of the Soviet Union, for example, during the nineteenth century when the Russian government deported Circassians to Turkey, Armenians migrated into the region and these migration processes continued during Soviet times and accelerated in the post-Soviet period. The post-Soviet period is also characterized by a return of Circassians living in diaspora. For example, one Adygh group (a total of 156 families) from Kosovo returned to Adyghea in 1998 (Smirnov 2006: 4). They were descendants of those who had left the Caucasus in the late nineteenth century and settled in the Ottoman Empire, which then included Kosovo. Although at present there are approximately a thousand repatriates living in Adyghea, their repatriation was not easy and they have encountered difficulties, such as finding employment.

Adyghea and its people: a historical background

The Circassians,[83] or Adyghs, as they name themselves, trace their descent from the indigenous people of the North-West Caucasus, which is their historical homeland, or *'Xekwzch'* (Old Country), as it is referred to by them (Jaimoukha 2001: 19). In the Soviet period, the North-West Caucasus was divided into many administrative units of different sizes. The majority of Circassians were found in four of these units, in each of which they were officially designated by a distinct name: Kabardinians in the Kabardino-Balkarian Republic, Cherkess in the Karachai Cherkess Republic, Adyghs in Adyghea and Shapsugh in their nominal area situated in Krasnodar krai on the Black Sea coast (ibid.). Overall, Adyghs are predominantly concentrated in their three titular republics: Kabardino-Balkaria, Karachai-Cherkess Republic and Adyghea.[84] Whereas 24.1 per cent of Adyghs live in the Republic of Adyghea, 25 per cent (50,000) of the total Adygh population, live in Krasnodar krai (Jaimoukha 2001: 21). Adyghs comprise only 0.5 per cent of Russia's population and about 7 per cent of that of the North Caucasus, and less than 15 per cent of the population of the North-West Caucasus.[85]

The Adyghs first emerged as a coherent entity in the tenth century, although references to them exist much earlier, since their ancestors are

---

83 The term Circassians, the English equivalent of the Turkic 'Cherkess', denotes all or part of the indigenous peoples of the Caucasus. There is no agreement as to which of those nations the appellation refers to, but three denotations are in use. The first, the most comprehensive, includes all the native peoples of the North Caucasus. The second use excludes the Eastern Caucasians, the Chechens and Dagestanis, and encompasses only North-Western Caucasians: the Adyghs, Abkhaz-Abazas, and the now extinct Ubykhs. The most restrictive sense refers only to the Adyghs, who are composed of many tribes who speak mutually intelligible dialects that make up Adigabze, the Circassian language (Jaimoukha 2001: 11).
84 There are no recent figures on the numbers of Circassians in the Caucasus, but according to Jaimoukha (2001: 21) the number could be more than 800,000 people. This number excludes approximately 50,000 Abazas living in the Karachai-Cherkess Republic. In addition, there are many Circassian communities in Turkey, Syria, Jordan, Israel, Egypt, Libya, Germany and the USA. Their precise numbers, however, are not known. According to Jaimoukha (2001: 23) their numbers could range between one to five million people. In this respect, the Adygh community in Turkey is the largest in the world and some estimate that their numbers could amount to more than four million people.
85 That the number is so small can be explained by a fragmentation within the Circassians as an ethnic group into several entities and nominal differentiations.

thought to have been tribes of Meots, Sindys, Acheis, Zikhis, Kasoges and Kerketys, who lived in the North-West Caucasus and along the Black Sea coast of the Caucasus since the first century BC (Smirnov 2006: 8). Their language belongs to the North-West Caucasian (Abkhaz-Adygh) group of Caucasian languages. The formation of the Adyghs evolved over centuries, during which Adyghs had close contact with other tribes mainly from Asia, such as the Cimmerians, Scythians, and Sarmatians.

Contemporary Russian-Adygh relations cannot be understood outside the history of the Caucasian War in the nineteenth century, which significantly changed the ethnic map of the North Caucasus. Even though Adyghs' first contacts with Russians date back to the tenth century, the eighteenth century saw a new stage in Russian-Adygh relations (Smirnov 2006: 10). This was the period when Adyghs and Russians became open enemies and armed opponents, caused by the Russian imperial policy in the entire North Caucasus. It took almost a whole century to completely subjugate the region, forcing many Adyghs to emigrate to the Ottoman Empire. Up to 1.5 million emigrated, leaving only 10 per cent of the Adygh population in the region (cited in Shami 1998: 623).[86]

When the Bolsheviks came to power, Adyghea launched a national movement aimed at creating an independent republic within the newly formed Soviet state; this was granted on 27 July 1922 when Adyghea became the Adyghea Autonomous Province within Krasnodar krai (Smirnov 2006: 13). During the early years of its autonomy, Adyghea lacked its own capital; its administration was located in the city of Krasnodar, the capital of Krasnodar krai. At that time, Adyghs predominated in the Adyghea Autonomous Province, but in the 1930s, the Soviet authorities began a programme of Russification and started to bring ethnic Russians into the region. This order was given under the pretext of providing the region with its own capital and eventually resulted in the domination of ethnic Russians over the indigenous Adyghs in the republic.

During Soviet times, despite the Russian majority, key government positions in the region were still occupied by Adyghs, enabling Adygh leaders

---

86   Shami's information is based on three different sources, Berkok (1958) and Karpat (1972, 1990).

to demand direct financing for Adyghea from Moscow, bypassing the Krasnodar administration. These attempts finally succeeded in the early 1980s and were strengthened by the federal law on the 'Adyghea Autonomous Region (*oblast'*)', adopted by the Supreme Soviet of the RSFSR on 2 December 1981 (Smirnov 2006: 13). Nonetheless, the break-up of the Soviet Union opened a new page in Adygh history, when on 28 June 1991 the Republic of Adyghea declared its sovereignty, separated from Krasnodar krai and drafted its Constitution on 10 March 1995. During these first years of sovereignty, the newly elected President and Communist Party leader, Aslan Dzhamirov, not only strengthened Adyghea's sovereignty, but also introduced a law on repatriation allowing the descendants of those deported at the end of the nineteenth century to return to the republic.

Islam - the religion of Adyghea
Under the rule of the Byzantine Empire, Christianity was widespread among Adyghs, but Islam started to penetrate Circassia (Adyghea) at the end of the fifteenth century when the Byzantine Empire was conquered by Seljuk Turks and consequently disappeared (Klimenko *et al.* 2009). Seljuk Turks and Crimean Tatars initially attempted to impose Islam on Adyghs by force, but encountered strong resistance forcing them to change their tactics. Thus, missionaries and merchants were sent to Circassia and, as a result of these efforts, Sunni Islam took root among Adyghs in the late sixteenth century. The acceptance of Islam by Adyghs accelerated the process of orientation towards Turkey, which was also facilitated by economic relations, including sea trade between the Turks and Ubykhs, an Adygh tribe that lived along the Black Sea coast. One Adygh historian, Samir Khotko, argued that there were two main reasons for the success of Islam in Circassia: first, the increasingly imperial policy of Russia in the South, which caused resistance from Circassia; and second, the Ottoman Empire's intense campaigns, which turned Circassia into a political, military, and economic partner by the beginning of the seventeenth century (Smirnov 2006: 9).

In Soviet times, only a small number of Adyghs continued to practice Islamic customs within their homes.[87] Many Islamic traditions either ceased to play an important role in Adygh society or were transformed, resulting in a so-called 'dirty' (*griaznyi*) form of Islam in Adyghea (Babich 2004: 68). Although Islam is more widespread in the Republic of Adyghea at present, Khanakhu (2001) maintains that the rebirth of Islam is not as significant as the rebirth of Adygh culture in the Republic of Adyghea. Islam traditionally has played a minor role for Adyghs. Instead, Khanakhu (2001) argues that it is the moral code of *Adyghage* based on long traditions that has retained its prominence for ethnic identification in contemporary Adygh society.

Adyghage – an ethical system based on long-standing 'ethnic' traditions is not peculiar to Adygh society. In other societies in the North Caucasus, cultural traditions have also experienced a renaissance. Such a trend is evident in the Republic of Abkhazia, for example, where the preservation of Abkhazian traditions occurs via '*Apsuara*' or 'mentality' (Sabirova 2008).[88] Like in other Caucasian societies, in Adygh society the traditional system of ethics and morals is a normative institution, which shores up solidarity, mutual understanding and recognition. The traditional system of morality and ethics is central to the preservation of Adygh ethnic culture and group belonging and is a category that defines Adygh ethnic identity.

Notwithstanding this, in the last fifteen to twenty years many more mosques have been built and the numbers of Muslim communities have increased in the republic. Currently, there are sixteen Islamic religious groups on the territory of the republic (Klimenko *et al.* 2009). In 1992, the first mosque was reopened and by 2004 thirty mosques existed and as many Muslim communities were officially registered (Babich 2004: 65). According to official statistics 103,000 Muslims live in the Republic of Adyghea and 160,000 Muslims in Krasnodar krai, among them 20,000 Adyghs (ibid: 65). While there are youth organizations in Maikop and Adygheisk, rural Muslim communities mainly consist of elderly people. Although one can observe a rise in practicing Islam, the religion has not gained a stronghold in Adyghea.

---

87   There are no exact numbers available on how many Adyghs continued to practice Islam during Soviet times
88   Like '*Adyghage*', '*Apsuara*' is an ethical system, a code of norms of traditional Abkhazian culture (Sabirova 2008).

According to Babich (2004), the reasons for this are two-fold: first, there are not enough spiritual leaders in Adyghea and not every community has *imams*; second and most importantly, most Adyghs are either indifferent to Islam or are against Islam altogether. The latter concurs with Khanakhu's (2001) argument that Islam has always played a minor role in Adygh belonging.

The process of Islamization in Adyghea has been strongly influenced from the outside (Klimenko *et al.* 2009), although not as significantly as in other republics, such as Karbadino-Balkaria and Dagestan (cf. Yemelianova 2001, 2005, 2007). The new Islamic leaders in Adyghea can be divided into three groups. The first group consists of Adygh repatriates, who returned from the Middle East to Adyghea in the 1990s and, in some cases, remain active. One example is Ibrahim Nikhad-khadzhi, who is *imam* of the mosque in Maikop and began his work with Adyghs in the early 1990s when he still lived in Damascus and received young people from the Caucasus (Babich 2004: 66). There are also other Adyghs from Syria, such as Faiz Autaev, who was the first to publish Islamic literature in Maikop. The second group of new Islamic leaders are Adyghs from Kosovo, who returned to their historic homeland in 1989, but received their Islamic education while living in Kosovo. According to Babich (2004: 67), the third group of spiritual leaders are those local Adyghs who received their Islamic education in the Middle East or the North Caucasus and started to play a significant role in religious life in the second half of the 1990s.

In recent years, some of the spiritual leaders of the Muslim community have attempted to introduce Sufi Islam. At the same time, they have resisted fundamentalist Islam, or Wahhabism, which is prevalent in the north-eastern Caucasus, in Dagestan and Chechnya (cf. Yemelianova 2007). This attempt to introduce Sufi Islam is supported by the Council for Muslims of the Republic of Adyghea and Krasnodar krai (*Dukhovnoe upravlenie musulman Adygei i Krasnodarskogo kraia*), although the majority of people prefer to keep Islamic practices as they have developed over the centuries in Adyghea. Generally speaking, the mufti of the Council think that Islam in Adyghea ('dirty' Islam), preserved from Soviet times, should be limited and Sufi Islam, which does not consist of Adygh and other traditions, should be spread amongst Adygh youth. According to Babich's (2004: 68) study, the introduction of Sufi Islam, for example, would mean a restriction on Adygh dancing culture, a prohibition on alcohol consumption during celebrations and a restriction on the old tradition of bride kidnapping.

Figure 2.5 The mosque in Adygheisk

Adyghea's current political situation
The political system in Adyghea is based on local self-government established according to long-standing traditions of communal life at the level of rural and urban councils (Khadzhebiekov and Poliakova 1994). Since the Republic of Adyghea came into existence, authorities in the republic have tried to create structures that are in line with traditional norms and which are accepted by the majority of Adyghea's ethnically diverse society. Thus, the legal, institutional, political and other functional characteristics of the self-

government system are rooted in the old customs of the republic's people (Polyakova 2002: 193). Traditional bodies, such as the Adygh mediation court, the village khases (village councils) and the council of elders have been used successfully to defuse ethnic tensions in situations that could have escalated into conflict. A political structure formed according to cultural traditions in order to manage cultural diversity is not peculiar for Adyghea only; other Caucasian republics have also tried to create political structures according to traditional norms. Dagestan, for example, is governed co-operatively by elites drawn from segmented kinship structures based on the tradition of *djamaats* (Ware and Kisriev 2001).[89]

Adyghea's recent history is largely defined by a struggle to keep its autonomy. The rationale behind the idea of subsuming Adyghea into Krasnodar krai is two-fold: first Adyghea is entirely surrounded by the territory of Krasnodar krai and the majority of the population are ethnically Russian; second and most importantly, are economic reasons. Krasnodar has been touted as an economic success story, with its Black Sea tourism industry and fertile soil, despite the fact that regional variation is stark; less fortunate districts are impoverished and suffer from high unemployment. Adyghea, by contrast, is the fifteenth most subsidized federal unit with 58.1 per cent of its internal budget coming directly from Moscow (Voznaya 2006).

Since Adyghea's independence, Krasnodar krai's authorities have opposed Adyghea's sovereignty, mainly for economic reasons. For example, immediately after Adyghea's declaration of sovereignty in 1991, questions of the ownership of ports, tourist areas and the two main roads that run from Krasnodar krai to the Black Sea coast were heavily debated. The Adygh government wanted a share of the profit that the roads generated for Krasnodar, which enraged the Krasnodar authorities. But conflict ceased due to good relations between Kondratenko, the governor of Krasnodar krai, and

---

89 A *djamaat* is a community organized politically and defined along territorial and historical lines (Ware and Kisriev 2001: 109). Typically, it is a village or a group of villages with an historical connection. Each *djamaat* consists of a few, and sometimes as many as ten, different tribal and ancestral structures, known as *tuhums*. Each *tuhum* is an extended and closely connected family. Governments of the *djamaats* traditionally consisted of councils of elders drawn from each of the constituent *tuhums*. This system of *djamaats* dominated Dagestani life prior to Tsarist and Soviet regimes.

Dzhamirov, acting President of Adyghea at that time (Smirnov 2006: 15). In the end, Adyghs were granted the right to sell their goods on the road, but all official profits would go to Krasnodar.[90]

Although at first the unification drive of Krasnodar krai's authorities was mainly for economic reasons, it quickly became part of Adyghea's rhetoric of identity politics, since for Adyghs it would mean losing their privileged standing. Murat Berzegov, head of the Circassian Congress, views the possibility of Adyghea losing its independent status as a breach of national rights (cited in Abelsky 2007) reminiscent of the period of the Russian-Caucasian War (1832-1864) and subsequent attempts by the Russian Empire to colonize Adyghea. In addition, Adygh elites stress that unification would mean the eradication of the republic.

The idea of subsuming Adyghea into Krasnodar krai re-emerged, however, in 2004 in the context of Putin's plans to streamline the Russian Federation by reducing the number of federation subjects by means of territorial mergers. On 29 December 2004, Alexander Tkachev made a statement in a press conference that it would be economically feasible to integrate Adyghea into Krasnodar krai. This statement was strongly opposed by Adyghs and drew strong protest from the Circassian Congress and Adygh *Khase* (Adygh Council). By the end of spring 2005, Russian officials stopped mentioning the possibility of unification in public, whereas in Adyghea, on the contrary, discussions on this issue continued. Nevertheless, in 2005, the Circassian Congress asked the Council of Europe, 'to immediately intercede concerning the situation in Adyghea to preserve its sovereignty' (Smirnov 2006: 16). In January 2006, some Adygh activists organized a picket in Maikop to preserve and strengthen the status of Adyghea as an independent entity in the Russian Federation.

Although Adyghea's integration into Krasnodar krai is opposed by the majority, especially by major Adygh/Circassian organizations (Circassian Congress and Adygh *Khase*), its inclusion is supported by the Russian population in the republic, especially the Union of Slavs of Adyghea (SSA), who argue for an inclusion on the basis of political factors, including alleged

---

90   This friendly relationship could be explained by the weakness of the Krasnodar authorities, which did not have Moscow's support at the time of the agreement.

discrimination against ethnic Slavs (Purdenko 2008, Sokolov-Mitrich 2007). Despite the fact that Adyghs make up less than a third of the population, the SSA argues that the titular nationality has taken control of policy, the economy and culture in the republic (Voznaya 2006). On 13 January 2007, the new President of Adyghea, Aslancheryy Tkhakushinov, was sworn into his new post and during his inauguration speech he clearly expressed his opposition to subsuming the two regions, stalling this idea for the moment.[91] The prospects of integrating Adyghea into Krasnodar krai at present are unlikely. As Voznaya (2006) notes that the federal centre is hardly interested in risking the destabilization of another part of the North Caucasus, irrespective of whether threats of ethnic conflict and strained internal relations from Adygh organizations are substantiated.

Adyghea's integration into Krasnodar krai could jeopardize some aspects of the republic's political structure based on traditional norms that enable ethnic minorities' political participation and is, therefore, a large part of the ethno-cultural associations' agenda. For example, the unification problem made the Circassian Congress a very influential body in Adygh society (Smirnov 2006: 18).[92] The rising strength and popularity of the Congress was only possible because of the full support it received from local authorities who had a vested interest in its activity. Together with the Adygh Khase (Adygh Council), the Congress mobilized the Adygh diaspora during the December 2004 and January 2005 crisis. In 2005, the Circassian Congress became the main organization openly fighting attempts to subsume Adyghea into Krasnodar krai.

The Adygh *Khase* is a close ally of the Circassian Congress, but this organization, at least its leadership, is more closely associated with the Adygh authorities. Unlike the Congress, the Adygh *Khase* has a well-developed network in Adygh villages, as well as in the diaspora. Following Tkachev's statement in December 2004, Adygh *Khase* organized a

---

91 'New Adygeya President Sworn In,' Radio Free Europe Liberty/ Radio Liberty, 16 January 2007. Online. Available HTTP: <http://www.rferl.org/newsline/2007/01/01-rus/rus-160107.asp> accessed 27 January 2007).

92 The Circassian Congress was founded by a group of Adygh intellectuals and former Adygh volunteers who had taken part in the war in Abkhazia in 1992-93, fighting for the Abkhaz.

Committee to defend Adyghea's Constitution and in May 2006 the organization, together with the Circassian Congress, held an Assembly of Adygh people in Maikop, which adopted a resolution that declared that Adyghs would boycott a referendum on the status of Adyghea (Smirnov 2006: 19). Nevertheless, the Adygh *Khase* is not as consistent and united in the struggle for Adygh sovereignty as the Circassian Congress.

Despite some differences, both the Adygh *Khase* and the Circassian Congress are close allies in defending Adygh sovereignty and have the same opponent – the Union of Slavs. The Union of Slavs of Adyghea was established in 1991 as an organization to protect the rights of the Russian-speaking residents in the republic. The leaders, Nina Konovalova and Vladimir Karataev, were deputies of the first Adygh parliament. Konovalova ran for Adyghea's presidency in 2002, but received only 10 per cent of the vote (Smirnov 2006: 19). The main aim of the Slav Union is to bring Adyghea back to Krasnodar krai since the Adygh government, as the organization claims, ignores the interests of the local Russians who constitute the majority in the region.

The situation started to change slightly when Vladimir Putin came to power in Moscow and Alexandr Tkachev was elected to the post of governor in Krasnodar krai. In 2005, on the eve of the upcoming parliamentary election, the Union and its leaders launched a large-scale campaign directed at the Russian population of the region, stressing the idea that all the problems of the Russians living in Adyghea could be solved if the republic was to merge with Krasnodar krai. During the last parliamentary elections held in March 2006, the Slav Union candidates were included on the list of the Party of Manufacturers and Entrepreneurs (PME). Despite some progress, Natalia Konovalova was the only leader of the Union of Slavs to be elected to the Adygh parliament. In total, PME and the Communist party, who also support the idea of a merger, received only 33 per cent of the seats in the parliament (Smirnov 2006: 20).

In conclusion, it can be said that the political arrangements in the Republic of Adyghea, based on old traditions, have left room for ethnic voluntary associations to actively participate in political discourse. This is especially accentuated by the long-standing debate on Adyghea's integration into

Krasnodar krai, where all major ethnic organizations are engaged in resolving this problem. Although there are many supporters of the idea of Adyghea becoming part of Krasnodar krai, the Circassian Congress and Adygh *Khase*, purely Adygh ethnic organizations, are most active in this process, since they strongly oppose such a possibility. Hence, the Union of Slavs and other political forces of Adyghea who side with the idea of a merger, expect support from the Russian authorities, which could be forthcoming at some point in the future, depending on Moscow's plans.

Conclusions
Both Krasnodar krai and Adyghea have political regimes that are defined by discourses of interethnic relations, although those discourses are different. In Krasnodar krai the political discourse is defined by the ambiguity of restrictive (discriminatory) non-Russian migration politics and the politics of cultural diversity. Such an ambiguity is a consequence of Soviet multiculturalism where cultural diversity was promoted on the basis of a primordial understanding of ethnicity, and each ethnic group was seen as distinct. In contrast, the political discourse in Adyghea is characterized by an ethno-nationalist ideology that reflects the interests of Adygh people, yet, at the same time, leaves room for the participation of ethnic minorities in political processes in this republic. The political discourses of Krasnodar krai and Adyghea have affected the relationships between different ethnic groups as well as identity politics at large. It has led to a strong sense of ethnic belonging for both Armenians and Adyghs. As for Adyghs; this is mainly inspired by the fact that they are a titular minority in 'their' republic. In contrast, Armenians in Krasnodar krai are considered only partly indigenous as a consequence of 'ethnic' categorizations in the political discourse and therefore are not fully included in the political discourse in Krasnodar krai. This official approach has spurred the formation of a strong Armenian diaspora in the region, so that many Armenians try to actively engage with Armenian community life creating their own space under these political conditions.

It is argued that this political background to the region is a significant dimension in the construction of Armenian and Adygh youth cultural identities.

Being situated in this particular ethnocentric context leads to a strong sense of ethnic belonging amongst young Armenians and Adyghs, which in part reproduces ethnocentric political discourses. A strong sense of ethnic belonging does not necessarily rule out cosmopolitanism as an identity resource for young adults. The influence of other dimensions involved in the construction of youth cultural identities, such as family and ethnic belonging, is examined in subsequent empirical chapters in order to obtain a complete picture of youth identity formation in this part of Russia.

3 Narratives of Translocation, Dislocation and Location

The previous two chapters established how - through discursive, legislative and policy frameworks - identity politics are formed at state, as well as regional, levels. The present chapter shifts the level of analysis to that of the individual and addresses the key question of this study – that of subjective definitions of ethnic belonging. By exploring various reference points for ethnic identifications among diasporic Armenian youth in the first part of this chapter, it is suggested that Armenian ethnic identifications are not 'fixed' but entwined within a complex web of diverse cultural attachments involving many 'routes' of dislocation, translocation or location. In contrast, in the second part of this chapter focusing on Adygh youth, it is argued that Adygh ethnic belonging is marked by essentialized narratives of 'roots' and location.

Diaspora and belonging: constructing a pan-Armenian identity[93]

As introduced in Chapter One, the concept of diaspora has been criticized widely recently. It is commonly accepted that the concept of diaspora implies that members of a diaspora retain a collective memory, vision, or myth about their homeland (Cohen 1997; Safran 1991). This collective memory constructs what Anderson (1991 [1983]) conceptualizes as 'imagined communities,' where people from different backgrounds and socio-economic biographies come to see (imagine) themselves as belonging to one community.[94] In the age of globalization, diaspora is comprised of ever-changing representations which provide an 'imaginary coherence' for a net of flexible identities (Hall 1990). Following these characteristics, it is beneficial to explore collective imaginations that form Armenian identity. Collective memory of the Armenian diaspora is understood as creating a sense of Armenian identity that does not only apply to Armenians in Krasnodar, but

---

93 Modified versions of the first part of this chapter on Armenians have been published previously (Ziemer 2009, 2010).
94 Although he applied the concept of 'imagined communities' to the nation-state, it is applicable to diasporic communities as well, as has been pointed out in other studies (cf. Panossian 2002, Vertovec 1997).

can be extended to other parts of the world, thus, constructing a sense of pan-Armenian identity. Yet, the degrees to which this collective memory is part of young people's ethnic identity varies.

Historical dimensions of Armenian diasporic belonging
For the Armenian diaspora in general, two major historical events underpin the contemporary sense of Armenian identity; the emergence of the Armenians as the first Christian nation and the 1915 genocide. The ancient history of Armenia traditionally forms the core of Armenian identity. The documentary basis for claims to being a 'chosen people' was established as early as the fifth century by the Armenian historian Agathangelos who described the Armenians' conversion to Christianity (Panossian 2002: 127). This status as the first Christian nation, and a chosen people, was propagated subsequently by Armenian historians (many of them priests) and the church itself (ibid.). Another key moment in the evolution of a distinct Armenian identity was the formulation of the Armenian alphabet at the end of the fourth century and the subsequent development of an Armenian literary tradition (Russell 2005: 39). For Armenian society, this resulted in a 'Golden Age' which began in the fifth century and lasted until the seventeenth century. Today, this period is remembered with pride.

Armenians have always emphasized Armenia's ancient history, so that the words 'Christian', 'first' and 'unique' have become deeply embedded in Armenian collective memory (cf. Panossian 2002; Payaslian 2008; Zekiyan 2005). In the course of history, Armenians used Christianity to set themselves apart symbolically from their neighbours and it helped them to resist assimilation by the Persian Empire. Thus, the collective memory of Armenians' conversion to Christianity marks a turning point in Armenian history and is one of the pillars of Armenian identity.[95] Overall, the memory of Armenians' conversion to Christianity indicates the desire to remain distinct and one of the most powerful means to reinforce such uniqueness is the idea

---

95 Nonetheless, among modern scholars there is a disagreement about when exactly Armenians converted to Christianity. The most credible of all dates is between 314 and 315, when King Trdat converted to Christianity. The other dates for Armenians' conversion can all be found in the period from 219 to 315. For more detail on this discussion see Zekiyan (2005) and Bournoutian (1993).

of Armenians as a 'chosen people', The narrative of the conversion to Christianity, however, was rarely mentioned by young Armenians, rather, it was the 1915 genocide that was frequently mentioned during interviews. The 1915 genocide, in which the Ottoman Turkish state initiated the killings of Armenians or their deportation to the Syrian Desert, is the most traumatic event in Armenian history and forms the other pillar of pan-Armenian ethnic belonging (cf. Aghanian 2007; Hovannisian 2007; Payaslian 2008).[96] It is now widely accepted (though still fiercely denied by Turkish sources) that around 1.5 million people were either killed or died of starvation in the 1915 – 1916 period (Alayarian 2008).[97] These mass killings affected every Armenian and so being Armenian, thereafter, meant being a survivor of the genocide, and a member of a community of sufferers, whose suffering continues to be denied by the perpetrators and their allies (Alayarian 2008). The genocide's psychological and social effects on the generations of Armenians after the First World War were devastating (Cohen 1996; Hovannisian 2007). The immediate impact on the surviving population consisted of traumatic emotional distress. No Armenian family was untouched by it. Over time, this mentality of victimhood accentuated by denial became a central element of Armenian collective consciousness and the main integrating force for the Armenian nation. As research participants are young and have not been directly affected by the genocide, one might expect that the memory of the genocide does not bear upon young people's identity. However, responses during the interviews suggest that, on the contrary, young Armenian adults are still engaged with and think about the genocide:[98]

---

96 There was, however, a prelude to the assault by the Turks during the First World War - when a pan-Armenian nationalist and revolutionary movement trying to reunite the three parts of Armenia was met by the Ottoman Sultan Hamid ('The Red Sultan') with massive violence in the late nineteenth century. Close to 300,000 Armenians were killed in Turkish Armenia between 1894 and 1896 (Cohen 1997: 44).
97 Alayarian's data is based on the Armenian genocide website of the Armenian National Institute, www.armenian-genocide.org. According to this Institute, the Armenian genocide falls into four stages: in 1894-1896 around 300,000 people died, in 1909 around 300,000 people died, between 1915 and 1916 1.5 million people died and from 1918-1922 about 300,000 people died (Alayarian 2008: 9).
98 Sargis's family is from a village near Erevan, the capital of Armenia. He came to Krasnodar in 2001, when he was 17 years old. For his parents it was important that he finished school in Armenia and enrolled at the Kuban State University in

Sargis: Of course, this question really, really disturbs me. Why? Because my forefathers, yes, my grandmother, my great-grandmother, they're from Western Armenia. They came under the yoke [Ottoman], they really did. They saw all the torture, and then the destruction of Armenians by the Turks. They saw everything, just as it was. Somehow they managed to escape with their family. But not all of them were rescued, only some. In the end, they [his family] managed to escape and they came from *there* [Armenia] to *here*, to Krasnodar krai. They lived for two years in Armavir [a town in Krasnodar krai], but then moved back to Armenia and lived *there*.

For Sargis (22 years), the direct bond with the genocide narrative is established through stories being told and retold in his family. According to Pratt and Fiese (2004), intergenerational transmissions, both material and symbolic, such as family stories or cherished possessions, educate succeeding generations about family culture, and shape individual and family identities. Manoogian *et al.* (2007) in their study of the role of Armenian-American women in passing on genocide stories to build family experiences, demonstrate a commitment from Armenian mothers to maintaining family cohesion and ethnic identity for future generations. Other literature on the Armenian diaspora also shows that history matters and that it nurtures ethnic identification (Aghanian 2007; Avakian 2000; Bakalian 1993; Talai 1989; Totten 2005,). Thus, the retelling of genocide experiences is an overarching, cultural narrative that defines family and ethnic group beliefs and identity.

For Sargis, the direct bond with the genocide narrative is also established through stories being told and retold in his family and, therefore, he knows about his forefathers' suffering from the genocide. The way he describes it, stressing facts with repetitions, indicates that this historical narrative is still part of his life and that he is emotionally affected by it. The narrative Sargis offers, stresses genocide and victimhood and the unsettled, nomadic existence of the diaspora consciousness. All are important elements of how many Armenians, not just in Krasnodar, view themselves. According to his descriptions, which are short and not very detailed, it becomes obvious that these are stories that have been passed on from generation to generation. In

Krasnodar to get a better education. His family came to Krasnodar for economic reasons, in search of a better life.

this respect, one could argue that what he describes are phrases from vivid folk memories of the genocide, which he had heard while growing up. These are narratives of victimhood that form part of his ethnic belonging. The memory of the genocide is part of his consciousness that creates a type of Armenian belonging for him. It is *there*, in Armenia, where the connection to the Armenian nation was established, which makes a difference to *here*, in Krasnodar krai, where he lives now.

Although Sargis discovered his grandparents' suffering from the genocide as part of the process of growing up in an Armenian family, not all Armenian families pass on those narratives from generation to generation, as the following excerpt shows. In such cases, it might well be the Armenian collective imagination that forms a young person's pan-ethnic belonging. Lusine became interested in the genocide question after regularly chatting on Armenian websites; otherwise she would not have known much about it.[99] For her as well, the connection to *there* [Armenia] makes a difference for her *here*, in Krasnodar and thus attracted her interest.

Ulrike: This means that you and your family were not affected by any of these conflicts or the earthquake?
Lusine: Not at all. No...The one thing, during the genocide, our grandmother was *there* and she escaped. She escaped to Tbilisi. Well, half of my relatives are in Tbilisi and half in Armenia. But then...Karabakh [she refers to the conflict]... we've been living *here* [in Krasnodar] for a long time and so we weren't affected.
Ulrike: What do you think about the genocide?
Lusine: I'm obsessed with it.
Ulrike: Simply, because your grandmother suffered ...
Lusine: Well, despite the fact that my grandmother suffered, my parents never talked about what it was [the genocide]. One and a half million [Armenians] were slaughtered. We just didn't know this. Just through the Internet, chatting, then I began [to find out about the genocide], especially as I'm a little obsessed with Armenia ...

---

99 In contrast to Sargis, Lusine's parents came to Krasnodar from Tbilisi thirty years ago, though also for economic reasons.

Later in the interview, Lusine (21 years) said that it was inevitable she would develop an interest in the genocide because there were no Armenian websites without at least one forum dedicated to the genocide. Checks showed that the vast majority of Armenian online chat-forums have sections dedicated to this issue. This is well illustrated by the major website *Armianskaia Internet Imperiia*,[100] since the genocide is dealt with in a broadly similar fashion across all the sites surveyed. On this website, themes dedicated to the genocide range from discussions on Armenians' attitudes towards Turks, discussions of books and films about the genocide and discussions on the recognition of the genocide by other states. In sum, the Armenian genocide is not only a family narrative that nurtures ethnic identification within many Armenian families, but there is also a broader interest among the Armenian diaspora to keep alive historical memory that forms a pan-Armenian identity. The memory of the genocide traverses geographical distance between Armenians in other parts of the world and is part of the diasporic 'collective imaginary' (cf. Aghanian 2007; Bakalian 1993; Bamberger 2000; Hovannisian 2007; Talai 1989; von Voss 2007).

Armenia's independence and Karabakh: narratives of translocation and dislocation
Alongside these historical narratives of the Armenian diaspora, there are narratives of recent events: initial victimization of Armenians in Azerbaijan, followed by Armenia's independence in 1991 and the 'victory' in the Karabakh war in 1994. These narratives are significant for pan-Armenian identification in Krasnodar and Russia on the whole, but also have an influence on Armenian people in diaspora in other parts of the world. Armenia's independence from the Soviet Union in 1991 was not a question the author raised in interviews or that interview participants addressed spontaneously. However, Armenia's independence is an event that is important for the whole Armenian community in Krasnodar and is celebrated every year. In conversations with research participants' parents and other adults, Armenia's independence was often addressed.

---

100 *Armianskaia Internet Imperiia*. Online. Available HTTP: <http://www.barev.net> (accessed 15 May 2007).

Both events, Armenia's independence and the Karabakh conflict, are closely entwined in the sense that Moscow's actions in the Karabakh conflict led Armenians to lose faith in the Soviet government. According to Suny (2005), Armenia had been the most ethnically homogenous of Soviet republics and its people were the most loyal of the Soviet nations. Yet, one could argue that perestroika left Armenia one of the most unfortunate economically – with nearly a quarter of the population homeless, victims of both political developments and natural earthquakes (Suny 2005: 122). On 23 August 1990, Armenia formally declared its intention to become a sovereign and independent state, with Karabakh an integral part of the new Republic of Armenia. The September 1991 referendum on secession from the USSR, the presidential election the following month and the December dissolution of the USSR allowed Armenia to achieve its independence relatively smoothly.

Every year, the Armenian community in Krasnodar celebrates Armenia's independence as a symbol of Armenian belonging. Usually, the celebration starts with a Church service and continues with traditional dances, reciting poems or singing Armenian songs by young and old, prepared by the whole community and Armenian voluntary ethnic associations. These annual celebrations are very similar in their format. Changes only take place with regard to who performs or where the celebration is held. In 2007, there was a celebration at the Armenian Church in Krasnodar, organized by the Centre for Culture and Education '*Narek*', whereas in 2006 it was organized by the *Armianskaia Pashkovskaia Obshchina* (APO). This does not mean, however, that the APO did not organize any events in 2007. In fact, in 2007, the APO went to the Armenian Church in Apsheronsk in Krasnodar krai, where its dance group '*Arin Berd*'[101] performed. Going to another town in Krasnodar krai is a sign of community spirit, creating stronger ties with other Armenian communities in the region. The following fieldwork diary excerpt gives an insight into how Armenia's independence celebrations are generally conducted.[102]

---

101 The dance group was named after the ancient fortress of Arin Berd in Armenia, which was the residence of the Uratu King Argishti in 782 B.C.
102 This excerpt describes the celebrations of Armenia's first independence in 1918, which lasted only two years. The format of these celebrations is very similar to that of Armenia's independence in 1991.

> ...When I got to the Church, the service was still being held [the service as mentioned above] ... We walked to the office building near the Church, where in front of the building was a square, where the celebration was meant to be held. I could see some kids in costumes running around. I felt sorry for them because the square where they were meant to dance was covered in puddles. The musician tried to set up his music system, but it took a while because of the weather. Then the rain started again and we went into the building ... Lots of kids were hanging around in the building. One of my friends suggested to the priest that we should postpone the concert until next week. His reply was that nothing will stop Armenians holding the celebration of Armenia's independence today. The rain stopped and the celebration began. The priest opened the celebration with a prayer and then the moderator continued in Armenian announcing who would perform. People gathered around in a circle and some very little girls started to dance some traditional Armenian dance, which was followed by older kids performing various traditional Armenian dances. While they were dancing, I could see joy on everyone's face; people took photographs or filmed the performances. The kids looked lovely in their Armenian costumes. In addition, poems or songs were recited in Armenian and Russian ... [Fieldwork Diary, Sunday, 28 May 2006].

This excerpt is valuable not only for its brief description of the celebration, but also illustrative of three other important points. First, the celebration is conducted on the grounds of the Armenian Church in Krasnodar and opened with a prayer by the priest, which highlights the importance of Christianity for Armenians and references the memory of Armenians as the first Christian nation and chosen people. Second, the priest's comment that nothing will stop Armenians holding the celebration today, also pinpoints the momentous nature of this celebration for Armenian community belonging. Although he said it jokingly, his comment had an underlying seriousness. Third, noteworthy here is that these celebrations are very similar to traditions that developed in the nineteenth century, when the first Armenian charities, and with them a sense of community, emerged in the region.

Figure 3.1 Arin Berd - Armenian dance group from Krasnodar during the 2007 independence celebration in Apsheronsk in Krasnodar krai

106 ULRIKE ZIEMER

Figure 3.2 Children performing traditional Armenian dance during the 2006 independence celebration at the Armenian Church in Krasnodar

Like Armenia's independence, the Karabakh conflict is an event that is important for pan-Armenian belonging. This narrative, however, also had a significant impact on research participants' personal experiences. The Karabakh conflict was referred to very often during interviews, since some of the interview participants were immediately affected by it, as their families had to leave Karabakh because of the war.[103] The aim here is not to discuss the reasons for the conflict or the conflict itself, as this has been done in other literature (cf. Chorbajian 2001; de Waal 2003; Kurkchiyan 2005; Laitin and Suny 1999), but to account for this event in terms of its impact on research participants. In many ways, this is a story about suffering and dislocation, when young Armenians had to leave their homes in early childhood and are

---

103 Eight out of twenty interviewees had been directly affected by the Karabakh conflict.

very unlikely to ever return. Such experiences led to difficulties in their understanding of home or homeland. It is also a story about translocation, in the sense that some of the research participants still maintain close ties with relatives in Karabakh.

The Karabakh conflict started on 13 February 1988, when ruling elites brought crowds on to the streets of Stepanakert, the capital of Karabakh (Laitin and Suny 1999). Their demonstration was an outburst of intense frustration, accumulated during the period of Soviet rule. Nagorno Karabakh was a small enclave in Azerbaijan with a population of 160,000 people, of whom 75 per cent were ethnic Armenians (Kurkchiyan 2005: 148). The demonstrators demanded that Karabakh should be separated from Azerbaijan and annexed by Armenia. This brief turbulence marked the starting point of the first violent conflict of the post-Cold War era and placed Karabakh at the centre of political developments in Armenia itself.

Shortly after the peaceful demonstrations in February 1988, riots broke out in Sumgait, an Azerbaijani city near the capital, and later in Baku itself. Thirty one people were killed, many were injured and thousands fled in panic (Kurkchiyan 2005:153-154). For Armenians the pogroms of Sumgait and Baku were proof that Armenians could never live under Azerbaijani rule and feel safe. Armenian accounts refer to these events as evidence of Azerbaijani ethnic hatred, of the genocidal tendency among 'Turks' that Armenians experienced in the Ottoman Empire in 1915, which Azerbaijani 'Turks' were now reviving (Laitin and Suny 1999:152). As such, Sumgait activated the historical memory of the genocide as well as of the mass killings of 20,000 Armenians by Azeris in Shushi, Karabakh in 1918-1920. It is important to note that although Azerbaijanis, are a different Turkic people than the Ottoman Turks, they are 'Turks' in Armenian popular understanding (Azeri is a Turkic language). In some ways, the Karabakh conflict is an event that is juxtaposed with the genocide in Armenian collective memory. In other words, for Armenians, the fast-spreading news of the Sumgait pogrom evoked collective memories and the agonizing personal distress of the genocide.[104] The

---

104 On 28 February 1988, the eighth day of the dispute, a three day assault began on Armenian residents in the Azerbaijani city of Sumgait, which could only be stopped by the Soviet Army's intervention. Thirty one people died, many were injured and thousands fled in panic (Kurkchiyan 2005: 153-154).

widespread assumption was that the ethnic cleansing that had been conducted with such marked efficiency in Western Armenia almost seventy-five years before was about to be repeated in the East. The Sumgait attacks were presented in Armenia as a 'Pan-Turkish threat to the whole nation' or as 'the Turkish model' for dealing with Christian Armenians (Kurkchiyan 2005: 154).

In the Armenian perception, the identification of Soviet Azerbaijan with Ottoman Turkey was quickly made – however misleading. According to Panossian (2002), Armenians attach different meanings to the Karabakh conflict. While some saw the struggle over the Karabakh enclave as a conflict between Christian Armenians and Muslim 'Turks', others perceived it as a continuation of the genocide of 1915, which expelled Armenians from their historic lands. In some ways, the Karabakh conflict is an event that is juxtaposed with the genocide in Armenian collective memory. In other ways, it is a conflict that led to strong Armenian nationalism, as the subsequent interview excerpt shows:

> *Lusine:* The problem in Karabakh and all the slaughter is because of the genocide. The Armenians themselves can't respond with such a mass-attack. Now they bomb Karabakh, now Shushi. They were slaughtering ... We have a town in Azerbaijan that Armenian terrorists destroyed. Armenians don't know anything about this. The town is called Shushi. But the Azeris mark the date of Shushi just as the Armenians mark the date of the genocide. Simply because of the genocide, the external Armenian hostilities against the Azeris and the Turks ... Turkey, of course, is too strong for the Armenians; they can't touch Turkey. If Turkey responds then the whole of Armenia will be destroyed. But Azerbaijan is more primitive, although the same Turks live there.

The aim of this discussion has been to explore the ways in which historical narratives bear upon the construction of young Armenians' identities. The introduction to this discussion argued that collective historical memory is one important dimension for creating diasporic belonging; yet in the age of globalization diasporic representations are no longer fixed. The point of departure is that these four narratives, presented above, create an overall

YOUTH IDENTITIES IN RUSSIA 109

sense of unity for the Armenian Diaspora. On a macro-level, they are a global force that creates a sense of belonging for all members of the Armenian diaspora in the world. In particular, the narratives of the first Christian nation and the 1915 genocide are overarching, cultural narratives, kept alive by intergenerational transmission and global technology, such as the internet. The Karabakh conflict and Armenia's independence are narratives in which a specific moment in the more recent past is emphasized with patriotism and pride. The Karabakh narrative in particular is closely linked to personal experiences of dislocation and translocation, which are discussed thoroughly in the next section on perceptions of home. Overall, all four narratives comprise important pillars of pan-ethnic identification.

Where is home? Perceptions of home

Where is home? On the one hand, 'home' is a mythic place of desire in the diasporic imagination. In this sense it is a place of no return, even if it is possible to visit the geographical territory that is seen as the place of 'origin'. On the other hand, home is also the lived experience of a locality (Brah 1996: 192).

So far, the discussion has conceptualized diaspora in general, and explored four different narratives that form modern Armenian consciousness in general and pan-ethnic belonging in particular. The pan-ethnic identification, although to different degrees, applies to all members of the Armenian diaspora, whether young or old or in different parts of the world. The pan-ethnic identification, however, becomes multi-layered when taking into account personal lived experience in the local context and in relation to what is understood as home or homeland. This is mainly spurred by either early childhood experiences of migration, experiences of transmigration or local rootedness. As Gilroy (1993) puts it, diasporic identification is simultaneously about 'roots' and 'routes'.

The subsequent discussion focuses on research participants' perceptions of homeland and belonging, which are two-fold. First, there is the perception of homeland, as where one was born – the place of emotional attachment. These perceptions embody aspects of translocation as well as dislocation. The second perception is that of home, as where one is living. On the one hand, this is the place of appreciation from those who have lived somewhere else in their early childhood years, the place where friends are and where they feel at home. Thus, for them it is the lived experience in a geographical place that matters. Those research participants, who have not lived or were not born in Armenia, did not see Armenia as their homeland. Armenia is either a place that is a symbol, that is idealized in their minds or it is simply considered to be their historic homeland. In this way, these young people emphasize the fact that some aspects of their ethnic belonging are 'imagined' as members of the Armenian diaspora.

'Home is where you are born'
At first glance, one might assume that the perception of home as the place where one is born is derived from the fact that the Russian word '*rodina*' has the meaning of 'being born' (*rodits'ia*).[105] It is suggested that this definition may have relevance, but perceptions of home are more complex.[106] These narratives of home are stories about translocation and at the same time about dislocation (cf. Brah 1996). Individuals with translocal identities might 'feel at home' in more than one place. They 'feel at home' in Krasnodar, even though they experience a desire for homeland, which is not necessarily Armenia. In most cases, but *not all* cases, it was research participants' parents who migrated to Krasnodar for economic reasons. Although Krasnodar is their home now, they express their love to their birthplace, where they came from. This is the place in their hearts and to which they feel they really belong. Krasnodar, in contrast, is just the place that gave them opportunities in life, as Seda (23 years) comments:[107]

---

105 The core root of both words is '*rod*', meaning origin or birth, but also kin, family or gender.
106 Eleven (of twenty) interviewees referred to home as the place where they were born and nine defined home as the place where they live. Of these nine interviewees, only three were local Armenians. The other six interview participants were born in another place. So, there is no clear evidence that it is necessarily related to the meaning of the word. In the majority of cases, this answer was given by those, who were not born in Krasnodar. Yet, some who were not born in Krasnodar suggested the opposite saying that home is where they live.
107 Her parents migrated to Krasnodar from Armenia (Erevan), when Seda was just two years old.

Seda: Well ... My homeland (*rodina*) will always be Armenia. I live here [Krasnodar], but, you know, somehow I'm torn between the two, because I really want to live *here* [Krasnodar], but have the opportunity to go to Armenia every six months. Because, I know that I couldn't live there. I couldn't live *there* forever, but I really like the city [Erevan] ... When you take a short trip *there*, the city strikes you with its kindness; it strikes you with its beauty and people ... you go *there*, just like when you go to a health resort, you can get some peace of mind. But to live *there* is sort of difficult.

Ulrike: Does that mean that Armenia will always be your homeland?

Seda: Yes, you can say that, my first homeland ... Russia is a country, which gave me life, where I live. But somehow I always consider Armenia my homeland. I live *here*, I study and work *here*, and I know, that I'll never go *there* [Armenia] for good. But I've got very good and warm feelings towards Armenia.

As the excerpt shows, for Seda, Armenia always comes first in the hierarchy of homelands. Armenia is where she was born. This is the place she adores, though she knows that it is almost impossible to go back there, due to difficult economic and social conditions in Armenia. Her feelings towards home can be classified as translocal, since the homeland is not lost as such, it is merely for economic reasons that her parents came to Krasnodar. It is the binary of 'here and there' that forms her dual translocal attachments. Her feelings towards homeland show emotional signs. This is where she feels at home and is the place she has warm feelings for. Her relationship to Russia is more rational. It is appreciative, but more distant: '*This is the country* [Russia] *which gave me life.*' Although showing some emotions towards Russia, she does not seem to display such warm feelings, when talking about Russia, as when she talks about Armenia.

Similarly, Sargis states that he can only ever consider Armenia his homeland. It is important to note that Sargis came to Krasnodar at the age of 17 and therefore has a close relationship with his homeland. Like Seda's parents, his parents also came to Krasnodar for better life prospects. In the interview, he expressed the desire to go back to Armenia to retire. Interestingly, for him another reason that Russia can never become his homeland is his nationality, which problematizes his connection to Russia, thus, reproducing Russia's identity politics which are based on an ethno-cultural understanding of citizenship:

> *Sargis:* Homeland? This is where I was born and where I grew up – this is my homeland (*rodina*). I was born in Armenia and grew up there. I'd never consider Russia my homeland (*rodina*), even if I've got citizenship. At the moment, I've got Russian citizenship (*rossiiskoe grazhdanstvo*), not Armenian. But I can't consider Russia my homeland ... for the simple reason that my nationality is Armenian. I was born there and grew up there. Homeland? This is my homeland – this is Armenia (*pause*).

To this feeling of translocation, one can add the feeling of dislocation in which one's senses having become dislodged from a given location (cf. Anthias 2006). Yet, dislocation does not necessarily mean that the 'diasporic homeland' is completely lost. Instead, it has become a homeland one cannot return to because of economic difficulties, as Seda has indicated and as Ashot (16 years) also explains:[108]

> *Ulrike:* Do you consider Krasnodar your home?
> *Ashot:* No, Karabakh is my home (*rodina*). I was born there ... Every year I go there. Every year in the summer, we go there for two or three months.
> *Ulrike:* Do you like it there?
> *Ashot:* Yes, I really like it.
> *Ulrike:* How come?
> *Ashot:* Well, it's ours. I love Karabakh more. Well, I couldn't live there, I couldn't live there.
> *Ulrike:* Why?
> *Ashot:* Well, because it's still very underdeveloped. It's like going from New York into the desert. And from Krasnodar to Karabakh it's the same. It's underdeveloped. Karabakh isn't a war zone anymore, everyone can go there. Well, it's just underdeveloped. Maybe after fifteen or twenty years there'll be something. I like to go there but not to live.

Like Seda, Ashot reveals some degree of dislocation, as he can never go back to Karabakh and live there because of the daunting life prospects. At the

---

108 Ashot was born in Karabakh during the conflict. His Dad came to Krasnodar first and his Mum followed when Ashot was six months old.

same time, like Seda, his identity appears to be translocal, as he maintains close ties with his 'homeland' by going back there every summer. Most importantly, for him 'homeland' is not the original homeland, Armenia, but Karabakh. Hence, Ashot does not have a classic diasporic identity that signifies a longing for return to the original homeland.

The questionable meaning of the original homeland for diasporic identification, is also exposed by those research participants, who have become fully dislocated after losing their 'homeland', as a result of ethnic conflicts. These are research participants who had to flee their homes (not in Armenia) during conflicts. For example, Lala (20 years) cannot clearly say where her home is, as the Baku she knew no longer exists.

>
> *Ulrike*: Where do you think is your home?
> *Lala:* I don't know; it's a difficult question.
> *Ulrike:* Krasnodar?
> *Lala:* No, and I don't like Erevan either. It depends how you understand the word homeland (*rodina*). Well, for me in a spiritual sense it's Baku, where I was born, but well Baku ... as it was ... doesn't exist anymore ... because the [Soviet] Union collapsed ... only Azerbaijanis stayed there. Well, the way Baku was at that time, there were lots of different nationalities ... It was a really well-developed city, like Odessa, but it's difficult to get it across to you. Moscow was nothing then. Baku was just a concrete centre, where all the amusements were ... And it didn't matter which nationality you were, which religion you had. Armenians with Azerbaijanis, who've been enemies all their lives, for centuries they lived together there, got married and had kids. And they were happy and satisfied with everything. I think, well, this Baku was an ideal place, where it would have been possible to live...

For Lala, the question of homeland is too complex and she is not able to give a clear answer. She sees Baku as her homeland because it was where she was born and because of the vivid stories her parents told her about Baku, but it is not the Baku that exists now. Therefore, the way Lala talks about Baku is to some extent idealistic.[109] For her, Krasnodar is the place

---

109 In 1989, her parents left Baku for Erevan. They lived in Erevan for a few years and finally resettled in Krasnodar.

where she lives, but not her home. Armenia, where she travelled to once, is just a place she knows about, but her personal experience did not create an emotional bond that made her consider Armenia her homeland. Thus, for her, it is all about a 'homing desire' (Brah 1996).

Lala is not the only research participant who developed a romanticized emotional relationship towards an 'imagined' homeland. Often the 'imagined' homeland is not Armenia as a historical homeland. Instead, it is the place where they were born, thus, invoking the notion of home as a lived experience of locality (Brah 1996). Yet, the notion of home as a lived experience of locality has to be understood in terms of narrativity, as sometimes it is parents' stories about the places where they were born that forms research participants' understanding of home and homeland. Mariam (19 years) has similar experiences to Lala; she is also from Baku and considers Baku her homeland, though she cannot remember Baku because she was too young when her family left the city:[110]

> *Mariam:* I think, probably, homeland (*rodina*) is the place where you are from. I've never been to Baku, but I'm drawn to it. I want to go there and have a look. Even when I hear national songs, it feels as if I'm drawn to it. I want to go to Armenia too, but I'm more drawn to Baku.

For both, Lala and Mariam, Baku is the lost homeland. This is the place they have an emotional attachment to, though they have never, or only briefly, lived there. Both have a complex relationship to homeland – their 'roots' are in Baku, but their 'routes' are very malleable. For Lala, homeland, the way it was does not exist anymore. For Mariam, although mentioning the place where her parents came from first in the hierarchy of homelands, it is also the historical homeland that has a meaning for her. She implies that she also wants to visit Armenia, referring to her pan-Armenian identity, but then returns to the importance of locality and talks about her feelings towards Baku. Thus, she juxtaposes her pan-Armenian identity with her localized Armenian identity.

---

110 Mariam was born in Baku, but when she was one year old her parents left Baku for Krasnodar because of the conflict.

'Home is where you live'
The complexity of home in the diasporic imaginary does not necessarily mean that diasporic subjectivity is 'rootless'. Brah (1996), for example, argues that the concept of diaspora offers a critique of discourses of fixed origins, while taking account of a homing desire. The homing desire, however, is not the same as the desire for a 'homeland'. She argues for a distinction between 'feeling at home' and declaring a place as home. Processes of diasporic identity formation are a perfect example of the claim that identity is always plural and processual. In this way, while for some belonging is created along ethnic lines of identification, for others belonging is created according to locality – lived experience. The subsequent discussion considers the understanding of home as where you live. It is the geographical location and the lived experience that matter to research participants. This is what Brah (1996) calls the 'feeling at home', as Sona (17 years) comments:

> Sona: I'm an Armenian patriot. I adore Armenia, because I'm an Armenian. I always remember Armenia. But my home (*rodina*) is Krasnodar. Because I was born here and I go to school here ... I don't feel foreign here, absolutely not. This is my home, but I'm Armenian.

When Sona talks about Krasnodar as her home it implies an image of 'home' as the site of everyday lived experience. It is a discourse of locality, the place where feelings of rootedness and everyday experience matter. Home here implies her networks of family, kin, friends and significant 'others'. It suggests a social and psychological geography of space that is experienced in terms of her home town. That is, a community 'imagined' in most part through daily encounters. As Brah (1996: 10) puts it 'this "home" is a place which remains intimate for its inhabitants even in moments of intense alienation from it – it is a sense of "feeling at home"'.

For some research participants, Armenia is the homeland, for others, Armenia is just a historical homeland, they happen to know about, but to which they have no immediate relation. Armenia for them is a distant place that does not matter as much as the place of 'feeling at home'.

> Khachig: Well, how can I put it, I live in Russia. I know that Armenia ... is ... sort of the historical homeland ... There are Armenian customs, but I don't adhere to them, because I'm Russian (*russkii*). I'm Armenian according to my documents, but in all honesty, I'm Russian (*rossiianin*). I love Krasnodar, this is my city ...

Here Khachig (18 years) clearly states that he has a distant relationship to Armenia. He says that according to his documents he is Armenian, but would prefer to be called a Russian citizen (*rossiianin*), since he is 'only' Armenian by birth; by lived experience he is something else. He talks about his identity in terms of citizenship and lived experience. Yet, he ethnicizes his identity, when he says he is Russian (*russkii*), which he is not in ethnic terms. Perhaps, it is here when he reproduces the political discourse that depicts 'citizenship' in ethno-cultural terms. He feels Russian (*rossiiskii*) as much as anyone else does. Nonetheless, describing Armenia as his historic homeland, he includes it as part of his identity.

Both, Sona and Khachig, were born in Krasnodar and one could argue that, they see Krasnodar as their 'natural' home without exception. Yet, for others, who were not born in Krasnodar, Krasnodar is their home, indicating that it is a subjective understanding that defines homeland/home.

> Anush: My homeland (*rodina*), as I've always seen it, my homeland, is the homeland where I live now. It's the homeland, which brought me up. It's the homeland, which has given me my education. My homeland is Russia.

Here, Anush (22 years) states that it is the lived experience that matters to her – she considers Russia as her home.[111] Yet, she continues by detailing her split diasporic relationship, referring to her pan-Armenian identity that has a 'fixed' origin to some extent. Although Armenia is not her homeland, she does make reference to it in the interview. To some degree, she stresses the 'fixed' origin when starting her sentence by referring to 'another' homeland (*drugaia rodina*).

---

111   Anush was born in Karabakh and came with her parents to Krasnodar when she was three years old.

Anush: I can't say that there is another homeland (*drugaia rodina*) that has made me the person I am. I really love Armenia. But for me, Armenia is not my homeland.

She loves Armenia, but not as a homeland, although it is still part of her identity. Overall, she implies a degree of uncertainty, thus, emphasizing the complexity of the meaning of homeland. Anush continues by idealizing the 'imagined homeland', even though her forefathers were not from Armenia. This suggests that for her, the two identity markers, one of location and one of translocation, are interlaced to some extent, creating a complex web of 'homelands' and identifications:

Anush: This [Armenia] is like a symbol for me. You know, it's difficult for me to explain. It was neither my homeland, nor the homeland of my forefathers ... It's difficult to say that this [Armenia] is my homeland. It's a symbol for me. It's such a love of mine, well, I've got so much love for Armenia ... It's like Armenians love the Ararat Mountain, although it's not their mountain. It's a Turkish mountain. But it's a symbol. In the same way, I love Armenia, although I wasn't born there. There is an Armenia and that's nice for me. It's nice that something from my state is still there, a place where you can go. ... The place where my relatives live [a village in Krasnodar krai] is also my home (*rodina*), though my little home. I've been here in Russia, since I was three years old. I have to say that. However much I make a big thing out of it and say that I'm not Russianized ... I am a little.

Armenia for her is a love she cannot explain and does not know where it comes from. To some extent, she infers that it is a love of 'fixed' origin, a love every Armenian should have or at least have experienced. Her understanding of homeland consists of a complex hierarchy, which was also communicated by Mariam earlier. First, there is Russia, she considers her home, whilst recognizing the difference of being Armenian in Russia. Second, there is Armenia, which for her is the 'imagined' homeland, as for most other Armenians. This is the homeland she adores. Third, there is her 'small' home, a village somewhere in Krasnodar krai, which is the place where her relatives live. Accordingly, she understands home (*rodina*) predominantly in terms of her lived experience.

The complex issue of understanding what research participants see as their home is crucial for identities. From the above discussion, we can see that research participants use home and homeland as ways of talking about their identity. These narratives are tightly interlaced with questions of national identity, culture and ethnicity. Although all research participants have Russian citizenship, it is not Russian national identity that is the all-embracing identity for them. While some identify with Russia, but cannot deny their Armenian roots (cf. Anush, Lala and Khachig), others strongly identify with the Armenian nation (cf. Sargis, Seda). This would confirm the proposition put forward in Chapter One that in contemporary Russia, citizenship is mainly defined in ethno-cultural terms. Most of them claim a link to an 'imagined community' which is both a 'national collectivity' and 'ethnic collectivity' (Anthias and Yuval-Davies 1992). Yet, it is not always Armenia as a primordial homeland. Along these lines, it is argued that research participants predominantly construct their identities in terms of ethnicity as well as geographical location.

Multifarious identities: between sameness and otherness
Following the discussion on the different perceptions of homeland, one might assume that Armenian identities in the Russian context are naturally constructed along a dual identification of Armenianness and Russianness. The picture is much more complex, however, and requires a multi-positioning of young Armenians' identity. Figure 3.3 below represents the complex web of identity markers and how they are interlaced. This diagram depicts the tightly intertwined identity markers and their subcategories that matter to research participants.

At first sight, one might think of young Armenian identities as hybrid identities that construct a space beyond and between binaries – a 'third space' (Bhabha 1990). In contrast to Bhabha's postulation of a 'third space,' it is argued here that most research participants have not created hybrid identities as such. Rather, in this context, it is suggested that research participants draw on cosmopolitanism as an identity resource.

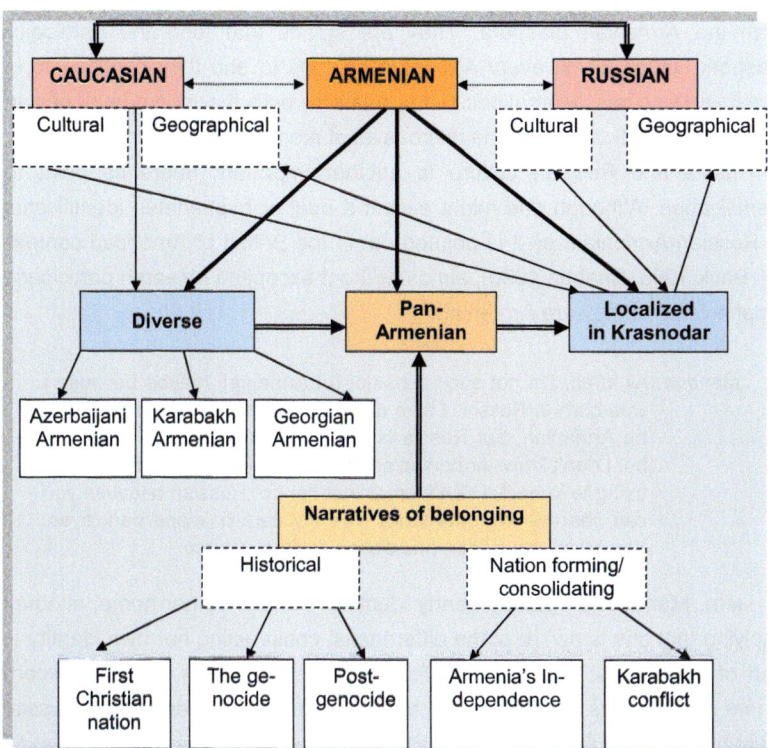

Figure 3.3 Armenian Identity Web

It is argued widely that cosmopolitan people can combine strong ethnic affiliations with an attitude that recognizes cultural plurality, making it easy to move around different cultural systems (Amin 2004; Appiah 1997; Lamont and Arksartova 2002). It is perhaps here where they use cosmopolitanism as a practice. While in some ways, young Armenians' identities indicate a sense of 'purity' or an essentialized sense of ethnic belonging, which places Armenian identity above every other identification; in other ways, they exhibit a complex interweaving of sameness and otherness.

The discussion on pan-ethnic identification and home has indicated that Armenianness is comprised of different levels, which are displayed in Figure

3.3. The very first level of identification consists of historical narratives that form the Armenian diaspora. They are stories that form the ontological diasporic space which every Armenian belongs to and they continue to be transmitted across generations. They relate to both the macro-level of pan-Armenian identification and the micro-level of more localized identifications.

Russia and Russian culture is another important reference point for identification. Although one might expect a dual or hyphenated identification of Russian-Armenian, as it is pointed out in the British or American contexts (cf. Back 1996; Bhabha 1990), almost without exception research participants emphasize that they are Armenian:

> *Manana:* All in all, I'm not such a patriot [of Armenia], maybe because I was born in Russia. I love my nation (*natsiia*) and I'm proud to be Armenian, but Russia is my homeland. I speak Armenian, but I don't know Armenian completely – I forget bits of it, but I'm trying to keep it. I don't forget that I'm not Russian because you can see this from my looks, like my dark hair and dark eyes. You know, any nation has distinguishing features.

Here, Manana (21 years) clearly identifies Russia as her home, although implying that she is aware of the differences, constructing her own identity as part of Russia, but different from Russians.[112] It is in this interview excerpt where she displays a strong sense of both cultures – Armenian and Russian – yet not implying the possibility of creating a hyphenated identity for herself. Her understanding of keeping the two cultures separate is also seen in her awareness of looking different from Russians, referring to racial ways of distinguishing herself from Russians. While her sameness is constituted by being part of the Armenian diaspora on an abstract 'imagined' level, she can only see otherness in terms of her local identity, where otherness is comprised of two different dimensions. First, otherness is depicted in reference to Armenia. Here, she insinuates that Armenia is part of the Armenian diaspora and the 'imagined' homeland, yet she has never been to Armenia and so indicates a distant, albeit 'idealized', relationship. Second,

---

112 Manana's parents came from Azerbaijan to Krasnodar before the conflict started. Manana was born in Krasnodar.

otherness is constructed in respect to Russians – as she looks different from Russians.

One explanation for a strong identification with Armenianness relates to a strong sense of primordial belonging. Armenianness is a primordial identity which has clear blood, kin and genetic characteristics, while Russianness is perceived as cultural affinity of location. Another explanation for a strong identification with Armenianness could be that research participants favour Armenian culture because of its political inequality with Russian culture (dominant culture). Denying a simple identification with Russianness can be seen as a tactic to challenge this inequality. Thus, Manana comes to see her identity in terms of two identity markers – that of Russianness (dominant culture) and that of Armenianness (subordinate culture). She is surrounded by Russianness in her daily life, though Armenianness creates a boundary for her that she cannot transcend, since she is aware of what signifies her in relation to the 'other', hinting at both racial as well as cultural boundaries. Nonetheless, she does not perceive this boundary negatively. By saying that *'any nation has distinguishing features'*, implying that racial and cultural boundaries are a matter of fact. It is argued that this awareness of cultural plurality and differences creates attitudes which inhibit the construction of hybrid identities, but enable individuals to move around easily between the two cultural systems.

The binary of Russian and Armenian cultural identities becomes more complex when taking into account the identification connected to the place of origin, in other words, sub-ethnic identification. Armenianness comprises different levels, that of pan-ethnic identification to which all Armenians belong, but also the more localized, yet diverse identity markers, depending on place of origin (Azerbaijani, Karabakh or Georgian Armenians, for example). There are cultural differences among Armenians from different places, seen, for example, in different Armenian dialects (cf. Talai 1986, 1989). This point of reference for identification is imposed by the diversity within the Armenian diaspora and when asking research participants about their ethnic identification, identity connected to their place of origin comes to the fore, while the pan-Armenian identity is emphasized mainly in relation to Russians, as Anush comments:

Anush: You know that the mentality (*mentalitet*) of Russians and Armenians, Caucasians, or especially of Armenians from Muslim countries, like me, is different ...You know, when lots of Armenians from Erevan came after the fall of the Soviet Union, we Armenians [in Krasnodar] could feel that ... but for Russians we're all the same. Russians don't care where we are from exactly.

Alongside the binary of Armenianness and Russianness, Caucasian and religious identifications are also significant. The geographical/cultural identification of Caucasian identity stands in contrast to Russian cultural identity. Often, research participants refer to their Caucasian identity, in the context of skinhead attacks, which will be discussed in more detail in Chapter Five. Skinheads do not distinguish between Armenians, Adyghs or Georgians, but refer to them as Caucasians. This Caucasian identity also comes to the fore in comparison with Russianness, generalizing that it is not only Armenians that are different from Russians, but all Caucasian people.

To sum up this complex picture of identity formation, it can be said that young Armenians' subjectivities are not only two-fold, but require a multiple positioning according to macro-levels of pan-Armenian identification and micro-levels of identification, such as sub-ethnic and geographical/cultural identifications. This complex web of identity markers does not create hybrid identities or dual attachments, as it is often claimed in the Western context (cf. Gilroy 1987; Bhabha 1990; Ali 2003). Instead, as has been demonstrated in this chapter, most young Armenian adults are inclined to see themselves as Armenian and almost without exception there is nothing like a hyphenated identification, such as Russian-Armenian. The strong identification with Armenianness accentuates a continuing sense of social difference or distance from 'Russian people', which is most likely imposed from above, by the identity politics of the region which has made ethnic awareness central for most people.

While there are many different ethnic cultures in this region, young Armenians predominantly find themselves positioned between two sets of cultural values – Russian (dominant culture) and Armenian cultural values. On the one hand, there is the social world of family and Armenian community. On the other, there is the Russian world which is experienced through institutions like education and the media. As a result of this awareness of cultural diversity, it is argued that young Armenian adults have begun to draw on cosmopolitanism as an identity resource that enables them to constantly translate between the different cultural systems. In the previous chapters, it has been demonstrated that the ethnocentric political discourse at national and regional levels is one dimension that poses a barrier to the formation of 'cosmopolitan' identities. This political discourse, however, is not enough to account for why cosmopolitanism as an identity resource has not gained a stronghold amongst young Armenians. In view of this, in ensuing chapters other social categories, like gender, are examined in more detail, to provide a clearer answer. The second part of this chapter explores the ways in which young Adyghs construct their ethnic belonging.

Homogeneity and location: an ethnic minority at home
Adyghs in the North Caucasus region are one of the oldest indigenous people in the region. As a result of the Russian-Caucasian War (1832 – 1864) numbers diminished, since many Circassians left the region for the Ottoman Empire. Because of this dispersion, the Circassians that remained in the region failed to consolidate a national identity, due to the physical separateness of the Circassian republics and the sparseness of population. With the collapse of the Soviet Union, the Circassians became merely the titular nationality in one republic (Adyghea) and two autonomous regions. The three nationalities that were formed, Cherkess, Adygh and Kabardinian are minorities in their nominated territory. Together with other national minorities, Adyghs also have experienced a resurgence of their national consciousness since the break-up of the Soviet Union. In some ways, this resurgence of national awareness is spurred by a 'national' history of over 200 years that has been marked by traumatic experience and resistance to Russian hegemony. In other ways, it is accompanied by the consciousness of being a small nation threatened by complete extinction.

Taking these factors into account, it is interesting to explore how young Adyghs construct a sense of ethnic belonging. While research participants live in Adygheisk, which is predominantly Adygh, many of them travel to

Krasnodar almost every day, either to work or to study. In this respect, young Adyghs often find themselves positioned within two sets of cultural values – Russian and Adygh. There is not only the social world in Adygheisk, family and the Adygh community, but there is also the 'Russian' world in Krasnodar which they experience through education and work. In line with the discussion on Armenian ethnic identities, Adygh ethnic identity is also explored as a particular kind of awareness among young Adyghs that constructs their ethnic belonging.

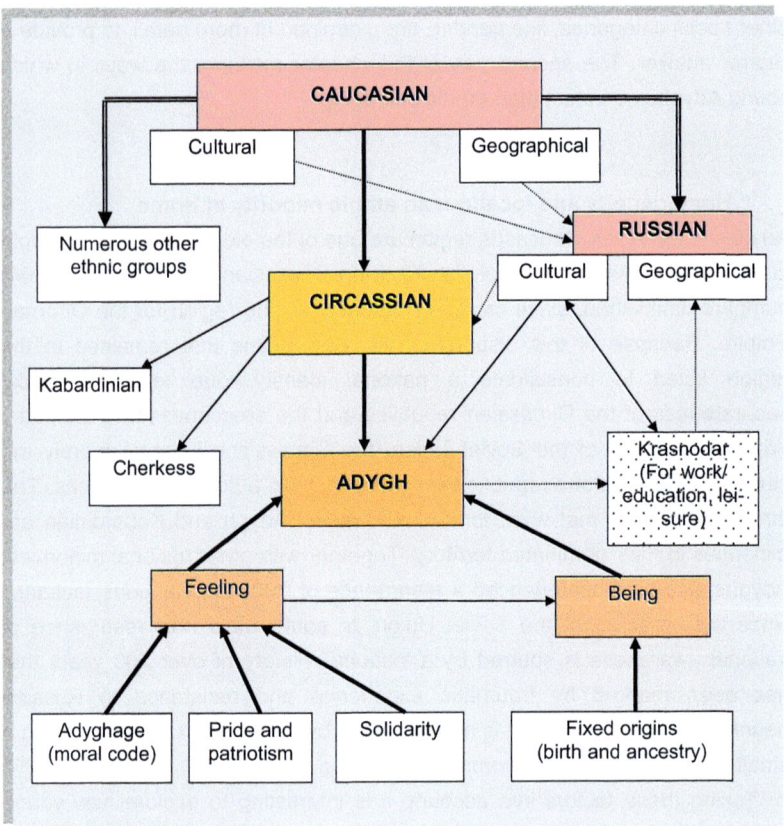

Figure 3.4 Adygh Identity Web

In this respect, two main identity markers are stressed in this section. First and foremost, there is the primordial identity marker of Adygh ethnicity. Adyghs are part of the Circassian people, which is an identity marker that is closely entwined with Adygh ethnicity. Second, there is the identity marker of belonging to the Caucasian people. Here, Caucasian identity is a combined marker of cultural and geographical identification. Both identity markers contribute to an identity formation process that is signified by the 'other', Russians, which are examined more closely in Chapter Five on youth cultural experiences and practices in the local context. Before embarking upon the discussion of these two major identity markers in detail, Figure 3.4 below represents the web of identity markers for young Adyghs in order to illustrate how their identities are formed.

The Caucasus: a geographical – cultural location of belonging
As Figure 3.4 illustrates, Caucasian identity is a very influential point of reference for Adyghs. For some, Caucasian identity is simply an identity that refers to a geographical space. For others, it is an identity that implies the historical and cultural processes that have formed this identity. One might even be tempted to call it a supra-ethnic identification, which depicts Adyghs as belonging to Caucasian peoples or to Caucasian civilization. In this book, this supra-ethnic identification is perceived as a social identity that mainly comes to the fore in relation to the 'other', Russians. It is an identity that is marked by difference and distinctiveness from Russians. It is used to distance oneself from otherness (Russians), but to share sameness with other ethnic groups. Thus, it is not only an identity that is distinct for only one group of people; it applies to all peoples with origins in the Caucasus, including Armenians.

While for an insider, Caucasian identity is a category of pride and traditional belonging, for an outsider (Russians, in particular), it is a term that has negative connotations, which have been constructed with the help of the Russian mass media that have created terms like 'a person of Caucasian nationality' (*litso kavkazskoi natsional'nosti*), which officially do not exist. The mass media significantly contributed to the rise of the so-called Caucasophobia in Russia, directed at people with Caucasian origins. The growth of Caucasophobia is mainly the result of the anti-Chechen campaigns by the Russian government during the first Chechen war, which were started following a Chechen terror act in 1994 (Iskandarian 1996).

From research participants' point of view, Caucasianness is an identity that is marked by pride and traditions, such as hospitability, as well as long-standing family traditions that are different from those in the West/Russia. In addition, it is a social identity that is entwined with value orientations, such as truth, honour, justice and wisdom. Caucasian identity, however, is not absolute. A person realizes him or herself through Caucasian culture, yet his or her ethnicity is something different and this has a substantial meaning for personal, social and political life. Caucasian identity is not inherited; it is a historical process that has formed a Caucasian personality.

Both Armenians and Adyghs belong to Caucasian people. For both, it is a social identity that comes to the fore when compared to Russians. Research participants, regardless of whether they are Armenian or Adygh, are deeply convinced that this Caucasian mentality is particular to them and sets them apart from the rest of the world, especially from Russians, who are living in close proximity with Caucasians. This was frequently communicated in my interviews in relation to Russians.

> *Fatima:* Adyghs are famous for being hot blooded, not only Adyghs, but Caucasians, well generally, *natsmeny*[113] sort of.
> *Diana:* Overall, lots of Russian girls like Adyghs [males].
> *Fatima:* Not loads, but almost all Russian girls.
> *Diana:* Not because they're Adyghs, but because they're Caucasian. They're attracted by their dark appearance; this is what Russian girls like a lot. I'm not saying this to get a compliment. I don't really know why I'm saying it. I sometimes think that this is because Russians have got their own mentality.
> *Fatima:* All in all, we're very hospitable.
> *Diana:* Russians are also hospitable, but not as much as we are. Hospitality goes without saying for us and has no limits. If someone comes to visit, we'd lay the table immediately and sit together for ages...

---

113 *Natsmeny* is short for *natsional'nye menshinstva,* a term that is widely used and translates as national minorities. In this context, she refers to all Caucasian people in this region.

In this dialogue, Diana (19 years) and Fatima (18 years) introduce three complex dimensions of what it means to belong to the Caucasian people. First and foremost, it is a gender dimension that Diana introduces, when saying that many Russian girls not only like Adygh men, but all Caucasian men. Diana's assertion exposes the flexible nature of Caucasian identity. Diana understands that for Russians it is not the ethnic identity, but the supra-ethnic identity that has a meaning, when saying that Russian women like Caucasians. In this way, she refers to the construction of Adygh identity within the public discourse, which often does not distinguish between the different ethnicities that fall under the term Caucasian.

Second, it is the construction along racial lines, that Russian women are attracted to 'Caucasians' because of their dark looks. Her understanding of Caucasian shows that she is aware that appearance is one marker that creates Adygh/Caucasian identity. In many respects, this is an identity marker of difference that has been created by the mass media in Russia and is closely entwined with racial terms, such as 'a person of Caucasian nationality' (*litso kavkazskoi natsional'nosti*), which is often used in the context of criminalization (cf. Roman 2002; Russell 2002). Third, there is the issue of hospitality that is different from Russians and is distinct for all Caucasian people. For Diana, it is not only hospitality on its own that is different from Russians, but it is a whole set of values, called *mentality* that is different. For Caucasians in general, and for Adyghs in particular, such customs and social norms have remained untouched in the course of history. For Adyghs, for example, hospitality is embodied in *Adyghage* (Adyghness), which is a category that defines Adygh ethnic identity and therefore could be considered an 'identity code' (Khanakhu 2001).[114] In many ways, Adyghness as an 'identity code' which is comprised of nobleness, good manners and hospitality.

To conclude, Caucasian identity is a social identity that is not absolute for one ethnic group. It is an identity that includes different ethnic groups with origins in the Caucasus. It is an identity that comes to the fore in relation to the 'other'. It is an identity that is marked by difference and distinctiveness

---

114 *Adyghage* is discussed in more detail in the context of Adygh gender relations in Chapter Four.

from Russians. Whereas in public discourse Caucasian identity is often portrayed in the negative, for an individual with Caucasian origins it is an identity marker that includes pride and tradition. In this way, young Adyghs, belonging to one of the oldest indigenous ethnic groups of the North Caucasus, have an awareness that naturally makes the preservation of traditions part of their ethnic identity. Young Adyghs' ethnic consciousness is thus fixed in traditions, myths and what one might call 'ethnic romanticism', whilst at the same time reproducing the political discourse of this region, which emphasizes the importance of one's ethnic belonging.

Adygh identity: feeling and being Adygh
Whereas the above discussion focused on the meanings of Caucasian belonging, the subsequent discussion examines the 'Adygh' dimension, and asks what young people mean when they claim to be Adygh. Part of the difficulty is that in the current political and cultural context, Adyghness is easily essentialized. Only in 1991, did Adyghea become a sovereign republic, with a distinctive set of national institutions and jurisdictions albeit based on long-standing traditions of local self-government.[115] Since its declaration of sovereignty in 1991, its status has been constantly contested by speculations about Adyghea rejoining Krasnodar krai. Despite Adyghea's geographical 'boundedness' and close contact with Russians, Adyghs perceive their identity to be largely indisputable and unproblematic. For most Adyghs today, Adyghness is a meaningful reference point vis-à-vis Russian identity. Commonsense terms such as birth and residence can be easily used to define ways of being Adygh. These are two obvious parameters, and a third one can be added – that of ancestry.

There are, then, in theory a number of ways to claim Adygh nationality. One way to explore Adygh nationality is to use the three dimensions of birth, ancestry, and residence. However, for Adyghs these can only be applied to a degree, stressing the primordial dimension of Adygh ethnicity. One can be a resident in the Republic of Adyghea, but not an Adygh. One can be born in

---
115 There are traditional bodies, such as the Adygh mediation court, the village *khases* and the Council of Elders, which have existed in Adygh society throughout history. For a more detailed discussion on the political system in the Republic of Adyghea, see Polyakova (2002).

YOUTH IDENTITIES IN RUSSIA 129

Adyghea, but not be an Adygh. The important consideration is ancestry; if one is born into an Adygh family, in Adyghea, then one is considered to be Adygh. Another way to explore Adygh identity is as a type of consciousness; it is a feeling that makes one Adygh. For example, Oksana is of mixed origin, her Mum is Russian and her Dad is Adygh:

> *Oksana:* You know, at times I feel ... I feel more Adygh, because I was born in this town, because I like Adyghs, their nation, their traditions. By the way, I consider myself more Adygh. Maybe I don't always behave like an Adygh girl. Sometimes because of what I wear, or because I always speak Russian, or maybe because of my Mum, people think I'm Russian. By the way, more often than not I think that I'm Adygh. In my passport I'm Adygh. In my passport, I put down that I'm Adygh.

Oksana (22 years) clearly states that she feels Adygh, despite her 'mixed' origins. She feels like an Adygh because she was born in Adygheisk. She refers to her being rooted to the place by birth as well as by place of residence. She derives her Adygh identity from this fact of being born there. Despite her reference to an essentialized view of ethnic belonging, she also implies that she might not be as 'proper' an Adygh as others, when she talks about her way of dressing and that she only speaks Russian. Nonetheless, to make up for the other half of her identity that is not Adygh, she displays a strong patriotism by stressing that she entered her Adygh nationality in her passport. The fifth paragraph (*piatyi punkt* or *piataia grafa*) in the passport was abolished by a law, passed in October 1997, and now the 'nationality' entry is by choice.[116]

From Oksana's definition, one can conclude that essentialized ethnic belonging that derives from history, ancestry and birth is equated with belonging as a type of consciousness, as a feeling. The question arises of how can one 'feel' an Adygh belonging? What does it mean to be Adygh? In the first place, research participants define Adygh belonging in terms of primordial ethnic belonging. Ethnic belonging by birth, however, is a

---

116 For more detailed discussion on the background to the federal decision to abolish the 'fifth point' in Russian passports and political reactions to this new law, see Simonsen (2005).

dimension that is taken for granted because they live in the Republic of Adyghea and there is no doubt about 'fixed' origins. When research participants were questioned about their awareness of Adygh identity the picture becomes unclear, as it is hard for many young Adygh adults to define exactly what is meant by Adygh identity. Nonetheless, this picture is predominantly coloured with pride and patriotism.

Ulrike: What does it mean for you to be Adygh?
Emma: I don't even know how to properly answer this question.
Pavel: I feel like an Adygh. I think, any person, whether he is Russian, Adygh or Armenian, should respect his nation, he should be proud of his nation. Personally I'm proud to be Adygh, and don't regret being Adygh.
Emma: I can't imagine being a different nationality, not because I'm against Russians and other nationalities. I just don't know, I don't know how to explain it.
Pavel: Well, our nation is close and united. Adyghs they're a very united people, they ...
Emma: There's only a few of us.
Pavel: We have, well, family roots, very, very interrelated and close ... through some sort of second cousin, third cousin ... very close. If there's trouble or some celebration, we always go to every relative. For us this is...
Emma: Anyway, it's the done thing ...
Pavel: For Adyghs, this is the done thing. For us it's not a custom, it's em ... em an old tradition that been around for ages.
Emma: And this is the way it was and always will be.
Pavel: The way it was and always will be.
Emma: So, I really like it when some event happens, whether it's good or bad.

This dialogue on how to 'feel' Adygh gives four major dimensions that mark their Adygh identity. First, there is that of 'fixed' or 'given' ethnic belonging that is taken for granted. This is pronounced when Emma (22 years) says that she does not know how to explain it. For her, it is just there and cannot be explained. Second, there is the pride and patriotism that everyone who is Adygh should feel Adygh, indirectly referring to *Adyghage*, which demands such awareness. Pride and patriotism, however, do not only qualify Adyghs. Such attitudes are widespread amongst Caucasian peoples generally, including Armenians, and have their roots in history and cultural traditions. For Adyghs, pride and patriotism are closely intertwined with solidarity. This solidarity has become stronger in the twentieth century because of the awareness that arose from political transformations of the early 1990s. It is the fact that they are *only a small people* that creates a certain pride and makes them voluntarily adhere to traditions in order to preserve their people. It implies a resistance to Western/global influences, when both, Emma and Pavel (23 years) say that *'this is the way it was and always will be'*. Most young Adyghs are proud of their traditions and have displayed similar attitudes. Taking all four dimensions together, then this is what it means to be Adygh. On the one hand, it is pride and patriotism, on the other hand, it is the adherence and preservation of long-standing traditions.

Conclusions
This chapter has explored the most basic dimension of the key question of this book that of subjective definitions of ethnic belonging. It has been argued in this chapter that young Armenian adults' identities are complex, while Adygh indigenous youth identities are constructed according to location and mainly two major identity markers (Caucasian and Adygh). Young Armenians' subjective definitions of belonging draw upon a variety of identity resources, such as the historical narratives of diasporic belonging, kept alive by intergenerational transmission or global technologies. These are stories about translocation that form diasporic belonging across the globe. Despite translocal dimensions of belonging, the discussion on the different perceptions of homeland has stressed that it is personal lived experience that most strongly influences subjective definitions of ethnic belonging. Research participants use home and homeland as ways of talking about their more localized identities. The different perceptions of homeland show that the primordial homeland, Armenia, as a cultural centre in the diasporic imagination is no longer applicable for Armenian youth on the whole.

This chapter has revealed that young Armenians and Adyghs have a strong sense of their ethnic belonging, which is partially a result of the regional political discourse that places emphasis on one's ethnic belonging.

Hence, one important identity marker for both young Adyghs and Armenians is constituted by Russians, as the significant 'other.' Following Lacan (2000 [1949]) and Althusser (2000 [1969]), identity is understood as a mirror image that only comes into being through social interaction or interpellation with the 'other'. It is the interaction with Russians that makes young Armenians and Adyghs keep a strong sense of their own culture, instead of creating a hybrid culture.

While young Adygh adults emphasize their 'fixed' origins, it seems as if young Armenians have begun to draw upon cosmopolitanism as an identity resource, when considering the subjective definitions of ethnic belonging. The discussion of young Armenians' complex constructions of identities has stressed that they keep a strong sense of ethnicity, but are able to recognize cultural diversity in their identity constructions. Crucially, this cultural diversity is not only recognized from the outside, but also from within the Armenian community in view of sub-ethnic differences. Accordingly, it is argued that, at times, cosmopolitanism becomes an identity resource to manage cultural diversity. At the same time, cosmopolitanism as an occasional identity resource serves to subvert the political discourse, something that becomes clearer when youth cultural leisure practices are examined in Chapter Five.

Most importantly, the strong sense of ethnic identification among young Adyghs and Armenians is evoked by the dynamics within their ethnic communities. In Chapter One, ethnic communities have been defined as collectivities which are articulated as ethnic by their group members for purposes of belonging. Hence, the next chapter examines thoroughly the ways in which the discourses within both ethnic communities bear upon the construction of young people's identities. The ensuing chapter on gender relations also demonstrates that besides ethnicity, gender is an influential category for the construction of youth cultural identities. It is through the intersection with gender systems of differentiation that ethnicity becomes essentialized.

4 Gendered Armenian and Adygh Identities

In this book identity is approached as a contextual and relational positioning rather than a fixed entity. In the previous chapter on ethnic identifications in general, and senses of belonging in particular, it has been argued that identity is constituted within particular contexts. Exploring how gender is constructed and displayed in both ethnic communities, this chapter argues that gender is a crucial identity resource for ethnic identification. Diasporic and indigenous identities are constructed through gender, and this chapter illustrates how research participants negotiate their identities in relation to both belonging to their ethnic communities and wider Russian society. At the same time, this chapter examines how research participants draw differently on ethnic identifications in order to overcome tensions and ambivalences in their everyday lives. Several sources emphasize that young women from ethnic minority groups negotiate between and transform fixed cultural norms (cf. Brah 1996; Mirza 1992; Mørk 2000). At the same time, this body of literature recognizes that the lives of these young women from ethnic minorities are inscribed by gender relations, class structures and racialized discourses.

Armenian traditions at the crossroads[117]

The social construction of gender and the idea of 'performed' gender identities provide a conceptual framework to understand the existence of multiple femininities and masculinities. A socially constructed gender identity can be understood as a product of social relations constituted through interaction within discourses of power. Gender identities are performed according to expected gender roles within society in general and ethnic communities in particular. Individuals perform gender identities in particular ways in order to express themselves and affirm as well as reproduce societal values via their social performance. Previously published studies on femininities and masculinities in ethnic/diasporic minority groups have

---

117   A modified version of the first part of this chapter on Armenians has been published previously (Ziemer 2010).

emphasized that gender is characterized by overlapping and complex dimensions of inequality that create multiple forms of femininities and masculinities that are both internally and externally relational and hierarchical (Archer 2001; Dwyer 1999; 2000, Qureshi 2004). Although femininities and masculinities are very complex, in Connell's view (1998 [1987]) their interrelation centres on a single structural fact – that is the global dominance of men over women.

The patriarchal paradigm exists in different forms in many societies, but has some common characteristics (cf. Therborn 2004). Broadly speaking, patriarchy can be defined as a 'system of social structures and practices in which men dominate, oppress and exploit women' (Walby 1990: 20).[118] Walby's (1990) definition, however, tends towards describing a set of practices in terms of their outcomes; that is the subordination of women. Such a dual-system approach prioritizes relations between men and women within the patriarchal system. Anthias and Yuval-Davies (1992) argue instead that patriarchal relations are not explicable by deploying the term patriarchy as a distinct social system. They contend that 'the social system cannot be divided into these different autonomous, but interrelated structures and that patriarchal social relations (in the descriptive sense) are endemic and integral to social formations with regard to the distribution of material resources and power' (Anthias and Yuval-Davies 1992: 109). The most significant characteristics of patriarchal relations for both ethnic communities studied here are: the division of gender roles and hierarchical power, the control of women's sexuality, and women's subordination to the rules of family and kinship relations.

The structural fact of men's global dominance over women provides the main basis for men's relationships to each other and their relationships to women, producing a hegemonic form of masculinity in society as whole. For Connell (1998 [1987]: 183) 'hegemonic masculinity' is always constructed in relation to various subordinated masculinities as well as in relation to

---

118 According to Walby (1990: 108), the main structures that comprise patriarchy are paid work, housework, sexuality, culture, violence and the state. The interrelationship between them creates different forms of patriarchy.

women.[119] Accordingly, hegemonic masculinities must embody successful collective strategies in relation to women in order to maintain their dominance. Given the complexity of gender relations no simple or uniform strategy is possible – a 'mix' is necessary (Connell 1998 [1987]: 186). Whereas Connell (1998 [1987]) writes extensively about hegemonic masculinity, he offers only a fleeting discussion of the role of femininities. Others, however, discuss a 'mix' of strategies that women use to negotiate their femininities in different, often contradictory cultural contexts. Having examined various strategies employed by young British Asian women to position themselves between two sets of cultural values, Qureshi and Moores (1999: 319) conclude that, for example, clothing is one form of strategy. Each style of clothing involves 'putting on' a different femininity and performing the situationally appropriate role.[120]

'Ia pokorna': patriarchy and traditional Armenian gender roles
According to Armenian tradition, Armenian women's life-cycle can be divided into four periods.[121] In every period of her life, an Armenian woman's positioning is oriented towards married life and child-rearing. The first stage, growing up as a child, is characterized by a modest life in her parents' home, where a daughter is under the control of male relatives and her father. The whole period in the parents' house prepares the daughter for marriage, which will determine her future life and status within the community. The second stage in an Armenian woman's life starts when she marries. Marriage carries a huge emotional weight in Armenian society as it is the culminating moment in a woman's life. This stage is also marked by a transition from being controlled by the father and male relatives to being controlled by the

---

119   Connell's notion of 'hegemonic masculinity' borrows the term from Gramsci's analyses of class relations in Italy and employs 'hegemony' to mean 'a social ascendancy achieved in a play of social forces that extends beyond contests of brute power into the organization of private life and cultural processes' (Connell 1998 [1987]: 184).
120   Young Pakistani women are shown to have a positive attitude toward traditional dress, which they routinely wear at home or at Pakistani community functions. These young women also establish boundaries by not wearing a traditional dress in particular educational contexts.
121   The knowledge of traditional Armenian gender roles has been obtained from Ishkanian (2004), Shakhnazarian (2005) and Ter-Sarkisiants (1998).

husband's relatives. The third stage is the stage of maternity and child-rearing. The fourth and final stage is the highest status of an 'older woman', for example, when she becomes a mother-in-law. This stage is perceived as a reward for a life devoted to serving the interests of the family (Shakhnazarian 2005: 57).

Similar to other diasporic communities across the globe, the family is a very important symbol of Armenian culture and retains its significance today.[122] The father is considered the 'keeper of the household flame' because he goes out into the world and works to protect his home and family. The mother is considered 'the hearth of the home,' selflessly supporting her husband and taking care of the home (Ishkanian 2004: 267). Consequently, the only female life-strategies that are approved and promoted are those which include the creation of a 'complete' family, marked by the presence of husband and children (Shakhnazarian 2005: 58).[123] This requires an Armenian woman to serve all members of her husband's family. Sacrifice and endurance are central categories for Armenian women. According to Shakhnazarian (2011), an Armenian woman's sacrifices correspond to romanticized and idealized cultural norms of Armenian women as victims; as passive, submissive, gentle and silent women.

While these norms are traditional and are thus subject to change over time, their basic tenets are accepted in the Armenian community in Krasnodar today. One could argue that the persistence of these patriarchal gender roles can be derived from a popular understanding that Armenian women have to be subservient to Armenian men. The idea of women being subservient is conveyed, for example, during Armenian wedding ceremonies, where the groom says to the priest 'I speak for her' (*Ia ruchaius' za nee*), while the bride says 'I am submissive' (*Ia pokorna*).[124] Although today, Armenian women

---

122 According to Ishkanian (2004: 267), family is central in Armenian culture due to Armenia's absence of history as an independent state. In the absence of statehood, the concept of 'nation-as-family' evolved in Armenian society.
123 Although Shakhnazarian's (2005) argument relates to Armenian Karabakh culture, the author's experience during fieldwork suggests this is still a widespread perception amongst Armenians in Krasnodar too.
124 The phrase '*Ia pokorna*' was mentioned frequently by female research participants, when talking about relationships between men and women or between boys and girls.

have many more rights and freedoms than in the past, these wedding vows remain central to the hierarchy of gender relations amongst Armenians. Armenian daughters are expected to be submissive to their fathers and are brought up according to the future role of wife and mother. Married women are expected to be good housekeepers and to put their husbands and children before their individual needs and feelings.

The gender order of the Armenian community in Krasnodar
The construction of history and culture is a major task facing all ethnic groups and consequently 'the past is a resource used by ethnic groups in the collective quest for meaning and community' (Cohen 1985: 99). A vital resource for constructing and maintaining ethnic group identity is the adherence to a particular gender order that relies on cultural traditions. Thus, the lives of Armenian women are inscribed by traditional gender roles that embody the boundaries of belonging and are produced in representations of group identity. By examining two major components of this gender order, this chapter seeks to highlight the constraints that the principles and standards of right conduct have for Armenian girls and young women. Armenian women are often defined by their social status, which is not class or financial means, but the role they assume in the societal structures geared toward the preservation of Armenianness in the diaspora (Peroomanian 2000). On the whole, with the 'Armenian' gender order within the community, Armenians as an ethnic minority are able to (re-)define their status in relation to the dominant group (Russians). The gender order, based on cultural traditions, helps the Armenian community to create a strong sense of group identity and to build a link to their pan-Armenian identification.

The first major component of the Armenian gender order is connected to the 'idealization' of Armenian women, where womanhood is presented as a repository of tradition and centres on home, family and child-rearing. Many studies on diasporic communities stress that women in these communities are seen as the 'keepers of the culture' (Billson 1995) and therefore women's moral and sexual loyalties are deemed central to the maintenance of group status. Within the Armenian community, women are perceived as being dedicated to their families and sexually restrained. As indicated above, there is a long-standing Armenian tradition that an Armenian woman's role is linked to reproduction – an Armenian woman is a good mother, a good housewife and also has to be beautiful.

Another major component of the Armenian community is the image of being a family-oriented community. Traditionally, Armenian families were characterized by big patriarchal family communities, although from the 1920s onwards Armenian families have become smaller due to large-scale rural-urban migration as a result of modernization processes in the Soviet Union (Ter-Sarkisiants 1998: 137-144). Nonetheless, the tradition of a close family itself and close kinship relations are still characteristic for Armenians in Krasnodar. Claims of family closeness are not unique to Armenians in Krasnodar, but also apply to Armenians in other parts of the world (cf. Bakalian 1993; Der-Martirosian *et al.* 1993; Peroomanian 2000; Talai 1986, 1989). Generally speaking, the close-knit family is considered to be a characteristic for all Caucasian peoples. Other studies on ethnic minorities in different cultural contexts have also stressed family cohesion. For example, the studies of Brah (1996) and Dwyer (1999, 2000) on British South Asians, the study of Mørck (2000) on Danish Asians and the studies of Qureshi (2006), Qureshi and Moores (1999) on Scottish Pakistanis accentuate the close-knit character of their family.

Both components of the Armenian gender order have clear gender implications for Armenian women. While both Armenian men and women identify the family system as a source of cultural pride, it is Armenian women who have the primary responsibility for maintaining family closeness and cultural reproduction. Even though research participants are aware of gender relations prescribed by traditions, they do not always agree with it:

> *Seda:* He'll [Armenian husband] never abandon you, never leave you, if you have kids, not like Russians. He'll always provide for you, but you have to obey him with everything. You haven't got your own 'ego'. If you try to show him that you're an individual, that you're a person, then he's not interested. He's interested in finding everything ready for him when he comes home, everything washed and the kids taken care of, that's all! But I want to show that apart from all this there is a person who still means something by herself, she still means something. Can

you understand? That she means something to the world in general and that she's maybe interesting not only because she's a good housewife and cook and so on.

In this excerpt, Seda (23 years) briefly describes the general gender order within the Armenian community, which is based on patriarchy and presumes that wives have to obey their husbands and are responsible for cultural reproduction.[125] The excerpt also shows that the construction of femininities always involves various processes of 'othering' – that is in relation to men, but also in relation to the majority culture (Russian culture). In this excerpt, Seda includes both processes of 'othering' in creating her femininity; that is in relation to men – Armenian and Russian men, but at the same time in relation to cultural expectations of Russian society (*rossiiskoe obshchestvo*) as well as Armenian society.[126] On the one hand, she explains her experience and declares her disagreement with Armenian patriarchal traditions; on the other, she juxtaposes Armenian culture with Russian culture, when she perceives Russians as lacking strong family ties. Russian men, in her opinion, do not hesitate to walk out on their wives, while Armenian husbands, would never desert their family. Nonetheless, Armenian traditions demand that women obey their husbands and do not develop themselves as individuals, whereas for her, Russian men would be interested in a woman's personality and thus give her the freedom to develop as an individual, rather than as an object for use in cultural reproduction.

From Seda's excerpt, one can see that Armenian gender order is constructed partially in relation to cultural traditions, but also as a product of 'othering' in respect to Russian society. The 'idealization' of Armenian women takes place by juxtaposing them to Russian society beyond the Armenian community. It is argued that Armenian women situate themselves as

---

125   Noteworthy here is that traditional gender roles still prevail in contemporary Russian society as a whole. A survey conducted by the Swiss Academy for Development revealed that of the 2006 respondents (aged 15 to 29), 79 per cent thought that men are responsible for the well-being of the family, while 80 per cent thought that the primary role of women in society is to be a good mother and a good wife (Dafflon 2009: 29).

126   For the ensuing discussion, the word Russian (*rossiiskii*) is used which is a civic term pertaining to Russian culture rather than an ethnic term.

everything that Russian women are not, and are imagined by Armenian men in this way too. Armenian cultural norms demand chastity before marriage. For Armenian men, women have to be chaste as well as dedicated to their families. This ensures group belonging for the community as a whole; in this way Armenian masculinity depends on Armenian femininity. The striving for this ideal effectively erases the Armenian 'bad girl', ignores competing sexual practices in the Armenian community, and uncritically embraces the embodiment of perfect womanhood and ideal femininity.[127] In the following interview excerpt, Sona talks about Russian women's premarital sexual experiences, which is the epitome of the 'bad' girl in the eyes of Armenian men. Here, the process of 'othering' comes into play – Russian women, according to Sona (17 years), are everything that Armenian women are not. They are, for example, sexually promiscuous.

> Sona: You see, Armenian men have the narrow-minded opinion that, you know, a Russian girl, if she sleeps with him before marriage, that means she's a tart. But in the culture of these people [Russian culture] it's not considered to be very wrong. Of course, it's not very desirable, but it's not a reason to call her a whore. At the end of the day, this is a free country. Yes, it's a different culture, completely different. Why don't you do in Rome what the Romans do, instead of judging people? You see, this [the idea that Armenian women should not have sex before marriage] isn't right, it's fundamentally not right.

Noteworthy here is that in contradistinction to traditional Armenian understandings; Sona does not perceive 'free' behaviour as bad – for her it is normal in contemporary society. Rather, it is the expectations placed on Armenian women she considers unjust, though she does not actively oppose these expectations. In other words, the Armenian community places expectations on women to ensure the reproduction of the Armenian community in its traditional patriarchal form. This, however, is increasingly difficult as the younger generation engages with the wider society and learns

---

[127] Tolman and Higgins (1996) show that parents in general have a two-fold understanding in relation to their daughters – that of a 'good girl' and a 'bad girl', While the 'good girl' is passive and a threatened sexual object, the 'bad girl' is an active, desiring sexual agent.

to accept gender behaviour that does not conform to traditions passed down within the Armenian community.

Young Armenian women positioning themselves
The gender order within the Armenian community is negotiated by Armenian women in individual ways and with complex strategies. These positions are heavily dependent on parents' class position[128] within society as a whole, and within the Armenian community in particular. The importance of the socio-economic background of parents is also vital for the ways in which young women position themselves in the British context, both for young women in general and for young women from ethnic minorities (cf. Dwyer 2000; Skeggs 1997). Young Armenian women's aspirations often contradict parents' perceptions. When this occurs some girls choose to conform to the 'ideal' Armenian woman, while others do so reluctantly or deny everything related to this 'idealization'. The question of the availability of resources is most important for understanding the diverse strategies for constructing individual positions. Those girls from a poorer family background are much more likely to follow the traditional gender order, since this increases their chances of finding a good husband in the future. In contrast, those young Armenian females from wealthier backgrounds are most likely to deny or subvert the discourse, as they have more resources to create a successful future for themselves. For them, the future does not only involve getting married.

Although the traditional gender discourse helps to (re-)define Armenians' status in Krasnodar, many female participants question this discourse, since it implies restrictions for them. As a result, a hierarchy amongst Armenian women has been created. Those young Armenian women, who have the resources to distance themselves from the traditional gender discourse within the Armenian community, sometimes look down on those women who do not. This hierarchy can be extended into the political sphere in Krasnodar, which

---

128 In this context, class is defined more loosely. During fieldwork, it was impossible to determine exactly how much money research participants' parents earned. Yet, close contact with research participants made it possible to understand the socio-economic differences between research participants according to the ways they spent their spare time, the types of clothes they wore, the types of mobile phones they had and whether they talked about going on holidays abroad etc.

distinguishes between local and non-local Armenians. In Chapter Two, it was suggested that the official political discourse artificially divides Armenian into new and old, 'us' and 'them', to justify discriminatory practices. Nonetheless, in a later paragraph, it will be shown that the 'real situation' is different from this official discourse. Female research participants also refer to this division between locals and non-locals, which the subsequent interview excerpt shows:

> Lala: What about the group?
> Ulrike: You said 'locals' – do you mean the ones who go to the Church [the Armenian Church in Krasnodar]?
> Lala: (*laughs*) Those who are a bit backward.
> Ulrike: Why do you think they are backward?
> Lala: Because I know what they live for. They live for the fact that they're at home, spending their time with their families. I remember the scene once when my birthday coincided with Easter, and we went to Church. Usually we go to Church at twelve at night at Easter. Well, we got together and drove to the Church, at twelve o'clock at night. Of course, without make-up, without anything, as we were – we got up and went. We arrived at the Church, but here they all were, as if I don't know, like a make-up stall, what a site! When I saw it, I was in shock. They were all overdressed. In Church, well, what nonsense!

During this episode of the interview with Lala (20 years), attempts were made to find out what Lala thinks about the division between locals and non-locals. When the Armenian Church is mentioned, she immediately makes the distinction between *progressive* and *backward* Armenians. Nevertheless, it is not entirely clear whether backward Armenians are 'non-local' Armenians. As this episode indicates, it is more about what she thinks about Armenian people going to the Armenian Church in Krasnodar. For her, Armenians, who adhere to Armenian traditions, are 'backward'. Here, she stresses that girls who go to the Armenian Church and dress up may be using the opportunity to meet someone and are thus following traditions.[129] Having a better social and class position, Lala's parents are well-off; she is not able to understand the

---

129 In the earlier discussion on Armenian traditional gender roles, it was indicated that a woman's beauty is an important aspect of Armenian tradition.

different cultural dynamics for some Armenian girls and does not approve of such strategies.

Later in a group interview with Lala and her friend, Lusine (21 years), they continue to elaborate on such differences and suggest a distinction between 'standard' (*standartnye*) and 'non-standard' (*ne standartnye*) Armenians. Lusine recounted an episode in her life, when one of her friends, a 'non-standard' Armenian, joked about the use of Armenian language. Following the story about her friend, we started talking about 'standard' and 'non-standard' Armenians and it became clear that 'standard' Armenians are negatively perceived by Lala and Lusine:

Lusine: She [her friend] doesn't think in the standard way either ...
Ulrike: What do you mean by 'standard'?
Lala: There are two types here in Krasnodar – the standard ones and the non-standard ones.
Ulrike: Are you non-standard?
Lusine: I don't know. I think, you have to define it ... This has to be defined by others.
Lala: Perhaps, we're the standard type ...
Lusine: (*interrupts*) No, I know a girl ... Ruzanna has a cousin. Her cousin is a girl, who's 21 years old. She isn't allowed to put make-up on. She isn't allowed to do this, even though her parents live in Russia. She isn't allowed to wear trousers. Her father drives her to university and then picks her up. She doesn't go anywhere and this lifestyle suits her ... She has to sit at home.
Ulrike: What do you think about that?
Lusine: It's bad.
Lala: You see, when you suppress a person, you kill their personality. There's nothing to talk about afterwards. If they haven't got any interests ... if she doesn't see anything and doesn't know anything.
Lusine: She doesn't see anything and doesn't talk to anyone. There's no development at all. But this is what she likes. I don't like anything that restricts me ... I don't like that, but she likes it. She thinks that's normal ... You can maintain traditions, I don't know, know one's language, observe one's traditions, at weddings, dances, yes, culture, well that's it. At present, in Armenia this [referring to this restricted lifestyle] doesn't exist. They [some Armenians in Krasnodar] live like they did fifty years ago, with the same beliefs. But when my Dad went to a

wedding in Georgia he was shocked. He said that in Georgia young people are more developed than we are here, because they don't have any restrictions. In Georgia, they say that people living in Russia can do anything they want, but why can't we do it? They're allowed to. But we haven't got that. Here in Krasnodar everything has come to a standstill. They say that we have to preserve our traditions and customs...

These two young women try to explain that 'standard' Armenians are those who adhere to traditions, which Lala and Lusine see as 'backward'. The 'non-standard' Armenians are those who are 'progressive' in the sense that they do not follow Armenian traditions uncritically. Nonetheless, when asked whether they would classify themselves as 'non-standard' Armenians, they cannot give a clear answer. For them, the backwardness implies restrictions for women, even though Lusine maintains that she practices some aspects of her culture. Both perceive the whole Armenian community in Krasnodar as backward, since the community tries to preserve traditions that even contradict cultural norms in Armenia, according to Lusine.[130] Lusine's understanding of Armenians in Armenia being much more 'progressive' than Armenians in Krasnodar suggests an element of idealization of the home country. For example, Zdravomyslova and Temkina (2007) in their study on gender problems in Armenia highlight the unequal nature of gender relations and demonstrate that traditions remain central to the construction of Armenia.

Lala and Lusine's classification strategy is subjective, especially considering Lusine's example of the girl with a restricted lifestyle. It is important not to privilege informant narratives. In practice, during fieldwork, there were no encounters with young Armenian women who indicated that they were happy just to stay at home. Thus, the stark 'standard/non-standard' or 'backward/progressive' distinction is better understood as a device to position the speakers. A more adequate classification of young women's strategies would include 'semi-traditional' and 'semi-modern' positionings. These subdivisions

---

130 At first, Lusine talks about Armenia, but then continues talking about Georgia, since her family is originally from Georgia. Earlier in the interview, she said that Armenia and Georgia are very much alike in her understanding and this explains why she always juxtaposes the two. Therefore, it is assumed that what she says about Georgia also applies to Armenia; she idealizes both.

were created by the author during fieldwork, as often research participants were 'traditional' in some ways, such as in their orientation towards marriage, but in other ways 'modern' in, for example, their choice of lifestyle. Furthermore, the term 'semi-modern' is applied in order to classify some girls who consider it possible to have a boyfriend and even sometimes to smoke, but intend to get married to an Armenian. This contradicts Lala and Lusine's 'non-standard' classification, since smoking is definitely 'non-standard' for Armenian cultural norms, while only considering an Armenian husband is 'standard' for Armenian cultural norms.

Returning to the question of the division between 'local' Armenians perceived as 'modern' and 'non-local' Armenians considered 'traditional', any correlation between Lala's and Lusine's classification and the 'real situation' could not be detected. Observation suggested that, in fact, it is socio-economic status that channels young women to position themselves in a traditional or modern way. This is illustrated by comparing three female participants, Anush (22 years), Armine (21 years) and Gaiane (20 years). All of them came more or less at the same time to Krasnodar, approximately eighteen years ago. Anush and Armine even emigrated from the same region, Nagorno Karabakh, whereas Gaiane emigrated from Armenia to Krasnodar. As explained in Chapter Two, according to the official regional political discourse, they are seen as non-local Armenians, since they only came to the region in the last twenty years. Despite all being from a similar 'non-local' background, they are not necessarily 'traditional'.

Anush and Gaiane can be classified as 'modern', as in many ways, and according to Armenian cultural norms, they seem to be 'non-standard'. For example, Gaiane plays beach volleyball in a mixed group in her spare time, although she knows that her relatives (not her parents) disapprove of such spare time activities. Like Gaiane, Anush also chose to participate in 'non-standard' activities. She has been clubbing and has travelled abroad on holiday with two other female friends, which caused disapproval amongst her relatives (although not her parents). In contrast, Armine conforms to Armenian cultural norms and would not consider participating in activities like playing sport in a mixed group or going on holidays abroad without her family. The difference between the three participants is their economic status, which influenced the way they positioned themselves. Whereas Gaiane and Anush are from families with a high economic status, Armine is located on the lower ladder of social hierarchy and therefore lacks the resources to distance herself from the traditional way of life.

Another important influence on how research participants position themselves comes from their parents' world outlook. This often results from their social and class position, but is sometimes related to their willingness to embrace and adjust to Russian culture. Research into family power-structure argues that the family is one of the oldest patriarchal systems. While power is important in families, Connell (1998 [1987]) also stresses the emotional pressure that families bring to bear on young people. It is often the emotional bond between parents and young people that leads them to follow parents' expectations. It is argued that parents' attitudes cannot only be explained through their economic well-being. Lala and Lusine, for example, are both from wealthy families, yet Lala appears to have chosen a 'modern' position for herself (although she would deny it) whereas Lusine's father still demands Lusine's adherence to tradition and she excludes the possibility of getting married to a man from a different nationality or of having a boyfriend before marriage. Overall, she is very critical of Armenian traditions. In terms of classification, she seems to position herself semi-traditionally.

To summarize the above discussion, the way young Armenian women position themselves and draw upon diasporic identifications varies considerably, depending on the socio-economic position of their parents. Those from poorer backgrounds are much more likely to choose a 'traditional' position for themselves, which incorporates a strong diasporic identification. These young women are most likely to be affected by the community's gender order and, thus, compliance may bring them real benefits by being publicly labelled as 'good girls'. Those young women, who have been classified as 'modern' and 'semi-modern' come from wealthier backgrounds and have resources that enable them to distance themselves from traditions they perceive as restrictive to their individual freedom. Finally, some young females choose a 'semi-traditional' position with stronger diasporic identifications. This position may be largely influenced by their parents' world outlook, which does not necessarily result from their better socio-economic position, but is more dependent on how far parents are willing to embrace and adjust to Russian culture. Overall, most of the young women in this research combine the two elements of compliance and resistance in their performances in order to ensure that they are seen as 'good,' but being able to be 'bad' sometimes. In this way, their strategies are very similar to that of young women or girls in Britain (cf. Griffin 1985; Lees 1993).

Maintaining cultural continuity: the question of endogamy
Having explored the positions young Armenian women chose for themselves, there is one important question that cuts across all positions – the question of endogamy. Whereas young Armenian men are relatively unrestricted in their choice of future wife, young Armenian women, especially from traditional ('standard') families, are under great pressures from their parents to marry within the community. Endogamy is one of the areas of major intergenerational tensions and many participants do not agree with this constraint. The 'dating' norms which govern young people's attitudes and behaviour in contemporary Russian society are different to traditional Armenian norms of dating. According to Armenian tradition, the perfect partner for a girl is someone from within her own ethnic, religious and class background, and elders (especially parents) have significant power in the selection of suitable partners (Bakalian 1993). The Armenian tradition of courting has been preserved to some extent, although this varies between families, as Mariam (19 years) explains:

> *Mariam:* A guy notices a girl and starts pointing her out to all his friends and relatives, asking who she is and whose daughter she is. You know, this is the way it starts. You find out who the father is. As much as one can ... It depends on social status. For example, if he hasn't got anything, of course, a rich daughter won't be allowed to become his wife. That doesn't really happen. He points to her; she points to him. Through so and so they get to find out all about each other. You know, you could say...they get to know each other without meeting up. They find out everything. Basically, it's like conducting a survey, who knows about this girl, what is good and bad about her, with whom has she been seen? You know, any scandal and all that.

They [Armenians] love this stuff, they, I don't know, they're just crazy about it, I don't know...

In many ways, this practice is a method of controlling daughters' behaviours, including restricting their independence and contacts. Often in ethnic communities, changes in female behaviour are resisted and interpreted as signs of moral decay and, thus, are carefully monitored and sanctioned (cf. Dwyer 2000; Qureshi and Moores 1999). The practice of choosing your partner has become accepted, although in the majority of cases it is necessary to get the approval of both families. If that approval is not gained, the chance of a happy marriage is reduced. Therefore, any young person, especially a young woman, when pressured by parents, tends to subordinate her own choice in favour of her parents' will. While these norms are in a process of transition within the Armenian community, young adults still struggle with their parents and cultural ideals. On the one hand, they feel obliged to please their parents, but at the same time they want to follow their heart and the norms of the larger society and assert their choice. This can create dilemmas for young women:

Armine: Whenever there is a problem, it's always resolved in favour of my parents.
Ulrike: Yes? Is that simply tradition?
Armine: Yes, ... I wanted to go out with a guy with a different religion. It was torture for me. But I listened to my parents; that's the way it was.
Ulrike: Did you split up?
Armine: Yes, because he was a Muslim. Yes, Dad isn't overly keen on them. You know, because there was a war in Baku, and they treated Armenians badly. You see, my Dad, uncle and cousin – especially men think very badly of Muslims. Well, they don't actually do anything, but a marriage with a Muslim is out of the question.
Ulrike: I've heard that. And so you listened to your parents and that was that?
Armine: Yes. He wanted to marry me and I wanted to marry him, but he has a different religion. I don't think religion is important for family life at all, but my Dad said, 'If you get married to him, I'll leave the house'. My Mum said that none of my relatives would come to the wedding and I'd be on my own with his relatives.

At the beginning of this subsection, it was argued that this issue cuts across social hierarchy. It also affects the so-called 'non-standard' ('modern') or 'semi-modern' Armenian girls. Whereas Armine has a lower social status and is from a poorer family, Narine (21 years), a wealthy 'semi-modern' girl, who goes out and has boyfriends, also talked about such problems:

> *Narine:* My Mum, you know, she doesn't mind. The main thing is that her daughter is happy. But my Dad wants him [husband] to be Armenian, so that I can continue the Armenian family, the Armenian surname and the lot basically. He's against it [a husband from a different nationality], categorically against it. Simply, I have to get married to an Armenian. Well, I went out with a guy for a year, but we split up ... My Dad was against this relationship because the guy was Russian and not Armenian. I got fed up with my Dad constantly saying it wasn't allowed, so I split up with him.

Here Narine communicates an idea that is implied in a well-known Armenian proverb: *'An Armenian isn't someone who has parents that are Armenian, but someone who has Armenian children'.* Although wealthy, local and fairly liberal, her father still wants to be a good Armenian and, therefore, determines Narine's choice of boyfriend and asserts his authority. Narine's strategy for overcoming this problem was simply to split up with her Russian boyfriend and to find an Armenian one. This strategy pleased her father, but at the same time accorded her the freedoms that are attached to having a boyfriend.

The Armenian community even attempts to preserve the tradition of endogamy at a wider, community level. A 'dating agency' (*klub znakomstva*) has been created in the Armenian Church in order to solve the perceived problem of the rise in interethnic marriages. It was not only my female participants who spoke about the problem of interethnic marriage. Most parts of the Armenian community consider the fact that many Armenian men marry Russian women to be a problem. This is the reason for the creation of this *klub*.[131] However, not all parents insist on endogamy. In many ways, this may

---

[131] A short interview with the head of this dating agency can be found in the Appendix 3.

be because parents perceive endogamy as backward and follow trends in Russian society (*rossiiskoe obshchestvo*), that is, that partners are chosen because of love. It may also be that they perceive disadvantages if their daughters marry Armenians:

> *Lala:* I know that my parents have a normal attitude to this question, because they can see that really there aren't any normal Armenian guys [in Krasnodar]. They're so primitive here [in Krasnodar], you can't imagine. As for the [Armenian] girls [in Krasnodar], well, girls I think are even more developed, than guys. Guys, how can I say it, they're so hypocritical. Because there aren't many of them, less than girls, they can have ten [girls] and at the same time try to pull the wool over their eyes ... So, I keep my distance from this.

Lala and her parents think that there are no 'normal' young Armenian men because young Armenian men are inclined to assert their symbolic Armenian identity in respect to Armenian women. During interviews female participants often talked about the special status of Armenian men, since there is a widespread opinion that there are less Armenian men than women. This, however, is contradicted by official sources; according to the 2002 population census, there are 141,501 Armenian men and 133,065 Armenian women in the region. The numerical predominance of men holds true for the younger generation; for the age category 20 – 24 years, there are 11,424 men and 10,733 women.[132]

The symbolic importance of Armenian men is more likely to be found in the patriarchal belief that every family should have a son (Ishkanian 2004). Consequently, Lala sees Armenian men as backward because they are conscious of their special status within their families. Young Armenian men are more likely than young Armenian women to insist on traditions in order to maintain their authority. This is not peculiar for young Armenian men; Alexander (2004), in her study, also argues that young men use their ethnic identity to maintain their masculine authority. For Lala, however, everything

---

132 Krasnodar krai Committee of State Statistics. *Natsional'nyi sostav i vladenie iazykami, grazhdanstvo.* Itogi vserossiiskoi perepisi naseleniia 2002 goda po Krasnodarskomu Kraiu, Tom 4, Krasnodar, 2005.

that is connected to the maintenance of traditions is backward, resulting in her conclusion that Armenian men are 'primitive'.

Although some girls are completely against marriage with an Armenian, other girls said that they were more inclined to marry an Armenian, even though they had a choice. The reasons they gave for this attitude were twofold: first, such girls tended to cite the issue of cultural difference; and second, they were concerned about how a husband with a different nationality would be seen within the community. Lusine, who has a very high status in the Armenian community, spoke about the difficulties an interethnic marriage would present for her.

> *Lusine:* Yes, my parents' approval means a lot to me. Because if my husband were Russian, with dark hair, and he came to our house ... Well, my parents, well, let's say, I convinced them about everything [so that her parents would accept him]. But if he stepped out into our Armenian community, then he'd feel depressed, no matter what, because everyone would give him funny looks. Over the years, everyone would get used to him, so he'd acclimatize and get used to it. He'd just be like a fish out of water. Everyone would give him funny looks. It would take ages for him to acclimatize and get used to it.

The question of endogamy is in transition, but still has a major impact on all young women. Generally speaking, Armenian traditions are at the crossroads between traditional and modern in so far as they are observed by choice and only sometimes by force. While some young women choose to adhere to Armenian traditions, others choose to distance themselves. In this way, young women's strategies are often contradictory, which means that they rely on performative resources in different ways and under different circumstances. While some choose to perform a 'standard' (traditional) position, which is supported by the Armenian gender discourse and helps to create one's status as superior to that of Russians and create a stronger sense of belonging, others choose a 'non-standard' (modern) position to live a life with almost no cultural restrictions. Nonetheless, the majority of young women choose positions in between, 'semi-traditional' and 'semi-modern', in order to ensure that they do not disappoint their parents and do not betray their cultural heritage, but at the same time are not estranged from Russian society.

Enacting and transgressing the 'ideal' Armenian
A symbol of diasporic identity: Armenian women's sexuality
Embodying the moral integrity of the idealized ethnic community, Armenian women are expected to comply with male-defined criteria of what constitute 'ideal' feminine virtues. Whereas some areas of patriarchal hierarchy have been challenged, such as endogamy, other areas, such as young women's chastity before marriage, have remained largely unchallenged. While the sexual behaviour of adult women is confined to a monogamous, heterosexual context, the sexual behaviour of young women is denied completely. On the one hand, it is used by Armenians to differentiate themselves from Russians and, thus, plays an important role in preserving their ethnic identities. On the other hand, the question of female chastity is closely linked to male dominance because masculine identities are dependent on female purity. There is a widespread perception that if parents, especially fathers, do not have enough authority over their daughters to make them 'proper' Armenians then they have failed to be good family men, as Anush explains (22 years):[133]

> *Anush:* I have the impression that the whole Armenian community is held up by the innocence of a girl. This gets the biggest interest in the Armenian nation because of the consequences. I'll tell you a little story. For example, a girl loses her virginity. There are another two sisters in her family. Her Dad and Mum have a good position. Everyone finds out about it. Her two sisters would already be under close surveillance because if one girl has already done it, then the second one and the third one could do it too. Her Dad loses his status as a good family man, because he didn't look after his daughter properly. If the girl can marry, then good. Thank God, if there is someone for her to marry. She'll give birth to a daughter, but this daughter will turn out like her Mum!

---

133 This belief is also conveyed in the Armenian proverb quoted earlier: *'An Armenian isn't someone who has parents that are Armenian, but someone who has Armenian children'.*

Ulrike: Is this peculiar for Krasnodar?
Anush: Yes, because it's a small community...You have to remember this. Men are obsessed with this virginity, I think.

In this excerpt, it becomes obvious that women's sexuality is about men's pride and honour. For Armenian men in general, it is about having authority over women; for fathers in particular, it is linked to honour and the maintenance of Armenian traditions. For women, it is about losing their reputation, when breaking 'Armenian' cultural norms. Many studies of ethnic minority groups have stressed that women's sexuality is one of the last bastions of tradition when families move to another country (Sahgal and Yuval-Davies 1992). This seems to be a common phenomenon for ethnic minorities regardless of country of origin, host country or religious background (Bakalian 1993; Bhattacharjee 1992; Pallotta-Chiarolli 1989). In this way, the family both demands and is a means through which sexual regulations reproduce collective belonging, both biologically and culturally. Female chastity ensures that, within the community, young women are not only seen 'biologically but also symbolically within the boundaries of the group' (Sahgal and Yuval-Davies 1992: 8).

Being chaste before marriage remains a routine practice, but also shows signs of becoming a reflexive practice. Some girls from middle and higher social backgrounds often relate negatively to this question, seeing it as unavoidable that they have to abide by the norms, at least officially. Nonetheless, norms are flexible and they can be transgressed in different ways. One way is through the surgical re-establishment of virginity. This is discussed as an act of betrayal, but at the same time it is considered as a means to have sexual freedom, but still abide by cultural norms.

Lala: Well about this, who goes out, who is seeing guys, well, to sleep or not to sleep with someone ... how can I put it ... there's a certain system, how girls do it, how they get around the system. There's even the issue of ... kind of – surgery to re-establish virginity. This is very widespread amongst Armenians, young women, because there are guys who want to get married, the majority of whom want a girl to be a virgin. A girl goes out and sees some guy. I'm not saying that this is bad. I think that at the age of 20, it is normal to have some sort of relationship; it's not that you're 13 and immature, right? Generally, she meets a guy and it happens or doesn't happen. Maybe she just went out, maybe it was just a drink, it's not important. She has this surgery, and during the wedding night, it appears that she's a virgin. That she was a virgin, right? This is very widespread. I heard this because some girls told me. They even just cut their fingers, so that there was some blood on the sheet, in short, to pretend there's some blood. In this sense, it's just to get around these traditions, although all do the same, we're all people, right? Everyone wants to relax, everyone wants to go out and enjoy themselves. We're all people; we all feel and fall in love, right?

Although these narratives are commonly accepted, research participants would deny these practices, often replying to the question of virginity by saying 'it goes without saying' (*samo po soboi razumeetsia*). Nevertheless, coexisting with the extreme practice of re-establishing virginity and observing complete chastity, there is the practice of having sex before marriage with a long-term partner. Although not publicly announced, this has become commonly accepted and normal practice. As this practice is commonly accepted, it gives young women the opportunity to adhere to Armenian traditions, at least to some extent; and at the same time to conform to cultural norms in Russian society (*rossiiskoe obshchestvo*). In the following excerpt, Lala and Lusine express both positions. Whereas Lala, who chose a 'modern' position for herself, wants to adhere to the middle-ground position, Lusine, who can be classified as 'semi-traditional', expresses Armenian traditional norms:

> Lala: Well, I won't tell everyone [about having sex with a long-term boyfriend], well do you know ... It's just for myself, how can I say it, I don't imagine [to be open about it]...
> Lusine: (*interrupts*) This is different for everyone ... I can't imagine that [having sex] before my wedding, I can't imagine it.
> Lala: But I, on the contrary, don't think that you should get married blindly. Maybe, you won't suit each other physically, this also happens.
> Lusine: Why blindly, we just talk to each other?
> Lala: Lusine, I didn't say that to you. If there's love, if there are feelings, you see, if there's concrete love straight away – how

can you be with him, just from a distance, I can't imagine this ... And, as a matter of fact, there's serious science showing that people can ideally suit each other, emotionally and all this...

Lusine: I can understand, this is all in my head ... I can't imagine it [having sex before marriage and in general] because it's deeply ingrained inside me. Not because I was brought up like that, I haven't developed the way I was brought up [she means that she is not completely 'traditional'] ... I have, how can I say it, a fear [of having sex before marriage and sex in general]. I'm so afraid, although at the same time I'm not afraid, I'm not 15 anymore. But it doesn't matter when you're told for your whole life that you can't, you can't, you can't [have sex before marriage], afterwards you don't even want to talk about it [sex] ... I just can't. Just because this is so deeply ingrained inside me that, I'll say, if you love me, let's get around it, without it [sex].[134]

Gossip as a means of social control

An influential dynamic in the lives of young Armenian women is gossiping. As the designated 'keepers of the culture' (Billson 1995), young Armenian women and their behaviour come under intense scrutiny, both from men and women in their community. For Armenian men, especially young Armenian men, gossiping is about demonstrating their ability to control their women and ensure female chastity. For the older generation on the whole, gossip is especially aimed at preventing deviation by younger ones.[135] Gluckman (1963) examines how far gossip can serve to protect the cohesion, integrity and continuity of social groups. For Gluckman (1963: 313), gossip is 'enjoyed by people about others with whom they are in a close social relationship'. Consequently, the right to gossip about certain people is a privilege for group members only. Gossip operates as a form of social control, in that those group members wanting to avoid being the subject of gossip will endeavour to

---

134 From puberty, Armenian children are taught that sex is a private act between two people and that it is a dangerous act. According to traditional Armenian cultural norms, sex is only sanctified by marriage (Ishkanian 2004: 271).

135 Tebbut (1995) and Harris (2004) explore the dynamics of gossiping in different cultural settings and times and have come to very similar conclusions. Tebbutt (1995) examines the issue of gossip in working-class English neighbourhoods from the late nineteenth through the mid-twenties centuries and Harris (2004) writes about the power of gossip to control gender relations in Tajikistan.

observe group 'norms'. Furthermore, competition for status and prestige between group members is regularly conducted and controlled through gossip (Gluckman 1963). This view posits group unity as the purpose of gossip.

The most common, and often bitter, criticisms that young Armenian women mentioned in respect to the Armenian community in Krasnodar, is that Armenians gossip excessively. Almost all young female participants referred to 'community gossip' and the negative impact it had upon their lives.[136] Following the processes of gossiping within the community, young Armenian women, especially those who position themselves traditionally or semi-traditionally, have much to lose by failing to perform 'ideal Armenian femininity'. In this sense, gossiping has sometimes the effect of limiting Armenian girls' spare time activities or free movements.

> Sona: Well, this gossip. Well, even if someone sees me on the street with a [male] friend, just a mate from school, then there'll be gossip. They'd say, 'But I saw her with a guy, they've already kissed each other'. Well, this is the gossip amongst Armenians, and you see, Armenian girls 'suffer' in this way, you could say (*laughs*).

In severe cases, for those who are brought up strictly, social activities thus centre on their home and family. Many girls assess critically how gossip can arise and therefore understand why their parents would not allow them to do certain things. How far they are affected by the community's gossiping is largely dependent on how far they are involved in community life and how they have positioned themselves. The following excerpt is from Gaiane. Gaiane keeps her distance from the Armenian community, has parents that are well-off and fairly liberal, so that she has more freedom to do what she wants – she chose a 'modern' position for herself. Nonetheless, she still struggles with relatives' opinions about her and what she is doing:

---

136 The act of gossiping also had an effect on conducting the interviews, as some female research participants were reluctant to divulge information which could be 'used against them' at some point in the future.

Gaiane: They [her relatives] can't imagine a different life; they don't understand that there's something better. Basically, I play beach volleyball, yes, my parents don't mind. Well, you see, kids do sport, girls rarely do sport. We've got a team of twenty people, six girls. I have relatives, when they found out, that I play volleyball, there was a big set out at home, 'How can this be? You're among men, this can't be! Have you gone mad? Don't go there anymore!'

Closely linked to the threat of gossip and the potential harm it can cause to the girls' reputation is the question of surveillance. For Armenian women, this involves a process whereby the awareness of surveillance becomes internalized by individuals and they practice self-censorship. This, however, is not peculiar for Armenian women only; Qureshi (2004) observes similar group dynamics amongst 'Edinburgh Pakistanis,' where young women also have developed a sharp sensibility as a result of the ever-present potential of being observed in public spaces. The awareness of surveillance contributes to the girls' intense consciousness of their appearance, behaviour and actions.

Armine: If you want to do something, the first question that comes up is: what will people say? I always, in everything that I do, my first question is, 'Oh, but what will people say, what will people say?' Even though, as a matter of fact, you do something for yourself, what difference does it make what people say?

During the interview, Manana (21 years) discussed how far gossip and surveillance affected her friend's ability to meet up with young men, as well as the strategies adopted to overcome this surveillance and gossiping:

Manana: She [her friend] even asked me today. She's also in touch with a guy from Moscow. Well, they're just in touch. He has already been to Krasnodar a couple of times and he's coming to Krasnodar again in a month's time. Well, she says, 'Find me a place, where I can sit and where I won't bump into any of my relatives'. You see, she constantly tries to avoid this situation, constantly [tries to ensure] that no one will see her. God forbid! Well, a female friend came to visit us a year ago and stayed in a hotel. Her parents knew that she was in the hotel, visiting a

> female friend. She was there in the hotel in Krasnodar for a week, but the friend only called into the hotel on the last day. The friend said that this is because you can guarantee that the moment she entered the hotel, thousands of her relatives would pass the hotel, see her and report on it. These relatives associate a hotel with some guy.

Whereas Armenian girls are especially affected by gossiping within the Armenian community, young Armenian men are not so affected, since they do not have to conform to the image of an 'ideal' ethnic subject in the same way as Armenian women do. As authority is granted to men in patriarchal societies, young men often receive special day-to-day privileges that are denied to young Armenian women. Some girls disapprove of the fact that even their younger brothers have more freedom than they do.

> Sona: I'll give you an example. We want to get ready to go out. My brother had gone already, and I say, 'Dad, I want to go out'. 'No', he'd say, 'You stay at home'. I'd say, 'But why do you allow Tigran to go out, but not me?' My brother is called Tigran. 'Why can he, but I can't?' 'Because you're a girl, you're Armenian, but he's a boy – he can. That's why'.

Young men asserting symbolic Armenianness

The above discussion focused on the constraints on young women in Armenian society and how they negotiate these constraints. The subsequent analysis turns attention to young men and examines the various ways in which they position themselves and construct their gender identities in relation to ethnicity and culture. To do so, it is important to note that this is mainly examined from the viewpoint of female participants. During fieldwork, it became clear that what the male interviewees said or did not say during the interview 'cannot be separated from their audience – from the relationships that sustain and support them, or from the patriarchal lens through which they are filtered' (Brown 1998: 91-92).[137]

In Chapter One, it was suggested that masculine identities are constructed through the negotiation of various power relations, with regard to both women and other men. Masculine identities are constructed through various positions

---

137 Although Brown's study focuses on girls, her proposition can also be applied to young men.

of self and others, particularly the interconnected social categories of gender, race and class (Archer 2001: 83). Research shows that men may construct masculine identities in relation to women, specifically the 'ownership' and 'control' of women; as Wetherell (1993) suggests, many masculine identities can be typified as formed around a discourse advocating the 'protection of femininity,' through which masculinity is constructed as powerful, defined through 'caring for' and controlling women (cited in Archer 2001: 83). Some Armenian girls, especially from very traditional families, are accustomed to such 'controlling' mechanisms, whereas others are unaware of them. Those young women, who grew up with such 'controlling' mechanisms, perceive this control as 'caring for' or 'protecting', as Temine (19 years) communicates:[138]

> *Temine:* Well, girls are not allowed to go out on their own, only with brothers and [male] cousins. I don't know; it may be tradition or something. Well, that's the way it is, that a girl always goes out with her brothers or [male] cousins. It's some kind of protection or something.

A number of writers suggest the link between ethnic minority masculinities as a form of resistance to racism, whereby attempts to assert patriarchal power may be a response to the powerlessness engendered by racist discourses (Wetherell 1993 cited in Archer 2001: 83). Alexander (1996), drawing on her study of British African-Caribbean men, challenges this by arguing that Black male identity should be seen as an extension of male power. Following Alexander's (1996) suggestion, it is argued that this can be equally applied to theorizing young Armenian masculinities. As proposed earlier, when discussing the question of female chastity, it is an issue that men use to display their male dominance. Whereas Alexander (1996) examines British African-Caribbean masculinities in relation to other men, this section explores how Armenian men construct their masculinities in mainly two ways – in relation to Armenian women and in relation to Russian women. Of course, constructions of masculine identities can be examined in far more complex ways than with these two dimensions, but as a female researcher, it

---

[138] Such behaviour is also typical for Armenian women in Armenia (cf. Zdravomyslova and Temkina 2007).

was not possible to go beyond this gender role to research, for example, young men's interactions with Russian or other Armenian men. Many female participants stress their dissatisfaction with young Armenian men. Armenian men are stereotyped as not being able to talk normally to girls, always being jealous and controlling and therefore constraining girls' freedom:

> *Armine:* Not long ago, I went out with an Armenian. That was some torture (*laughs*). Even when you talk with him, you've got to think of something to say. You say something and he's offended, he just can't understand. He had this weird, mad jealousy. I couldn't go anywhere. He didn't allow me to go to my dancing classes, 'You can't go to your dancing classes, you can't go there and perform, that's impossible'.
> *Ulrike:* Do you think that all Armenian men are like that?
> *Armine:* Yes, the majority are very demanding, they're very jealous. I even have [male] cousins (*laughs*), yes, I've got a cousin who's seeing a girl, and he tells her how to dress, that she can't wear a short skirt, trousers and boots and all that. He controls her in this way.

Young Armenian men assert their dominant role by trying to insist on traditions that are out of date. These are 'symbolic' patriarchal norms they try to mobilize in order to bring across the image of a 'real' Armenian man and maintain their hegemonic masculinity. They display stereotypical behaviour for Armenian men, which in the above excerpt, according to Armine is jealousy. It is also argued that these young men 'display' such masculinities to young Armenian women owing to a cultural influence on, what may be termed, hegemonic masculinity. In this case, it is closely linked to their special status within families and their upbringing as 'proper' Armenian men. As Qureshi (2004) maintains, gender identities are performed for different 'audiences' and in her study, she applies the concept of 'segregated audience', which means that young people apply different strategies for different audiences. In this way, it becomes obvious that Armenian women choose a certain strategy which is mainly defined by their diasporic identity. For girls, young Armenian men's gender identity is defined as follows:

> *Manana:* In general, [Armenian] guys haven't really changed their opinion about [Armenian] women. For them, a woman must be a good housekeeper, a good mother, good looking and good in bed.

More evidence that young Armenian men assert their symbolic identity is provided by the issue of multiple girlfriends. According to tradition, Armenian men's sexual behaviour is free and Shakhnazarian (2005) asserts that having sexual relationships outside their marriage or more than one serves to boost Armenian men's status amongst their friends. Here, Russian women come in useful for Armenian men. Armenian women are untouchable for Armenian men before marriage. They are the ones they have to 'care' for, while Russian women are perceived to be promiscuous. This perception sometimes creates a barrier between Armenian girls and boys, which is difficult to understand for Armenian girls:

> *Armine:* All the guys have lots of girlfriends ... Well, you see, it's not comfortable for us, especially when you talk to guys. For example, one of my parents' acquaintance, he says, that he's afraid of approaching an Armenian girl of getting to know her and seeing her. I don't know why, but they're afraid of seeing an Armenian girl, but don't explain why. They've got so much freedom to do what they want.

While Armenian men display a 'symbolic' gender identity towards Armenian women, characterized by traditional attitudes and 'caring for'/'protecting,' Russian women are used to boost their status amongst their friends. As Armenian women are culturally precious, it is Russian women who fill the gap and are used to raise their status amongst friends and satisfy their sexual desires, as Ani (22 years) explains:

> *Ani:* They're just blokes, just blokes, and they're allowed everything. Nevertheless, Armenian guys never stay on their own. If he goes out in town, in his car, it's not even important which type of car. If he wants to get to know a girl, on the street or somewhere, any girl wouldn't mind. Which means, it's easy for them with girls, with any girl. Armenian guys use the fact that they're in demand. They also know how to present themselves, they begin with lots of compliments and what girl ever tires of this?

To conclude, young Armenian men display different ethnicized gender identities that conform to Armenian and Russian cultural norms. Their performance of ethnicized gender identities in different situations for different audiences enables them to overcome the cultural gap between what they are supposed to do and what they want to do. For young Armenian women, performances of gendered identities are different in so far as the majority of them chose to reaffirm some norms, but at the same time oppose established norms, although in most cases this simply means being very critical of them. Discursive power, arising from a coalescence of the traditional gender discourse and social control, with the help of gossip and surveillance, comes to bear upon their gendered performances in certain situations. Their strategies for performing discursive constructions of how women are supposed to be are not always the same and vary by the degree to which they choose to oppose or reaffirm what is expected of them.

Adygh gender relations and tradition

Culture and tradition are as important for the Adygh community as they are for the Armenian community. In contemporary Russian society in general, and in Adygh society in particular, a renaissance of ethnic culture has taken place. This also has an impact on Adygh gender relations. While the Armenian community uses the maintenance of traditions to form ethnic group belonging and to define their status in Russian society, Adyghs use traditions to define their ethnic minority status in 'their' republic. Although Chapter Three presented an argument that young Adyghs are always placed between two different cultural systems, Russian and Adygh, gender relations are constructed largely according to Adygh cultural traditions via the moral code *Adyghage* (Adyghness), which was never completely eradicated during Soviet times. The subsequent discussion looks at traditional frames that form gender relations in Adygh society. Akin to the gender order in the Armenian community, a historically evolved complex moral system has similar effects on Adygh gender relations in contemporary society, as shown in the material that follows. Furthermore, compared with the Armenian community, Adygh society also has a culturally developed control mechanism that makes it hard for young women, as well as young men, to diverge from general norms in society. In contradistinction to Armenians, it is contended that most Adygh women choose to comply with Adygh cultural norms, since compliance gives them the advantage of a clearly defined group belonging and the sense of being a 'real' Adygh woman. This is especially important given the minority status of Adyghs in 'their' republic.

Culture as morality: a legacy of gender relations
As stressed in the previous chapter, the issue of *Adyghage* (Adyghness) has retained its prominence in contemporary Adygh society and is central to the preservation of Adygh ethnic culture and group belonging. It is also a category that defines Adygh ethnic identity and therefore is an 'identity code' (Khanakhu 2001). Another concept that is closely associated and often overlapping with *Adyghage* is *Adygh Khabze* or *Adygh Nemys*, which is roughly rendered as 'Adygh Etiquette'. Customs and social norms are enshrined in the orally transmitted rigid and complex code of Adygh Etiquette and have developed historically in Adygh society 'to ensure that strict militaristic discipline is maintained at all times to defend the Circassian lands against invaders' (Jaimoukha 2001: 172). *Adyghage* and *Adygh Khabze* are cultural and social obligations transmitted from generation to generation, which direct an individual in Adygh society in his or her thinking and actions.

As in the Armenian community and in other Caucasian ethnic cultures, these norms include a clear separation of gender roles. Within family life, housekeeping is the task of women and women are seen as mothers and wives. As in the Armenian community, in Adygh society it is women who have the primary responsibility for maintaining family cohesion and cultural reproduction. In Adygh tradition, women are perceived as mothers, as the keepers of the home (*khranitel' domashnego ochaga*) and the main organizers of the intra-familial relations and networks (Shogenova 2004: 121). Women are considered to be the beginning of all beginnings in the social world and are referred to with great respect. This is communicated in many Adygh proverbs: 'There is nothing in the world that did not originate from a woman' (*Net v mire nichego, chto ne nachinalos' by s zhenchshiny*) or 'There is no question higher or more important in the world than the woman question' (*Net v mire voprosa vyshe i vazhnee, chem vopros o zhenshchine*). Most importantly, even in contemporary Adygh society many of these symbolic roles for women have been preserved and young women do not oppose them.

Alongside clearly defined gender roles, Adygh family relations remain strictly regulated. Many of the characteristics of traditional Adygh family life are similar to those of Armenians and other ethnic cultures in the North Caucasus. The head of the family is always the husband and he has full responsibility for the well-being of family members. This clear division of gender roles within Adygh society has contributed to the maintenance of tradition within families. It is derived from the understanding that men are the 'workers' (*truzheniki*) and 'providers' (*dobytchiki*) in many North Caucasian societies (Khanakhu 2001: 45).[139] Khanakhu (2001) argues that even today men's role as 'provider' hinders the rise of feminism in the North Caucasus. It is worth noting that contemporary socio-economic realities have undermined this conservative family structure, as Adygh women sometimes appear as the only material 'provider' in the family.

The norms of 'Adygh Etiquette' assert a tremendous influence on Adygh men so that a man's failure to enact any of these norms may result in his non-acceptance in Adygh society. According to these norms, a real Adygh man should be a patriot of his homeland and all his actions should be directed to the service of his people. He has to be very courageous, strong-willed, decisive, resourceful, responsible, and prepared for self-sacrifice. These norms represent the 'ideal' Adygh man, of course, but at the same time they generate a sense of group cohesion and cultural belonging. These norms place certain cultural expectations on every young man; to perform a masculinity that conforms to cultural values within Adygh society. In Adygh language, there are even set phrases which describe one's degree of conformity to *Adyghage*. For example, 'He has got *Adyghage*' (*Adygag'e khel'shch*) or 'He has got little *Adyghage*' (*Shlag'ue khel'k'ym*) (Shogenova 2004: 61). Thus, young men's status in society seems to be determined by their successful conformity to *Adyghage* and *Adyghe Nemys*.

---

139 Although not discussed in detail in earlier sections of this chapter, this understanding also applies to Armenian culture.

These norms for men also bear significantly upon gender relations. As in Armenian society, the father of a family is the defender of his wife's and his family's honour and is, therefore, compelled to ensure his children's conformity to Adygh values. In contrast to Armenian culture, there is an element of reticence in gender relations in so far as it is not considered appropriate to show any affection for wives or children. At the same time, it is not appropriate to talk negatively about wives or other females within the community. Patriarchal elements in Adygh society are conveyed via conservative family structures, as discussed earlier. There is, however, some evidence that classical Circassian society was initially matriarchal and was only later transformed into patriarchy when the physically stronger males gained more power (Jaimoukha 2001: 165). As fathers are the head of the family, they also have the responsibility for bringing up their sons and transmitting their values to their sons. Following this tradition, young Adygh men often see their role as protecting or controlling their sisters or female cousins, as their fathers have taught them. Alii (20 years) indicates this during our interview:

> Ulrike: What do you think about Adygh culture?
> Alii: I'm really into tradition.
> Ulrike: Seriously?
> Alii: Yes, I'm very demanding on my family, my sisters and [female] cousins. I stop them doing lots of things.
> Ulrike: Do you think that's good?
> Alii: Of course, it's good. I'm reasonable in what I forbid; it's within a certain framework, according to tradition. Well, I don't stop them doing everything, but really, just what isn't right. I forbid, how can I say it, certain behaviour. I tell them what they can do.

This excerpt might make one think that Adygh women and girls are oppressed and controlled. This is not the complete picture. Spending an evening with three Adygh girls, we became engrossed in a conversation about general gender relations in Adyghea. The following fieldwork diary excerpt describes how Emma, one of the girls, thinks about gender relations in Adygh society:

...Emma had a lot to say concerning Adygh gender relations. She reckons that many people have the wrong impression and think Adygh women are oppressed and have no rights at all. She thought this is mainly because they still have a traditional family structure in many ways. The husband is the head of the family and the wife does all her duties without questioning him. However, Emma said that an Adygh woman does not get angry with her husband, not because she is afraid of him, but because she respects herself. It is not in her genes to express herself like this with her husband. Despite some sort of emancipation, according to nature an Adygh woman should be feminine, charming, mild and if she wants, delicate and weak. She never competes with her husband. Adyghs have a proverb: 'What you cannot get with good, you cannot get with bad' (*Chego ne dob'esh'sia dobrom, togo i zlom ne dob'eshsia*) [Fieldwork Diary, Thursday, 8 June 2006].

Nonetheless, later in our talk it becomes clear that nowadays it is difficult to keep such traditions if one, for example, considers Russian fairytales on television. How can parents explain Adygh codes of conduct to their children, when a *babushka* in a fairytale rudely shouts at a man and kicks him out? This is definitely hard to explain to children in Adygh society, as it does not conform to Adygh norms. Hence, it is suggested that many traditional norms have remained, but are not always fully observed. Often participants complain that Adygh traditions are gradually disappearing. Inevitably, the decades of Soviet rule produced major changes in Adygh society. These not only include demographic population changes in the republic, but also changes in women's outlook. Nevertheless, the underlying gender identities that privileged male power and a hierarchy according to age appear not to have changed. It is the maintenance of these traditional gender identities that has allowed the preservation of some basic Adygh traditions. Noteworthy here is, that the changing nature of Adygh traditions is repeatedly criticized by men, since they are the ones who appear to lose out in this process (Zdravomyslova and Temkina 2001). Often it is Adygh men, who insist on traditions, whereas Adygh women are more relaxed about it:

Ulrike: What traditions, which you liked, don't exist anymore?
Baizet: Reticence, but reticence in the way that you force yourself to think; nowadays many girls have become morally degenerate (*raspushchennye*). But this depends on the family. There are girls from normal families, who aren't allowed to do many things. But there are girls, who want more and don't listen. They go out and do what they want. Well, by morally degenerate (*raspushchennye*) I don't mean that all of them are tarty and go out a lot, but they've no manners or sort of vulgar manners. I mean their manners are provocative.

Adygh masculinity depends on Adygh femininity. On the other hand, this excerpt describes a naturally occurring process of cultural transformation, which started when Russians first invaded Circassian land. Although, Baizet (20 years) is very critical of Adygh girls, he seemed to ignore that in other ways Adygh women quite firmly retain the belief that it is important to keep their own customs and not ape those of the less constrained Russian women:

Diana: If a girl stays out late at night, she's not allowed to smoke, to drink, hang around with guys. She's just not allowed to go out. There are restrictions.
Ulrike: What do you think about that?
Diana: Given contemporary life, it's not right, but if everybody were to observe traditions, then, yes, I'd like it. Generally, I really like Adygh traditions. The fact is they're disappearing.
Fatima: If you mean whether or not it's appropriate. Well, generally, an Adygh girl shouldn't, according to Muslim rules, go to a nightclub, have a good time there and express herself there. It's considered to be improper ... I agree with my parents, well, with my Mum, whether I like it or not, I was born Adygh. I live here and in any case, I have, whether I like it or not, to accept it because really I intend and plan to get married to an Adygh. Well, if your husband is Adygh, everything, they say, will be alright. It's inappropriate as a way of life [going clubbing, smoking etc.] and it's necessary to watch oneself, like an Adygh...

Marriage and endogamy: choosing their calling

When looking at attitudes towards marriage amongst young Adygh adults, it becomes evident that participants of both sexes do not feel as much pressure from the community, as young Armenians do. It is more a matter of choice which is acknowledged by both young men and young women:

> *Oksana:* I don't intend to get married, so far I don't want to, I want to achieve something and do something first.
> *Ulrike:* But to whom would you like to get married?
> *Oksana:* Adygh or Russian, I don't know, the main thing for me is that it would be a man [not a woman]. A while ago, I thought that I'd only get married to an Armenian. Now I've decided that he will be Adygh. It doesn't really matter. Even getting married to a Russian would be ok. The main thing for me is that it's a man who'd love me, respect me and understand me.

> *Ulrike:* Will you get married to an Adygh or is that unimportant?
> *Murat:* That's a difficult question. It depends how it works out.
> *Ulrike:* It doesn't matter to you?
> *Murat:* Not really, it depends how it works out.
> *Ulrike:* You see, some say it doesn't matter; others say they'd only get married to an Adygh.
> *Murat:* But what if you fall in love?
> *Ulrike:* That's why I'm asking.
> *Murat:* If it's love, why not get married. For example, my uncle ...he married a Russian.
> *Ulrike:* But you'll lose your tradition?
> *Murat:* No. She'll take on my traditions. She'll take them on a hundred per cent.

Though more inclined to endogamy, which is inspired by patriotic 'save the nation attitudes', their open attitudes could be explained in several ways. First, the moral system of *Adyghage* teaches children tolerance, understanding and humaneness from an early age. Second, whereas in the Armenian community the perfect partner is supposed to be confined to one's ethnic, religious and class background, in Adygh society such aspects are not as important. Khanakhu (2001), for example, even argues that the meaning of social stratification and wealth were eradicated during Soviet times. Nonetheless, fieldwork experience has shown that some are wealthier than others and status matters, although this did not appear to affect attitudes towards marriage. Finally, they do not feel as much pressure because marriage is not perceived as a means of maintaining a sense of ethnic belonging, which stands in contrast to Armenian perceptions on marriage. Indeed, even though Adyghs are the 'minority' in the Republic of Adyghea, they remain very conscious of the fact that it is 'their' republic. Although there is an element of choice concerning endogamy, some research participants displayed a certain conservatism instilled via their up-bringing:

Ulrike: When it's time for you to get married, will you get married to an Adygh or doesn't it matter?
Ruslan: (interrupts) To an Adygh. Yes, it does matter, only to an Adygh.
Ulrike: Why?
Ruslan: Because that's a tradition in our family. An Adygh should get married to an Adygh. This is an unwritten rule. That's very traditional. This unwritten rule is centuries old.
Ulrike: But what if there is this beautiful Russian girl in Adygheisk...
Ruslan: (interrupts) No. Even if she's good-looking, if she's Russian, it matters, it won't happen.
Ulrike: And what if you fall in love?
Ruslan: No, not for me. Maybe for some other guy. I want to continue the tradition.

Ruslan (21 years) can only explain his intentions by referring to family traditions and his own belief in Adygh traditions. Time and again, during fieldwork, it seemed that Adygh ethnic belonging is experienced as a privilege because they are only a small people. It is a privilege young people love to emphasize and adhere to. In a similar way to Ruslan, young Adygh women sometimes enjoyed performing their traditional roles. This might be explained by two facts: this performance enhances respect in society (by following *Adyghage*), and, most importantly, it is doing your bit to 'save the nation' by only considering an Adygh husband and insisting on Adygh traditions.

The patriotic attitudes go even so far that some aspects of Adygh traditions are romanticized amongst young Adyghs. For example, if one considers the tradition of 'bride stealing', which a suitor can use when the bride's parents do not allow him to take their daughter as his wife. The suitor could then abduct his beloved from her parent's house on a set date and time. This tradition has been preserved; indeed, it has become a kind of 'cult', since young men like to abduct their beloved just for fun:

> *Renata:* I'd like to be stolen and also I want to wear a traditional sai at my wedding. Oh, I've dreamt so much about it.

As one can see, Renata (18 years) transforms 'bride stealing' from an act of resistance to parents into the ultimate 'romantic wedding' dream. This romantic notion of bride stealing is common among female research participants suggesting that it has become a 'cult' amongst young Adyghs, which reinforces their ethnic belonging. Another important marker of Adygh culture is considered to be respect for older people (a norm shared with Armenians). But, since it cuts across all Caucasian peoples, it might be considered more accurately as an indicator of regional belonging. Many incidents during fieldwork suggest a revival, or at least the strong maintenance, of traditional hierarchies of age and gender:

> *Artur:* We Adyghs have a custom, well unwritten, it's not like a law, our Constitution is unwritten, but they teach you from birth to respect the elderly.
>
> *Zarema:* When I walk together with my younger brother and father, then my father walks between us. I walk on the right, one metre behind him, and my brother walks on the left, but even further from my father. If I'm one metre behind, then my brother is two metres behind. This is an old custom. When Adyghs rode on horseback, the younger ones had to maintain a distance from the older ones – the length of half a horse...

At first glance, one may assume that Zarema (19 years) said this during the interview to impress the interviewer. However, many participants communicated the unquestioned persistence of some traditional elements and hierarchy in Adygh (or wider Caucasian) gender relations. Social control in the Adygh community is maintained not, as amongst Armenians, by gossip, but by the so-called 'culture of shame' (*kul'tura styda*) (Khanakhu 2001: 51). If a girl fails to conform to Adygh norms, she may ruin her reputation. This control mechanism also applies to men, however, as illustrated by Madzhid

(21 years) in his account of an incident that had occurred in the village (*aul*) of his relatives.

> *Madzhid:* Well, about ten years ago, or maybe less, when some guys had a fight, one guy thrust a knife into the other guy and cut him. The whole *aul* and the elders got together. They got together in the centre of the *aul*, where festivities take place. They put down big benches and 200 to 300 people stood there. They got together. The elders and young people sat together. Well, they began to discuss what the guy did and how he did it. Is it good or bad? But before this incident the guy had done other things as well. The first time they forgave him, but this time, when he did something bad again, they kicked him out of the *aul*.

To conclude the discussion on Adygh gendered identities, one can say that gender relations are structured to maintain and reinforce group belonging and cohesion. Although Adygh gender traditions were undermined in the Soviet period, some basic aspects have been preserved and retain their influence. The privilege of male power over women has not changed significantly. Most participants choose to conform to Adygh cultural norms as a means of ensuring their inclusion in the Adygh community. Often adherence is motivated by patriotism, a desire to 'save the nation'. Although the ethnic community discourse is strong, it is not strong enough to preserve traditional gender identities fully. There are some expressions of mixed cultural identities, especially in relation to attitudes towards marriage and the choice of clothes and lifestyle. In these matters, young Adyghs do not necessarily conform to the community's cultural expectations.

Conclusions

This chapter has focused on the ethnicized gendered identities of young Armenians and Adyghs and has shown the ways in which the formation of group identity is woven through the formation of the particular subject positions of young men and women. For both young Armenians and Adyghs ethnicity becomes essentialized through its intersection with gender systems of differentiation. This discussion has drawn on the concept of performativity to stress the mutual constructions of ethnicity and gender through performative acts. In addition, it has been shown how the gender discourse and ethnic conventions relate to each other in their concurrent performance. In both communities, ethnicized gender identities are formed through deeply held ideas and are products of a patriarchal order. It is argued that gender and ethnicity are dependent on each other for their mutual construction.

This chapter has stressed how the performances of young Armenians and Adyghs can reaffirm ethnicized gender roles, but also oppose established norms. Whereas for young Adygh women compliance with Adygh cultural norms is almost universal, for Armenian girls compliance or resistance is largely influenced by socio-economic positions and parents' world outlook. Young women's identity performances are constructed at the intersection of discourses of parental authority, male dominance and the needs of the community. At the same time, these identity performances are constrained by the symbolic importance of female 'purity' and its significance for ethnic belonging. For both Adyghs and Armenians, whether men or women, the relationship between 'performers' and 'audiences' significantly affects the performance of their identities in different situations.

The last two empirical chapters have concentrated on how young people's identity constructions are shaped by their membership of a particular ethnic community. In the final empirical chapter, the ethnographic investigation moves the analysis to the significance of place for the construction of youth identities. In the next chapter, youth identity formations are not explored from within their respective communities, but from the outside world, as attention turns to the question of how far the political discourse and attitudes of the Russian population influence the construction of social and cultural identities among young Armenians and Adyghs.

5 Situating Youth Cultural Practices and Experiences in the Local Context

Recent years have seen an increase of interest in the study of the complex relationship between youth cultural identities and place. In Britain, this type of research has been conducted primarily in cities with multi-ethnic communities in order to examine ethnicity and changing youth cultures (Back 1996; Gunter and Watt 2009; Nayak 2004). Alongside this work in Britain, changing youth cultures and place have been examined in the peripheries (Pilkington *et al.* 2002; Pilkington *et al.* 2010; Salo 2003). All of these studies recognize the complexities of young people's cultural experiences in a global world and universal explanations have been replaced by a concern to acknowledge differences and the plurality of voices. At the same time, the importance of place and neighbourhood for the formation of youth identities is accentuated (Back 2007; Gidley 2007; Nayak 2003, 2004; Taylor and Addison 2009).

These discussions on the ways in which young people inhabit the spaces of the city, show that multiculturalism and interethnic dialogue exist alongside 'stark new divisions and old hatreds' (Back 2007: 52). Back (2007: 52) argues that the ways young adults inhabit spaces in the city can be described as tactics young people use to 'live with and through difference' and 'make bearable what is unbearable'. Young Armenian and Adygh adults' everyday lives are also marked by such a dual experience. While their leisure spaces are characterized by inclusive notions of ethnic plurality and tolerance, individuals are sometimes racialized/ethnicized when they pass through public spaces. Public spaces are understood as complex systems in the formulation of youth histories (MacDonald and Marsh 2005; Robinson 2009). These are spaces that young people use in response to their own needs and constraints. The main argument in this chapter is that young people are not just passive recipients of everyday racism, but have routinized their responses to racism and xenophobia in their everyday practices.

Youth at leisure[140]

Questions of youth and leisure are central to the debates on place and the ways young people inhabit places. Most studies on place and youth cultures provide a notion of place which cannot be imagined outside of its relationship with other places, outside of the 'wider world' (cf. Pilkington *et al.* 2011; Skelton and Valentine 1998; Yoon 2003). Yet, in these studies it is also shown that local cultures have not been entirely replaced by global change and that place is as important as ever (Back 1996; Nayak 2004; Pilkington and Johnson 2003). Youth identities require space of their own in which to assert themselves and are also tied to the specificities of particular locations. Nonetheless, the emphasis in this chapter is not so much on a place for oneself as it is on a place to go to and be with friends. Place is understood as a space in which young people can meet and be with others; in short, a chosen space. Leisure places are social spaces, where relations are not marked by familial obligations, but friendship.

The sociological theory of Pierre Bourdieu is of particular significance for discussions on youth spaces and leisure activities. Bourdieu (1989) discussed a 'social space' in terms of a metaphorical space. This space always has a material and physical manifestation, but is not inevitably determined by it. For Bourdieu (1986, 1989), in the social 'metaphorical' space the different forms of capital – cultural, economic, social and symbolic – one can draw on come to have meaning and validity. Social space is closely linked to Bourdieu's (1977) notion of *habitus*, which describes the way in which individuals develop attitudes and dispositions and engage in social practices.[141] He understands individuals as 'knowing subjects', who are neither 'pushed' in a certain direction by external social structures, nor completely free to act in ways they want to. For Bourdieu (1977), social actors are both inventive and strategic in the way they do things. Social actors take into account objective constraints and internalize social structure and then externalize social structure through social action. Like Bourdieu, in this chapter, it is presumed that when a young person enters a 'social space',

---

140 A modified version of this chapter has been published previously (Ziemer 2011).
141 A young person acquires a habitus through his or her upbringing and education.

such as a park, club or even their home, the individual not only embodies a certain number of different capitals, but is also strategic in the use of spaces.

The politics of friendship patterns
A large part of young people's leisure time is spent with friends and family. Friends play an important role in the process of growing up and sometimes are more important than the family. Friendship is a term that implies cooperative and supportive behaviour and a specific interpersonal relationship between people. It is also a part of young people's lives that creates a sense of belonging. Existing research on friendship patterns amongst young people from ethnic minorities in Britain stresses that same-ethnic friendship networks have the potential to create community and group consciousness, which may in turn encourage social and political mobilization (Parker and Song 2006).[142] At the same time, ethnically segregated networks are criticized as being 'too cohesive' and 'excessively bonded' hindering full integration (Reynolds 2007). For the subsequent discussion, however, the focus is not so much on questions of same- or mixed-ethnic friendships, but on what basis these friendships are formed. The main argument for this subsection is that friendships are not first and foremost ethnicized/racialized, but rather gendered. Accordingly, the subsequent discussion analyses the different notions of friendship and friends for both young men and women.

The majority of research participants form friendships based on residence and leisure activity as well as their place of study. For young Adyghs, this means that most of their closest friends are from Adygheisk and in particular from their immediate neighbourhood; the street or block of flats in which they live. As most of them had entered college or university (mainly in Krasnodar or Maikop[143]) at the time when this fieldwork was conducted their circle of friends included those from university or college as well their school friends. Often this is the period when young Adygh adults form friendships that cut across ethnicities, because in Adygheisk friendships are predominantly same-ethnic, since Adyghs are the ethnic majority in Adygheisk. For young Armenians, friendships are formed in the same way. Often the closest friends

---
142 Nevertheless, the formation of friendships and its significance for the growing-up process is still a relatively new research area (cf. Reynolds 2007).
143 Maikop is the capital of the Republic of Adyghea.

are from school; those they grew up with in their district (*raion*) – but new friends are made later, for example, at university.

Friendships are formed primarily on the basis of common interests, rather than ethnic belonging. This is pointed out in other works on ethnic minority groups. Ali (2003) examines the different music tastes of children, stressing that friendships are negotiated according to likes and dislikes of popular artists, rather than on an ethnic basis. In her research, she shows that the social geography of the children and the demographics of the area in which they live are most important for friendships. Similarly, Wulff's (1995) study suggests that friendship is more about a 'micro-culture', where people share localities and certain momentous events that create a bond. Nonetheless, Reynolds (2007) contradicts these findings with her research on friendships amongst young Caribbean people in Britain. Her findings show that, although respondents have mixed-ethnic friendships, these are only categorized as 'casual friends' or 'acquaintances,' while 'best friends' or 'closest friends' have the same ethnic background. She proposes that these same-ethnic friendship bonds among young Caribbeans are reproduced and facilitated by social capital during the transition to secondary school and adulthood.[144]

In contrast to Reynolds (2007), and in line with Wulff's (1995) and Ali's (2003) analyses, this study maintains that it is not only ethnicity that dictates friendship bonds. Larger forces have an influence on the ways young people form their friendships, but it is life circumstances combined with shared values and same interests that come to the fore when choosing friends. Like Wulff's (1995) and Ali's (2003) participants, research participants also form ethnically mixed friendships and do not attach significance to ethnicity in the formation of friendships, as Madzhid (21 years) tell us:

Ulrike: Tell me about your friends.
Madzhid: I've got friends everywhere and lots of them, Russians, Armenians, Georgians, Dagestanis.
Ulrike: How did you get to know each other?

---

[144] Social capital has become an increasingly influential concept in the study of friendship. It can be broadly defined as 'the values that people hold and the resources that they can access, which both result in, and are the result of, collective and socially negotiated ties and relationships' (Edwards *et al.* 2003: 2 cited in Reynolds 2007: 386).

Madzhid: They're all here [in Krasnodar].
Ulrike: Are they from your department?
Madzhid: No, why? They all study in different departments.

Noteworthy here, is that the question of friendship often led research participants to talk about the different nationalities of their friends. Such a reaction can be explained in two ways. First, research participants often thought that the researcher was only or mainly interested in nationality issues and, therefore, answered the researcher's question with reference to the different nationalities of their friends. Second, awareness of one's nationality is strong in Russia. In Chapter One, it was argued that ethnicity is routinely used as a marker in Russia, as a result of Soviet multiculturalism and nationalities policies. After the collapse of the Soviet Union, state and regional political discourses were inhabited by discourses of 'ethno-territoriality' and nationalism and have not lost their significance today (cf. Pilkington and Popov 2008; Popov and Kuznetsov 2008; Wolczuk and Yemelianova 2008). Hence, in this region, like in other Russian regions, the awareness of one's nationality is encouraged by a regional political discourse that emphasizes the importance of ethnic belonging. However, while nationality is recognized and referenced routinely, this does not mean that friends are chosen according to nationality:

Lusine: ... I only hang around with Armenian friends. I don't choose my friends, I met them because of my attitude to life and interests. It just happens that I have only Armenian friends, it's just life.

Lusine (21 years) only has Armenian friends, she says, because of life circumstances, the environment she grew up in etc. but she did not choose them herself. Earlier in the interview, for example, she said that in her class at school there were twenty five pupils and seventeen of them were Armenians. The demographics in her school and immediate neighbourhood had, thus, determined that most of her friends are Armenians. The opposite process is described by Lala (20 years), whose friends are mainly Russian, although, for Lala too, the choice of friends is determined by the demographics in her school.

Lala: I was the only Armenian [in the class]. I had good, close relations with everyone... You know, my friend Lusine [her close friend quoted above] went to a school where her class was mainly Armenian. I was shocked at that.

Friendship choice is, therefore, determined primarily by the particular ethnic composition of the school attended.[145] Whereas Lusine happened to be in a class, where there were more Armenians, for Lala it was the opposite – a class where she was the only Armenian. A similar process was described by Adygh participants, whose school was predominantly comprised of Adyghs.

Demographics and the politics of place exert a crucial influence on friendship choice. In the British context, it is argued that friends are chosen according to ethnicity, when young people from an ethnic minority feel that they are perceived as hostile in the school environment (George 2007). Here, friendship groups function to support each other in a hostile environment and express a high degree of racial consciousness (George 2007; Mirza 1992). The research conducted for this book, however, suggests that friendships are not necessarily formed according to ethnicity. Rather, when it comes to choosing their friends, it seems that young people draw on cosmopolitanism as an identity resource. By this, is meant that they remain connected to their cultural heritage, but simultaneously draw on the region's long history of cultural mixing. It is argued that they manage to subvert the dominant identity politics of the region (by choosing friends not according to ethnicity, but according to interests and values).

While ethnicity is not considered crucial in the choice of friends, friendship patterns vary between young men and women. Whereas young men develop large circles of friends, young women often have deeper and more lasting friendships. This is noted in other research on friendship among young people (cf. Wulff 1995). It is argued that males tend to 'do things' together, rather than spending time talking about their inner lives (Messner 2001: 254). Research participants confirm these patterns of friendships. Whereas young men talk about friends in general terms, as Madzhid has described above,

---

145 In Krasnodar, all schools are ethnically mixed; but the precise nature of 'ethnic mix' varies from school to school.

girls, like Oksana (22 years), distinguish and describe what a friend means to them.

> Oksana: I've got two [female] friends who are reliable and whom I trust. When we went to school, naturally I had lots of friends ... I think that since school I've kept close with two friends ... who support me, not only help me in difficult situations, but also make me happy without being envious, and help me at any time. If I call at night, in the morning ... they always help me. I'm really happy to have friends like this.

The above discussion has explored the ways in which young people form friendships. Friends are an important part of young people's lives and are significant in the creation of a sense of belonging. The main proposition for this discussion has been that young people are social actors that cannot act completely free from external social structures, but form their identity in a process of choosing from what is available in their surroundings. It has been shown that it is not so much ethnic belonging that determines the choice of friends, but life circumstances, such as place of residence or schools' demographic structure. It is gender differences that are the most important factor in the formation of friendships as well as for explaining the ways young adults choose spare time activities; this is discussed below.

Gendered leisure practices: the different meanings of guliat'
The word *'guliat'* has different meanings in everyday Russian language. One of the most popular meanings is 'to party' or 'to have fun' (Pilkington 2002: 151).[146] The meaning it is focused on here is the meaning of 'having fun' together, which can include all types of leisure time activities - from spending time at home to going out with friends. This analysis shows that in many situations *'guliat'* has different meanings for young men and women from both communities. What the meaning *'guliat'* has in common for both men and women is 'having fun' and spending time with friends.

---

146 It translates literally as 'to go for a walk,' but can also mean 'to walk around in the city centre,' 'to go clubbing,' or 'to go out' in general (often implying alcohol use). It can also mean a casual relationship between a man and a woman.

For young men from both ethnic groups, leisure time activities are very similar, except that when young Adygh men intend to go out on a 'big night', it means that they have to go to Krasnodar or Maikop.[147] Beyond these 'nights out', Adygh research participants spend their spare time sitting on the bench in front of the fountain in the centre of Adygheisk, hanging around in their cars and talking, or sometimes going to a café or a beer bar (*pivnyi bar*). Whereas Pilkington (2002) suggests that in the 1990s young people in the provinces could hardly dream of having their own car, this is not the case in the Krasnodar region today. Not everyone has a car, of course, but those who do, make use of it to get to places or use it to get friends together as a leisure place in its own right when it gets colder. Thus, in winter, hanging out for young men in Adygheisk either means spending time in one's car or sometimes spending time at home when parents are away.

> *Ruslan:* Well, how can I put it, we're a little everywhere. Maybe we sit in a café somewhere. Maybe we play billiards for a bit. We just go somewhere and play billiards. Friends meet us somewhere, or we just hang around in the flat. We sit all day on these benches near the fountain[148] or in the car. We park our car here and sit and watch. We wait for something interesting to happen. Sometimes one of our friends gets married, so we have some fun (*poguliaem*) at the wedding ... In winter when it's cold, we hang around in the house or somewhere in a café. We also hang out where they play billiards. Or, maybe, again we just come here and hang around in my car. Sometimes we go to Krasnodar ... the only thing is that in winter, we don't stay for long in any place, it all depends on money.

---

147   There is almost no cultural infrastructure in Adygheisk, except one café and two *pivnye bary* (beer bars).
148   This was the place where the author conducted most interviews with young Adyghs, including the interview with Ruslan. This is also the place where the author got to know most of Adygh research participants.

YOUTH IDENTITIES IN RUSSIA 181

Figure 5.1 Young men hanging out on the benches near the fountain in the centre of Adygheisk.

Figure 5.2 Young men hanging out in their cars in the centre of Adygheisk

YOUTH IDENTITIES IN RUSSIA 183

Figure 5.3 The main street in Adygheisk

For girls spare time activities only slightly vary between Armenians and Adyghs. In summer, the leisure activities for female Adygh research participants are not much different from young men. They get together in groups, walk up and down the main square or simply sit on the bench near the fountain in the centre of Adygheisk or just in one's yard (*vo dvore*).[149] When they want to 'go out clubbing', to the cinema or bowling, they go to Krasnodar or Maikop. Often, they are joined by their course mates from Krasnodar on these occasions. This development, of their course mates from Krasnodar joining them, is emphasized here as it implies an 'ethnic' mixture, illustrating that ethnicity is not important for leisure time activities.

> *Diana:* In the summer, we met up nearly every day. This summer, lots of us got together (*sobralis' kompaniei*). We had a great time together (*guliali*).
> *Fatima:* We were just chatting. In the evenings, friends came and we hung around in our yard (*vo dvore*).
> *Diana:* You know, where I live, there's a yard and we always hung around there. Lots of my friends joined us.
> *Fatima:* Friends, like Slavik, Rusik, Emil'...

As this interview excerpt with Fatima (18 years) and Diana (19 years) indicates, often leisure is spent together in a mixed group, including young men and women, although there are other spare time activities for young men for which they prefer male company. Male research participants prefer their male company when they want to drink or go out clubbing. On the whole, they consider this to be a 'man's thing'. Fieldwork observations revealed that amongst Armenians, it is not as common to spend time in a mixed group of young men and women. Generally speaking, there are only a few places where a 'mixed company' is accepted. For younger Armenians, under twenty years of age, these are gatherings in the park or discos, organized by the

---

149 Getting together in one's yard was also a common youth cultural practice in the 1990s (Pilkington 2002). While for Pilkington's participants, spending spare time in one's yard often implies use of alcohol and smoking, for Adygh research participants this is not necessarily the case. In winter, it becomes more difficult, but they still gather in each others' homes.

YOUTH IDENTITIES IN RUSSIA 185

community (*obshchina*).[150] Once they are older than twenty, young men and women start to separate and not to spend so much spare time together as, at this age, university or college demands hard work. As a result, leisure time becomes restricted to seeing just one's 'very best' friends. For Armenian girls, nevertheless, getting together with best friends remains similar to the practices of Adygh girls. Going to the cinema or bowling is also attractive to them, although they are most likely to do this in a girl-only group. Overall, *guliat'* for Armenian girls generally means meeting up with friends and talking over a cup of tea or walking around in the city centre or in parks.

The vernacular culture as a medium to reach the 'global'
In the introduction to this chapter, it was suggested that the global is strongly mediated by the local. For research participants, especially young Armenian women, the local is comprised of two different facets; on the one hand, it is their ethnic community; on the other, it is comprised of their engagement with wider society. Chapter Four demonstrated that the young generation's engagement with wider society has led young women to learn to accept gender behaviour that does not conform to traditions within the Armenian community. Such stark divisions also come to the fore in leisure practices. In the subsequent discussion it is argued that young Armenian women use Russian culture as a vehicle for engagement with the 'global'.

One example of this contradiction is the leisure practice of 'going clubbing'. The above discussion has shown that, for most young women, *guliat'* generally means meeting up with friends and talking over a cup of tea or walking around in the city centre or in parks. 'Going clubbing' is not that attractive for most of them, mainly because of their cultural up-bringing; sometimes parents would not allow them to go clubbing.[151] Often, research participants described their leisure time activities as *'this is all that we can do.'*

---

150 The regular Armenian dancing classes in the Centre for National Cultures and the *Armianskaia Pashkovskaia Obshchina* (APO), which were mentioned in Chapter Two, however, are mixed.
151 Of 15 female interviewees, only one goes clubbing regularly. Another twenty-year-old female said that she used to go clubbing when she was about 16 years old, but considers herself to be too old now. In addition, three interviewees had been clubbing more than once, but said they were not too keen on it. The remaining 10

> Armine: You know, here in Krasnodar you can't really do much. We don't have much to do.[152] There's only *Krasnaia ulitsa* [the main street in the city centre]. You can go clubbing or sit in a café somewhere. But as I'm not allowed to go clubbing, all we can do is walk up and down *Krasnaia ulitsa* or hang out in the park.

In this interview excerpt, Armine (21 years) raises two important issues concerning her spare time activities. First, she refers to the local conditions in Krasnodar, emphasizing the fact that Krasnodar is only a small town compared to Moscow or Saint Petersburg and, thus, lacks space and sights that are important for her definition of *guliat'*. On the other hand, although there are clubs and bars in Krasnodar, this is not a spare time option for her because of parental restrictions. Girls, like Mane (19 years), who experience parental restrictions, often describe themselves as very domestic and say that they do not like clubbing anyway:

> Mane: We go out, but I'm someone who likes to be at home. I'd rather be at home, than out. Sometimes we go to a café or walk along *Krasnaia ulitsa*.
> Ulrike: But if you go out do you go clubbing sometimes?
> Mane: No, we don't go clubbing. My parents don't allow it and I don't really want to go. It's just not my thing.

Seventeen year old Sona claims that the biggest problem for Armenian girls is that they cannot go out the way they want to.

> Sona: You know, Armenian girls have the problem that they're not allowed to go out that much. They can't go here, they can't go there. They can't dress how they want. This doesn't apply to everyone, but most. Ninety nine per cent of the girls have this problem. Sometimes you're not even allowed to go out with your brothers or [male] cousins.

---

interview participants were not allowed to go clubbing, but at the same time they said that they do not feel the need to go and that it is not appropriate.
152 For her *guliat'* embodies the meaning of sightseeing or simply walking around and looking at something interesting.

However, this is not the norm. Some, of course, experience restrictions in respect to going clubbing, but this is not necessarily different from any other families in Russia. It is rather about the relationship between parents and children and is, therefore, related to gender, given that fathers often are more protective of their daughters than they are of their sons. Here, it is not so much ethnic belonging that matters, but the traditions that circulate within the community. As stressed in the previous chapter, by and large parents' attitudes towards daughters going out depends on how far they are involved in, and affected by, the community. Nonetheless, on a broader level it depends on parents' world outlook. One of my research participants told me how she understands the whole situation:

> *Anush:* Well, he [her Dad] was a bit worried. There were all these perceptions that Armenian girls are not allowed this and that. He also followed them, like a proper Armenian, like a proper Armenian Dad (*laughs*). When he came to understand that he can trust me that I wouldn't do anything bad; all his perceptions just changed. Everyone deals differently with this. You see, I think that you shouldn't look at it from the viewpoint that she's an Armenian and so it's like this or that she's a Russian so it's like that. It's the family that has the biggest influence overall.

As Anush (22 years) indicates, it is also influenced by the extent to which fathers are willing to adhere to traditions or consider traditions important. For many fathers, attitudes have changed and letting their daughters go out is not unusual. In the interview excerpt below, Lusine (21 years) maintains that it also has to do with how far fathers are willing to assimilate Russian culture. The previous chapter has shown that Lusine is one of those girls, who associates 'modern', 'progressive' attitudes with 'Russian', but 'traditional', 'backward' attitudes with 'Armenian' culture. This, however, is an issue that cannot be proven. Cultures cannot be delineated along ethnic lines only, but are fluid and ever-changing (Gilroy 1993).

Generally speaking, parents who follow traditions and oppose 'global' influences restrict their children more. In this context, 'global' influences can be equated with Russian influences. Parents who are more open to global influences are less restrictive. While it could be argued that those parents are de-traditionalized in the sense that they ignore traditions, it is maintained that these parents and their children embrace a kind of cosmopolitan existence in that they draw on several cultural traditions, which to some extent is a 'traditional' aspect of Armenian and Adygh culture in this part of Russia. These young people are able to use the vernacular culture, predominantly Russian, to engage with the 'global'.

> *Lusine:* Because I've already said, my Dad is a very modern person (*sovremmennyi chelovek*). He's lived here for about twenty years. And he can see ... I think that only stupid people don't completely accept Russian laws. If you can see that you live in this world, you live in this society; you can see that this society lives according to certain laws. It doesn't matter; you can bend the rules sometimes. Well, an intelligent person understands this. My Dad's an intelligent and educated man. He knows that until you're intelligent enough to work it out for yourself, he has to impose [these rules] on you. And then, you can see how great it is when he allows you [to go out] ... I remember when I was allowed to go out, I was so happy, I felt so adult-like, so happy that my Dad trusts me, that's great!

Most interesting in this interview excerpt is that, as discussed above, Lusine's perceptions are based on a distinction between Russian and Armenian values. It is argued, however, that a large part of leisure and socializing originates from global influences that are reworked in the local context. It is not strictly 'Russian' to go to leisure centres or clubs - these are global institutions of consumption that can be found in most parts of the world.[153] Hence, the Russian (vernacular) culture is used as a vehicle of engagement with the 'global' and a site of everyday resistance to parental restrictions.

> *Manana:* You see, what you have to understand about tradition (*speaks very quietly*) is that, if an Armenian girl goes to a café or restaurant then that's considered bad ... Armenian girls can only go out when there's a wedding, so that they can meet someone. Well, I don't think it's right. This isn't really right. To

---

153 During fieldwork, the author was struck by the design and structure of the biggest leisure centre in Krasnodar, which was no different to a leisure centre in England.

be honest, I think it's completely wrong. But, I'm trying to be good...although sometimes I have to lie to my parents (*laughs*).

Figure 5.4 Ploshad' Revoliutsii (Revolution Square) at Krasnaia ulitsa in the centre of Krasnodar

Figure 5.5 Krasnaia ulitsa in the centre of Krasnodar

Leisure and public spaces

Central to leisure time is the negotiation of public spaces. While public spaces can be spaces for leisure characterized by 'ethnic mixture', they can also be spaces where young Armenians and Adyghs encounter xenophobia and racism. These encounters are examined in more detail in the subsequent discussion, which explores urban space as a site of 'inclusion' for young people. Some of the places examined here are public spaces, such as formal meeting places of the Armenian community, for example, of the Armenian Church or the Centre for National Cultures in Krasnodar (*Tsentr natsional'nykh kul'tur Krasnodarskogo kraia*), others are more informal, such as ethnically coded 'park gatherings'.

There is a lack of infrastructure for youth leisure in Adygheisk. There is only one café and two bars in the town, and girls would never go to the bars, as they are considered inappropriate places for girls. Once a month, there is a disco in the *dom kultury* (house of culture), organized by the town's administration. This disco is looked down on by anyone older than twenty. Those older than twenty usually have at least one friend with a car and are able to drive to Krasnodar or Maikop to go out on a big night.

For young Armenians in Krasnodar, finding places for leisure activities, such as clubbing, is not difficult. Krasnodar's infrastructure is well established and new bars and clubs and other leisure centres seem to open every couple of months. Although these places are there, and most of the young men make use of them, the majority of Armenian girls reject these places, as it is considered inappropriate for a girl to spend her time there. Armenian girls repeatedly talk about bars and clubs as inappropriate for women because 'they are dangerous': a site of 'drugs, criminals and prostitutes', In this context, girls have produced maps that document contours of safety and danger. Yet, these maps do not merely correlate to gendered or ethnic identities, but show the ways in which young people combine available forms of social knowledge in the use of spaces (cf. Back 2007). Although bars and clubs are often rejected, leisure centres are popular amongst girls, as they provide the opportunity to go to the cinema or go bowling.

One aspect of this 'rejection' of bars and clubs as a chosen space of youth sociality comes from a resistance to global or 'Russian' influences.[154] Another cultural aspect can be found in a different meaning of space. Armenians and Adyghs have close kinship relations and it is not unusual to invite someone home.[155] Even when parents are at home it appears that young people do not feel the need for privacy. One's room or kitchen is private enough to have a friend around. In the technological age, the internet and mobile phones provide another means to create a space, where one can communicate with others. Most research participants had access to the internet and phones at the time of my fieldwork. Compared with young people in the 1990s, when it was important for them to claim their own space by spending their time in public spaces of the city (Pilkington 2002: 142), for young Armenians (as well as Adyghs) today there are many more opportunities to claim their own space.

For both young Adyghs and Armenians 'going to the park' is still part of their leisure strategy. While for some Armenian girls 'going to the park' is a strategy for overcoming 'restrictions' and participating in a mixed company, for others it is simply a chance for a 'healthy walk'. In Krasnodar, there are many parks and young Armenian women often choose the park closest to where they live. Nonetheless, it is commonly accepted that there are also some parks that have become 'ethnic territories'. The *Park 40 Let Pobedy*[156], for example, is the park where many young Armenians get together. There is also *Park Gor'kogo* (Gorkii Park) which is considered to be Adygh territory and, finally, there is *Park 30 Let Oktiabria*[157] which is 'Georgian territory'.

Although stories about 'ethnic' gatherings in parks were encountered among research participants, they are more popular among teenagers. Those older than twenty talked about, but had lost interest, in these types of gatherings. When asking why these parks were ethnically coded, research participants said it was by chance, although they also noted that a few years

---

154 It is not that all global influences are resisted, but those that are perceived to be 'negative'.
155 In fact, close kinship relations are a cultural characteristic that cuts across all Caucasian peoples.
156 Literally translates as '*park in commemoration of the 40 years of victory*'.
157 Literally translates as '*park in commemoration of the 30 years of October*'.

ago many Armenians had lived in this district (*raion*). On the subject of the 'Adygh park', the majority of research participants said that this park has become their place because the park was closest to Adygheisk. Interestingly, none of the girls from Adygheisk are attracted to this park; it is described as a boy's thing. Although at times these accounts suggest a certain gendered use of parks, their ethnicized use does not appear to represent a form of racism, but reflects a pragmatic use of what is available.[158]

> *Murat:* On bank holidays we drive to *Park Gor'kogo* in Krasnodar.
> *Ulrike:* What is so special about this park that you go there?
> *Murat:* It's close for us for hanging out (*tusovat'sia*). And, how can I put it; there aren't any parents there (*laughs*). It's better to hang out (*tusovat'sia*) there.

In this interview excerpt, Murat gives two main reasons for using the park for getting together – its closeness to Adygheisk and to get away from parents' control. In addition, it is maintained that it is also a means of getting away from communal control within Adygheisk. Adygheisk is a small town where everyone knows each other. The same applies to young Armenians gathering in parks; the park provides an opportunity to be together, talk and listen to music. The music played on those occasions includes Russian and Armenian pop music as well as international pop music.

While young Adyghs' spare time options are either at home in Adygheisk or going bowling or to the cinema in Krasnodar or, for young men, going clubbing or hanging out in the park, for young Armenian adults there are some additional choices for specifically ethno-cultural leisure activities.[159] Armenian ethno-cultural institutions are important for those who feel the need to engage actively in one's ethnic culture. However, such endorsement of one's ethnic culture does not necessarily inhibit the formation of cosmopolitan practices. Parekh (2000b) maintains that despite cultural diversity, we live in a culturally structured world, where cultural identity retains its significance. In Chapter Two, it has been demonstrated how public discourse is structured

---

[158] In contrast to this research on young Armenians and Adyghs in Russia, Back (2007) uncovered forms of racism in the use of parks in his research.
[159] This is obviously not important for young Adyghs, since they live in their 'own' republic and comprise a majority in the town of Adygheisk.

around ethnicity and ethnic awareness in Krasnodar. Amin (2004: 11) suggests that cosmopolitan practices are also accompanied by 'ethnic loyalty as a source of communal security and cultural nourishment'. In this way, and as the discussion so far has shown, young people's leisure practices are ethnically structured, but not ethnically exclusivist, and include strategies that draw on cosmopolitanism as an identity resource.

One such ethno-cultural space is the Armenian Church in Krasnodar. Of course, not every young Armenian person goes to the Church and those who choose not to go do so for personal reasons, rather than as a conscious denial of their Armenian identity. The Church is the site of a range of cultural events, in addition to Church services. The Church is a place where young people can have fun and in the summer they may just hang around by the bench and fountain in front of the Church.

Another ethno-cultural space is the Centre for National Cultures in Krasnodar (*Tsentr natsional'nykh kul'tur Krasnodarskogo kraia*), which gives young people an opportunity to hang out on their own and engage with their own culture, by offering Armenian dance classes or Armenian language classes.[160] Chapter Two discussed the political implications of the Centre in the context of the state discourse promoting cultural diversity. Some local human rights activists would argue that the Centre is a state-sponsored institution mainly trying to disguise the real problem faced by minorities from this region. Ignoring the political implications of this Centre, when asked why they come to the Centre and why they want to learn Armenian dance or Armenian language, research participants often replied that it is important to observe one's tradition and nowhere else do they have such an opportunity apart from at the Centre.[161] While some of the girls told me that they wanted to come to this Centre because it was the only place (other than school and

---

160 There are many other organizations which organize Armenian cultural events and Armenian language classes, where young people can go, such as *Armianskaia Pashkovskaia Obshchina* (APO). The role of Armenian voluntary associations has been discussed in Chapter Two.
161 That they chose this Centre for language and dance classes was largely dependent on geographical location. The APO is reasonable far away from the city centre. As some of the girls lived in an opposite *raion*, attendance to dance or language classes in the APO could have involved a journey of more than an hour.

college) that their parents allowed them to go to, other girls maintained that it was important for them because of the feeling of belonging.

> *Sona:* ...there are only a few Armenians in Russia and they're under pressure... and we're all friends ... The Centre is really good for getting together ... lots of people can hang around together. Well, everyone is united in one place ... there's a disco for everyone ... and we can hang around with friends and get to know the new ones. Well, that's so cool...

These spaces give young people a sense of belonging and the opportunity of experiencing Armenian culture in their daily practices. By and large, going to these places is a matter of choice for young Armenians; some feel the need to experience their own culture, others avoid them. Yet, these places, as befits the regional political discourse, are not ethnically exclusive. Whoever is interested can come along:

> *Manana:* ... It all depends who wants to come along. Actually, I asked her [the Russian girl] why she'd be interested in Armenian traditional dancing. You know, she said that her boyfriend was Adygh and that's also a Caucasian nation. And then, she told me that's why she's here because it's just interesting for her...

These leisure spaces are simply not reducible to ethnic identities, but depend on the ways young people form social knowledge. The options for leisure spaces that are produced here, illustrate young people's individual choices and at the same time constraints, sometimes resulting from parents' restrictions. While in some ways Armenian culture is re-imagined in these localized ethno-cultural leisure places, in other ways it is a means for young women to overcome parental restrictions by using them to gain contact with young Armenian men and vice versa.

Figure 5.6 Teenagers dancing during a celebration on the grounds of the Armenian Church

Figure 5.7 Arin Berd, practising for their next dance performance

At first glance, it seems that these leisure places are characterized by intercultural dialogue and that ethnicity does not matter. The discussion of these leisure spaces has illustrated that in many instances leisure spaces are structured ethnically and in their use of them young people reproduce the politics of cultural diversity, in which all ethnic groups are equal, yet viewed as distinct entities. In their leisure practices, it seems as if young people draw on cosmopolitanism as an identity resource and form spaces that are not ethnically exclusive and are free of racism. Such instances can be viewed as the result of the historical tradition of cultural mixing in the Caucasus region.

Routinizing difference

In Krasnodar, I just know that there're many people who say that, well, Russians are the good ones, all the other people are the bad ones, and they should leave. I just know this because I've heard it very often (Anahit, 15 years).

The previous part of this chapter discussed ethnically structured leisure practices, demonstrating that while young people reproduce the political discourse of cultural diversity at leisure, leisure spaces and practices are not racialized or ethnically exclusive. This part of the chapter explores the ways in which individuals sometimes become racialized/ethnicized when passing through public spaces. A number of studies in the Western context emphasize that the politics of cultural diversity not only embody interethnic dialogue, but also rigid divisions (Back 2007; Nayak 2004). One explanation for this might be the politics from above, where communities have been ethnically segregated. In research on Russia, the majority of literature on Russian everyday racism and xenophobia focuses on its causes and origins (Roman 2002; Russell 2002). There is only a small amount of literature that analyses the experience of everyday xenophobia (Pilkington and Yemelianova 2003). The subsequent analysis focuses precisely on the ways young people experience xenophobia and racism as part of their everyday lives.

Everyday xenophobia and prejudice in contemporary Russian society
In most societies, xenophobia, intolerance, everyday racism and prejudice have become important phenomena and policy issues as the processes of globalization bring with them increasing flows of migration and intermingling of different cultures. Pusic (1995) argues that xenophobia arises as a consequence of building and rebuilding states with new forms of citizenship at a time of deep economic crisis. Others maintain that xenophobia and intolerance arise due to discontinuities in people's biographies in transition from one regime to another, which increases their sense of insecurity (Nassehi and Richter 1996), or due to the lack of civil society and an established free press (Spülbeck 1996). All of these general conditions are typical of contemporary Russia and Krasnodar krai.

Essed (1991) argues that everyday racism is a multi-dimensional phenomenon that is characterized by repetitive and recurrent familiar practices which are inherent in society's culture and have to be seen as more than structure and ideology. In this way, it is difficult to identify precise causes of xenophobia in contemporary Russia. However, it is necessary to mention at least three specific factors which play or have played a key role in explaining the rise of xenophobia among Russians and were discussed tacitly in Chapter One and Two. One contributing factor is the decrease of the ethnically Russian population, combined with positive population growth rates of Caucasian peoples, such as Chechens, the Ingush and Azeris (Dubas 2008, Vishnevsky 2005). In this situation, xenophobic attitudes amongst the ethnic Russian population can be understood as a way of safeguarding their status in Russia's multi-ethnic society.

Another contributing factor is the presence of immigrants, especially those of non-Slavic origin, in contemporary Russia. Russia has become a major in-migration destination, with a documented net gain of 5.8 million people, 1989-2004 (Heleniak 2008: 34). It is estimated that every year approximately 4.6 million people come to Russia to work illegally, and nearly 80 per cent of the illegal workers come from the CIS countries (Dubas 2008: 35). Hence, migration has become an important topic in Russian politics today and the presence of immigrants provokes tensions in the Russian population. Finally, the conflicts in Chechnya and the fact that the Chechen conflict spread to other regions of Russia through attacks against civilians[162] also played a crucial role in the rise of xenophobic attitudes in Russia.

One important concept included in the various dimensions of everyday racism and prejudice is that of the 'other'. The relationship with the 'other' is important for the construction of 'self'. This relationship has been central to the psychoanalytic conception of identity. According to Lacanian psychoanalysis, identity starts developing at 'the mirror phase', when the infant recognizes him or herself through the image of the carer which acts as the 'other'. When the child moves into language and the web of social relations surrounding the child becomes bigger, 'it finds the image of selfhood to which it will aspire in the desires, speeches and rituals of those others with whom it comes into contact and on whom it depends' (Bowman 1997: 44). Elaborating on Lacan, Althusser (2000 [1969]) suggests that identity occurs through the interpellation of the self into the discourse of others. Moreover, Griffiths (1999) contends that anyone separate from one's self can be seen as the 'other' and becomes part of the process of locating one's own place in the world. The relationship between self and others influences identity processes and self-awareness (Griffiths 1999). In this way, othering processes can also be understood in terms of power relations (Bhavnani 2001). Othering processes can include differentiations according to biological, cultural, religious, linguistic or territorial differences. These markers of difference legitimize exclusion and/or subordination of minority groups in society.

For contemporary Russian society, the process of 'othering' is multi-dimensional. The image of the 'West', and in the 1990s in particular a disassociation with Sovietism, have led to a revival of the Russian idea and Great Russian Chauvinism among nationalist-patriotic or extremist movements when forging Russian national identity. Conversely, perceptions of non-Russians and what it is to be 'Russian' are as important for these processes of 'othering'. In just two to three years after the 1991 break-up, xenophobic attitudes in Russia increased by 1.5 times on average (Gudkov

---

162 For example, the explosion in residential buildings in Moscow in 1999, and the terror attacks at the Dubrovka theatre in 2002, at the school in Beslan in 2004 (Dubas 2008: 37).

1995: 15), in recent years the level of everyday xenophobia has decreased, according to the Public Opinion Foundation in Russia.[163] In 2002, for example, every third survey respondent (32 per cent) stated that they experience irritation or hostility in relation to representatives of another nationality; in 2004 and 2006, only 29 per cent and 21 per cent respectively stated the same.[164]

The concepts of 'one's own' and 'other,' of 'ours' and 'not ours' are deeply embedded in one's consciousness. There has always been a sense of 'us versus them' (*'svoi'* versus *'chuzhoi'*) in the ethnic Russian population, with 'us' being positively regarded, 'them' negatively (Sikevich 1996). Of course, this differentiation is not peculiar to Russians. In Chapter Five, for example, a similar differentiation within the Armenian community was discussed, where the distinction between 'us' (Armenians) and 'them' (Russians) within Armenian traditional gender order, is part of a process to reassert their status as a minority group versus the majority within the political discourse. Hence, a sense of 'us versus them' is universal of human social interaction, as indicated by Griffiths (1999) among others. In the case of Russian ethnic identity, while having a long historical tradition in the ethnic Russian consciousness, this dichotomy can refer to the division between ethnic Russians (*'russkie'*) and non-Russians (*'inorodtsy'*) or to the division between Russians and peoples outside of Russia (*'inostrantsy'*), especially the West (Sikevich 1996).[165]

While hostile attitudes among Russians towards non-Russians have historical roots, the rise of xenophobia can be derived from these historical roots and current conditions. Some argue that manifestations of xenophobia

---

163   It is important to note here that the Public Opinion Foundation (FOM) is a state-controlled institution.
164   Public Opinion Foundation, 15 - 16 April 2006, Online. Available HTTP: <http://bd.fom.ru/report/cat/societas/nation/xenophobia/of061623> (accessed 24 October 2007). The data is based on a representative survey of 1500 respondents in 100 survey sites covering 44 regions of Russia. The statistical error does not exceed 3.6 per cent.
165   Earliest references to non-Russians (*inorodtsy*) can be found in Russian fairy tales where one often encounters amusing variations on the theme of 'ours' and 'not ours'. In fairy tales, devils are euphemistically referred to as 'not ours'. For instance, 'and then those [devils] who were not ours flew in' (cited in Sinyavsky 1990: 483-484).

among Russians are most often linked to a sense and awareness of their own impoverishment and inferiority (Malashenko 1999). Although the inferiority complex has decreased since 2004, the tendency to blame 'others' for perceived misfortune remains pertinent, as Table 5.1 shows below:

Table 5.1: Are people from 'non-Russian' nationalities guilty of Russia's many misfortunes? (% of survey respondents)[166]

	2004	2005	2006	2007
Agree	42	37	34	32
Disagree	52	57	58	58
Don't know	6	6	8	10

Similarly, others argue that in times of turmoil individuals tend to feel the increasing need for an 'image of the enemy' (*obraz vraga*) (Sikevich 1999). Nevertheless, these reasons do not seem to be enough to explain the rise of xenophobia as part of Russian national identity. As demonstrated in Chapter Two, and as pointed out by Essed (1991), structural factors are as significant as the ideological factors (Althusser) that interpellate individuals to concrete subject positions. Therefore, xenophobic attitudes in this part of Russia can also be explained by the specific political discourse and political anti-migratory regime in Krasnodar krai, as well as in the whole of Russia.

Encountering everyday prejudice and racism
Fieldwork has shown that Armenian and Adygh youth are disturbed by the open, everyday prejudice in Krasnodar, especially as most of them feel that this is the place where they belong, where they feel 'at home'. Being treated as the 'other' can happen in any daily situation, for example, in shops or on public transport, as Armine (21 years) explains:

> *Armine:* Sometimes when I use public transport ... You know, Armenians are always guilty ... that's not comfortable, when

---

[166] Levada Center, 28 August 2007. Online. Available HTTP: <http://www.levada.ru/press/2007082901.html> (accessed 24 October 2007). The data is based on a representative survey of 1600 Russian citizens.

they insult your people, but you can't be rude because your upbringing doesn't allow it. You're standing there and you're listening, pretending that people don't say this sort of thing about you.

Physical appearance affects the way young men are treated by public bodies such as the police (*militsiia*). One consequence is that young Armenian and Adygh men are more likely than Russians to be stopped by the police. Police checks in turn are a consequence of the new passport and registration regime and the limits on freedom of movement introduced after the collapse of the Soviet Union. The Russian *militsiia* routinely stop individuals on the street for identity checks and do so overwhelmingly on the basis of appearance (Ossipow 2003). Nevertheless, this has become so routinized that Sargis (22 years), for example, dismisses it by saying '*that's the way it is*'.

> *Sargis:* You see, you're walking along the streets, one [of us] is Caucasian, and the other two friends are Russian. A policeman [*militsioner*] approaches us and, of course, only wants to see my documents. You show him your student card, but that's not enough. Well, then he'll take you to the police station. Well, that's the way it is...

A different appearance not only affects one's treatment by the *militsiia*, it also can lead to rejection by Russians. In general, such attitudes are strongly influenced by Russian media's negative depiction of people of Caucasian origin (cf. Roman 2002; Russell 2002). In Krasnodar krai, in particular, such attitudes were formed as a result of the region's political discourse that stresses the threat of illegal migration for the region's stability, especially in relation to people with Caucasian origins, portraying them as 'not local'. This rejection can even lead to overt everyday racism in the form of openly derogatory comments directed towards the non-Russian persons:

> *Sargis:* ...you're sitting somewhere and they say you're *chernyi* (black), why did you come here? That doesn't make you feel very comfortable.

The term *chernyi* in this context is a derogatory term and applies to any Caucasian person. Research participants complained that the Russian population does not even distinguish between the different Caucasian ethnicities; for them Caucasians are just collectively seen as non-Russians, differentiated from Russians by characteristics such as different appearance or language. Thus, everyday racism is addressed in general to anyone who looks or speaks differently, Khachig (18 years) describes.

> *Khachig:* It's just that many don't distinguish, well, they see a non-Russian face and call them either Adygh or Armenian, whatever suits best. Everyone is lumped together under one nationality.

These are just a few examples of recounted incidents that make young Armenians feel excluded. As a response, some young Armenians choose to silently accept these incidents of everyday racism and refrain from openly reacting to them. In this way, it seems that they are able to defuse them. Others, however, respond more actively, by emphasizing their own ethnic belonging during everyday interactions. Sona, for example, describes a form of active response:

> *Sona:* Despite the fact that we live in Russia, it doesn't matter ... if I have contact with Russians, it doesn't matter ... when we go out somewhere, to a café, and they're playing music there anyway, I always have my CD with Armenian music with me, and put it on so that everyone can listen to it. With Russians, when we talk, it doesn't matter, they always respect me, and they respect Armenians. I make sure that they always respect the Armenian nation (*armianskaia natsiia*).

Whereas Sona (17 years) maintains that it is important for her to acknowledge her nationality (even though she thinks it is insignificant for forming friends), Gaiane (20 years) considers it important, not to display too much of her nationality in everyday interactions at university. She thinks that this is not necessary because it serves no purpose in everyday interaction. Nonetheless, her position may be interpreted as a strategy for maintaining her ethnic identification, whilst being selective about those situations in which to display ethnic belonging.

> Gaiane: Why do I have this attitude [not to display too much of her nationality in everyday interactions]? Because I live amongst Russians anyway. I live in Russia. No one says that I'm Armenian because I don't give anything away. I keep my nationality (*natsional'nost'*) to myself. I express my nationality only when I'm with other nationalities ... I never speak my mother tongue in public places because that's uncivilized, just uncivilized (*nekul'turno*). In the presence of a person who can't understand my language, I'll never speak in my language ... if I speak to my Mum on the phone I speak Armenian.

At the same time, Gaiane criticizes young Armenian men, who like to display their nationality and thus often create negative stereotypes.

> Gaiane: But our Armenian [lads] what do they do? In the car, the window is open, their music is so loud in the car that you can hear it three kilometres away. But why? Excuse me, but if I was Russian, I'd hit him myself. It's irritating.

This behaviour is not unusual for young men. Other published research shows that young men like to adopt certain 'racialized' styles to show their 'desired' masculinity (cf. O'Donnell and Sharpe 2000). Sewell (1996) maintains that some African–Caribbean boys express their disillusionment and opposition to school in terms of black 'nationalist' ideology, which is often articulated in music, dance and demeanour. Furthermore, O'Donnell and Sharpe (2000) show that Indian and Pakistani boys, as well as English and African-Caribbean boys, often cited national or ethnic heroes and rituals, such as sporting and musical rituals, as reference points for a desired masculinity. Nonetheless, the exposed self-defined 'masculine' behaviour of some young men encourages resentment and the formation of stereotypes amongst the Russian population. These stereotypes, as Khachig earlier indicated, cut across all Caucasian ethnicities. In 2007, it was reported that 30 per cent of survey respondents considered the 'provocative behaviour' (*vyzyvaiushchee povedenie*) of national minorities to be the cause of nationalism in contemporary Russia, as demonstrated in Table 5.2.

Table 5.2: What is the main reason for nationalism in Russia today? (% of survey respondents)[167]

	2002	2007
National prejudice of the Russian population	7	8
Provocative behaviour of national minorities	25	30
Poor living conditions in Russia	34	31
The authorities can't deal with the outbreak of nationalism	12	12
The authorities are interested in the exaggeration of nationalism	7	9
Don't know	15	10

Another commonly accepted aspect of everyday prejudice relates to the treatment of members of ethnic minorities in the education system:

> Emma: In some of the institutions of higher education, there are people teaching, who don't like *natsmeny* [national minorities]. And they always pick on you and don't always let you pass your exam. ... Can you imagine, once the Dean of the University said to my cousin that he should leave and work at the market...
>
> Anahit: Actually, we've got a teacher, who's my class teacher ... well, she's perhaps one of those teachers who doesn't like *natsmeny* ... One time we had to make a big poster, and one girl wanted to use one of those glittery pens to make it all sparkly ... but the teacher said, 'Well, I don't need this Armenian sparkle here!' Can you understand? The teacher really said that. No one said anything. But why did she say it?
>
> Manana: One day, I went to the library in my district (*raion*) ... the librarian looked strangely at me and was very unfriendly. When

---

167 Levada Center, 25 July 2007. Online. Available HTTP: <http://www.levada.ru/press/2007072500.html> (accessed 24 October 2007). The data is based on a representative survey of 1600 Russian citizens. The statistical error does not exceed three per cent.

I wanted to get a book, she looked at me and said, 'I thought you lot couldn't read Russian. Don't you want to go back to the market and sell things? Why would you want to come to this library?'

Whereas in Britain, for example, such attitudes are regarded as unacceptable, the public discourse in Krasnodar makes them ordinary and everyday. While in Western democratic societies, young people might be encouraged to seek legal redress against such examples of open discrimination, in Krasnodar young adults appear to accept that: *'That's the way it is'*, and that there would always be people who did not like *natsmeny* (national minorities). While this may suggest that Armenians in Krasnodar are passively accepting racial discrimination, it may be argued that their response is deeply infused with Armenian tradition, which teaches that rudeness and conflict are inappropriate.

One aspect of everyday prejudice that stood out amongst Adyghs was the rejection they experienced when speaking their native language in the city of Krasnodar.[168] Speaking Adygh on public transport often evokes resentment amongst the local population. It is here that Russians distinguish between 'them' and 'us', by defining the Russian nation by language. At the same time, identity markers of difference are defined in geographical terms – Krasnodar is 'our' place, while Adyghs are not from this town.

>*Murat:* Well, we're Adyghs. They don't want us to speak Adygh [in Krasnodar]. I had this situation, we went home from [football] training in the *marshrutka* [fixed-route taxi]. And we were talking in Adygh. A *muzhik* [bloke] sits opposite us in the *marshrutka* and says to us, 'If you want to talk, then speak in Russian. You're in our town. Speak Russian'. ...There are just some people who don't like other nationalities.

Being Armenian or Adygh, 'non-Russian' or 'Caucasian' is sometimes seen as problematic when seeking work. For Adyghs, this is, however, more

---

168 Young Armenians in Krasnodar are fluent in Russian and are more likely not to be able to speak Armenian than Russian. Therefore, language as a dimension of everyday racism was not mentioned by research participants.

a question of getting a *propiska* (residence permit) in order to be able to work in Krasnodar, as Allii (24 years) explains:

> *Alii:* It's difficult to find work in Krasnodar. First of all, because you need a *propiska*, a Krasnodar one. Well, you can find a job [as an unskilled worker]. Without a *propiska* you can only find a job as a manual worker. You can find a job somewhere in a warehouse. ... if you want to find work in Krasnodar, you have to have a *propiska*.

For Armenians, discrimination in the labour market was mainly communicated by Armenian parents, but not by research participants themselves. There is the perception that discrimination in the labour market occurs on the basis of surnames, since surnames, like physical appearance or language, are a marker of ethnic difference.[169] Often, participants would deny there is discrimination in the labour market according to ethnicity, but would confirm that attention is paid to surnames within the krai's administration structures.

> *Ulrike:* Have you heard that there are problems with surnames in Krasnodar, as in if you have an Armenian surname you have less opportunities?
> *Khachig:* Well, less opportunities for what? Let's say, for career advancement in the administration, maybe ... But for ... well, let's take the SBS [a big leisure centre in Krasnodar], who are the owners? Armenians, well, now Muscovites, now Muscovites buy up everything here. The *Siti-Tsentr* [a big shopping centre], you know, the founder of *Siti-tsentr* is an Adygh. The [owner of the] restaurant *Roial'* is an Adygh, not Armenian. *Urartu* [a restaurant] on *Seleznaia* street [*ulitsa*] an Armenian. *Vip-klub Maksimus* on *Turgeneva* street [*ulitsa*], an Armenian ... Here [in Krasnodar] practically all those enterprises are owned by non-Russians...

Although Khachig by and large rejects the claim that there is any general discrimination on the basis of surnames in Krasnodar, it is generally accepted

---

169 As this was not on the agenda amongst research participants, the author addressed this question in particular, since parents were keener to talk about the problem of discrimination according to surnames.

by members of ethnic minorities that it is hard for individuals from ethnic minorities to get work in local administration offices.[170] Generally speaking, it is an unwritten law that *natsmeny* (national minorities) cannot get employment in the city's administration or only with great difficulty. However, many research participants stress that the issue here is not only one of discrimination, but also money.

> *Emma:* In Krasnodar nationality [*natsiia*] plays an important role. There's a big wall between yourself and employers; your nationality [*tvoia natsiia*] plays an important role.
> *Oksana:* Well, this wall immediately disappears, if you can put money on the table.

Some Armenians have changed their surnames,[171] for example, changing *-ian-* to *-ov-*, if they think they may have problems to find work.[172] The question of changing surnames was even addressed in a newspaper article (Galatsan 2006). However, this article does not talk about why some people from ethnic minorities consider changing their surnames in order to get a job in the regional administration or other governmental offices and, thus, appears to suggest that it is more a personal choice (to get a better 'karma') than a consequence of structural circumstances.

When asked about this issue, most research participants said that they would never change their surname because they are proud to have an Armenian surname. But when talking to parents, some of them admitted to me that they had thought about it because they know that it would improve their children's job prospects. One parent even admitted that his daughter would get on better, if she could get married to a Russian. This is an

---

170 The author's fieldwork experience suggests that Russians also recognize this type of discrimination.
171 Statistics to verify these comments were unavailable, due to the reluctance of the local authorities to divulge this information.
172 The name changing issue is difficult to prove, but does seem to have a long history. One local scholar suggested in an informal discussion that in the Soviet Union many people changed their names to disguise their ethnic origins. He claimed that, for instance, Lenin and Trotskii had changed their names to disguise that they were Jews and Stalin changed his Georgian name.

important issue, since in most cases parents prefer their daughters to marry an Armenian in order to carry on traditions.

Dealing with racist attacks
In addition to these incidents of everyday xenophobia and discrimination, research participants also mentioned incidents of racist attacks and often talked of the threat of 'skinheads'. In the period, 2004-8, a total of 58 violent attacks were recorded in Krasnodar; of which four were murder (Kozhevnikova 2009 cited in Laryš and Mareš 2011: 139). Of these attacks, the bulk (34) occurred in 2004 with 11 recorded in 2007. Although the Krasnodar administration seemed to have established a sufficient regime to avoid such incidents (there were only two recorded racist attacks in 2008), the problem is nonetheless very real for many of these young people. For example, in December 2010, a young Armenian was stabbed 16 times in the city centre of Krasnodar, although the incident was subsequently dismissed by the authorities as a case of football hooliganism.[173]

In particular, the problem of skinheads is stressed in this part of the chapter mainly for two reasons: first, because this is a problem that affects the whole of Russia and has received substantial media coverage (cf. Raskin 2006; Shargunov 2002). According to the SOVA Center, the informal neo-Nazi skinhead movement is one of the largest in the country, with 50,000 followers and approximately 10,000 to 20,000 active members.[174] In 2007, there were 327 racist attacks, which is an increase of 42 per cent in comparison to 2006 (Autalipov 2009). The number of racist attacks did not decline in 2008, when 87 people were killed and 378 injured (ibid.). In 2009, 71 people were murdered and 333 injured (Laryš and Mareš 2011). Second, when asking research participants about experiences of discrimination, this was the first issue they raised.

The Armenian community in Krasnodar krai has suffered violent racist attacks in the past, beginning in 1996, with sporadic violence by Cossacks

---

173 Armenian News. 22 December 2010. *Criminal who Stabbed Armenian Teen 12 times Detained*. Online. Available HTTP: http://news.am/eng/news/42597.html (accessed 12 January 2011).
174 SOVA Center. Online. Available HTTP: <http://sova-center.ru> (accessed 7 January 2008).

against Armenian businesses, homes and cultural monuments (Giragosian 2002). In April 2002, an Armenian cemetery was vandalized, which was an incident that attracted substantial media coverage, but in the end was dismissed as an isolated action of 'football hooligans' (Demchenko and Petrosian 2002). For young Armenians and Adyghs, however, this story is a story about skinhead violence, which elicited ethnic solidarity among *natsmeny* (national minorities) as a response, as Temine (19 years) describes:

> *Temine:* When skinheads in Krasnodar ... demolished an Armenian cemetery, many of our lads together with Adyghs went to kick their arses ... a cemetery is the most holy place. Everyone helped. They really beat them up. They named a place and then they had a fight ... I know that they got what they deserved. It's outrageous that these skinheads demolished the headstones of our forefathers. It's terrible....

This solidarity evokes an identity that is ethnically inclusive, rooted in a Caucasian identity that posits ethnic difference as insignificant and envisages all *natsmeny* as affected by the problem. In Russia today, skinheads have become a kind of 'folk devil' because of media coverage. In this way, an everyday fear has been created, which has become routinized and generated common perceptions of skinheads among young people regardless of whether they are formed via direct or second hand experiences. The examples below show the extent to which these young adults use generalizations, such as 'they are criminals,' 'they attack every non-Russian'.

> *Manana:* ... because I know that skinheads attack everyone who's not Russian and I'm not Russian. You can see that in my appearance. If you like, I've got dark hair and brown eyes. Well, any nation has got distinct characteristics, such as Armenians, Georgians or Adyghs ... It doesn't matter really, but they only attack non-Russians ... I knew a girl who was in a *marshrutka* [fixed-route taxi] and fell asleep, woke up because everyone around her started screaming. It turned out that skinheads had set her hair on fire.

Sargis: ...they are criminals. No one pays attention to them. So we all got together ... they just want to wind you up to start a fight, well you see ... they say a few words ... they're getting more insulting ... and then bang ... if you're in the tram it's better to just leave...

This everyday fear even means that young Armenians would stay at home on Hitler's Birthday because they know that it would be too dangerous to go out on the streets. As one Armenian girl told me in an interview:

Armine: ...Well, they say, that for non-Russians it's better not to leave the house on these days [she refers to Hitler's Birthday in April] because they're like cockroaches ... Imagine fifty skinheads and you're a girl on your own...

From this example it becomes obvious, that Armine has already taken precautionary measures not leaving the house on Hitler's Birthday but not all her ideas are based on personal experience, as in 'they say', but, presumably, what she had heard on TV or had read in the press.
The stories, which are examined here, construct identity in a cross-national sense. This is when all ethnic minorities are united.

Manana: Well, in Russia, it doesn't matter, there are only a few Armenians, it sort of means that they're under pressure. You're in your homeland, but, it doesn't matter, you're still under pressure ... well, we're all friends ... Caucasian people ... like brothers and sisters ... that's normal for us ... we're all united...

This last interview excerpt, demonstrates the relational nature of identity rooted in the interplay between structure and agency and discourse and practices. Young people perceive skinheads as a threat to ethnic minorities and respond to this threat by taking precautionary measures. The appeal to 'Caucasian brotherhood' in this interview excerpt can be read as a response to this external threat; a redefinition of 'us', through the supra-ethnic category of 'Caucasian', in relation to the 'other', When talking about skinheads, the young adults' Caucasian identity comes to the fore, but not their Armenian or Adygh ethnic identity. Research participants seem to know that skinheads do not distinguish between different ethnic peoples, thus, do not take it as an attack against their Armenian or Adygh ethnic belonging, but rather take it as an attack against various ethnic groups. Hence, it is not all about ethnic identity, but more about the supra-ethnic (Caucasian) identity, because for skinheads, all Caucasians become the same. Here it is an inclusive identity, referring to all *natsmeny*, despite cultural differences, negotiating identity not in an essentialist way, but a shared identity, that of being a minority in general.

Conclusions

This chapter has explored the complex relationship between youth cultural identities and place. It has been argued that for research participants the notion of place embodies a dual experience of interethnic dialogue and inclusive notions of ethnicity as well as racism. The question of place, however, is complex and cannot be reduced to ethnic identities. Young adults are social actors who form social knowledge and internalize objective constraints and social structure and in this way strategically use place. Internalizing the social structure of cultural diversity, young Armenian and Adygh adults reproduce the regional political discourse of cultural diversity and discrimination. It has been demonstrated that leisure sites are ethnically structured, but not ethnically exclusive. It seems that at leisure, young adults are most likely to draw on cosmopolitanism as an identity resource. It is not that these young adults draw on different identity resources to overcome ethnic and racist boundaries in their strategic use of leisure spaces, but rather that they work within these ethnic and racist boundaries.

Friends are an important part of young people's lives and are important in the creation of a sense of belonging. It has been suggested here, however, that it is not so much ethnic belonging that determines the choice of friends but rather life circumstances, such as place of residence or schools' demographic composition. Research participants form friendships on the basis of shared values and interests and express a policy of ethnic equality by not attaching any meaning to ethnicity and thus not racializing or ethnicizing those relationships. In contrast, this chapter has shown that gender differences are vital for the formation of friendships.

Although not consciously ethnicizing their leisure practices, individuals sometimes encountered racism in public spaces. Indeed, such encounters were so routine that racism is met with a certain degree of acceptance. It is suggested here, however, that apparent 'silence' might be better understood as a quiet reassertion of ethnic belonging that undermines the dominant political discourse. To conclude, young Armenians and Adyghs move within an ethnically structured local context that is defined by stark contradictions; racism and xenophobia exist alongside cultural diversity and interethnic dialogue. They manage this process, often by drawing on cosmopolitanism as an identity resource. Yet, they do not actively transcend ethnic boundaries, but rather relive and reproduce these boundaries.

6 Conclusion: Youth Cultural Identities Revisited

This book has explored the complex processes of identity formation and cultural experiences amongst young Armenians and Adyghs in Southern Russia. It has been demonstrated that young Armenians and Adyghs are not able to traverse the boundaries of ethnicity and racism/xenophobia, but rather have developed strategies that enable them to manage their ethnically structured environment. Cultural identities of young Adyghs and Armenians in this part of Russia are constructed through complex processes of interacting social categories of sameness and difference that are inscribed in the local context. It has been shown that the construction of youth cultural identities in Southern Russia is a complex multi-dimensional process that cannot be reduced to ethnic belonging only. The analysis has also revealed that geographical peculiarities of place and the differences to other societies cannot be generalized, but serve to move academic practice forward as those peculiarities are accounted for.

This study has inevitably required the application of concepts from different subject disciplines and theoretical paradigms. One vital concept used to theorize youth cultural identities in this analysis is cosmopolitanism. Cosmopolitanism has been employed to challenge conventional sociological, as well as popular and political, conceptions of diasporic and indigenous identities. It has been shown that cosmopolitanism should be seen not as an 'identity', but as a strategy for managing cultural diversity. Cosmopolitanism is understood as the result of a long history and tradition of migration and cultural mixing in this part of Russia. Living in a culturally diverse society can create cosmopolitan experiences, since it compels individuals to constantly manoeuvre within different cultural systems (Werbner 1999; Lamont and Arksatova 2002). It is argued, however, that in view of the specificities of Krasnodar krai and the public discourse on ethnicity in contemporary Russia, cosmopolitanism has its limits. Primordial 'loyalties' are frequently articulated in public discourse in Russia and, thus, have become part of an everyday reality that is significant on the individual level for the construction of social identities. In this way, cosmopolitanism as an identity resource is still in its infancy in the post-Soviet cultural space.

This book has stressed the significance of the post-Soviet regional context for understanding processes of youth cultural identity construction in the Russian Federation. Young Armenians and Adyghs are subjected to the identity politics in their region and reproduce as well as normalize the political discourse in their everyday practices. Both Krasnodar krai and Adyghea have ethnocentric political regimes, although the political discourses differ slightly in both regions. In Krasnodar krai, the political discourse is defined by an ambiguity of restrictive (discriminatory) non-Russian migration politics and the politics of cultural diversity. This ambiguity implies an ethnic hierarchy where some ethnic groups, which are considered native, are favoured at the expense of non-Russian migrants and ethnic minorities. In contrast, the political discourse in the Republic of Adyghea is characterized by an ethno-nationalist ideology that leaves room for the participation of ethnic minorities in political processes in Adyghea. Both ethnocentric political regimes are the result of Soviet multiculturalism, where cultural diversity was promoted on the basis of a primordial understanding of ethnicity. Hence, in post-Soviet Russia in general and in Adyghea and Krasnodar krai in particular, individuals often articulate and envisage their identities in ethno-cultural terms and therefore cannot be understood completely without considering the Soviet legacy of multiculturalism.

In contradistinction to studies in the Western context, this study has demonstrated that a culturally diverse locality does not necessarily lead to the formation of 'new ethnicities' (cf. Back 1996; Ali 2003). Instead, both young Armenians and Adyghs keep a strong sense of their ethnic belonging, which in some ways reproduces that very regional identity politics. Young Adyghs' strong sense of ethnic belonging is underpinned by their indigenous, albeit minority status, in the region. At the same time, their sense of ethnic belonging is constructed through patriotic attitudes, the result of Adyghs being only a small people. Young Adyghs derive their sense of belonging from two major identity markers that are both rooted in geographical location – Caucasian and Adygh identity. Nonetheless, Caucasian identities is a supra-ethnic identity that mainly comes to the fore in relation to the 'other',

Russians, and is used to distance oneself from otherness (Russians), and to share sameness with other ethnic groups, including Armenians.

Similarly, young Armenians' identities are not multifarious in the sense that they construct a 'third space' (Bhabha 1990), but instead their sense of belonging is articulated predominantly through Armenianness. Like Adygh identity, Armenianness is understood by the young people in this study as a primordial identity which has clear blood, kin and genetic characteristics. Their narratives of belonging are diverse, however, and cannot be generalized for all Armenians in Krasnodar. Instead, each young person's family history and individual narratives (which are different for each individual) have to be considered thoroughly in order to understand how young people form a sense of belonging. This confirms the proposition stated in Chapter One that all identities are narratives and through narrative we come to know, understand and make sense of the social world and can form our social identities. It is lived experience and feeling 'at home' that matters to young Armenians and, therefore, belonging to a specific geographical place is significant for identity formation.

This research has revealed the significance of place relations for youth cultural identities. For both young Armenians and Adyghs, the notion of place embodies a dual experience of interethnic dialogue and cultural diversity, as well as racism and xenophobia. One important aspect for the formation of youth cultural identities is the significant 'other'. In the empirical chapters of this book, it has been argued that it is the interaction with Russians (dominant culture) that makes Armenian and Adygh youth keep a strong sense of their own culture instead of creating a new (hybrid) culture (cf. Hall 1996b).

At first glance, it seems that leisure places are characterized by intercultural dialogue and ethnicity is presented by young people as unimportant to understanding their everyday experience at leisure. Youth cultural leisure spaces, however, are structured ethnically and in their leisure activities young people at best partially reproduce the politics of cultural diversity, whereby all ethnic groups are equal, but viewed as distinct entities. At leisure, nonetheless, young people have begun to draw on cosmopolitanism as an identity resource and form spaces that are not ethnically exclusive and are free of racism. Such instances might be viewed as the result of the historical tradition of cultural mixing in the Caucasus region.

The book has demonstrated that friendships are primarily not ethnicized or racialized, but rather gendered. Whereas young men often form large circles of friends, young women are more likely to have deeper and more lasting friendships. Overall, the choice of friends is determined by life circumstances, such as place of residence or schools' demographic structure. Young Armenians and Adyghs view their friendships as based on shared values and interests, rather than ethnic belonging. The performance of the social category of gender, however, leads to some rather rigid divisions within youth cultural leisure practices. Especially for young Armenian women, locality is experienced at two levels; on the one hand, that of the ethnic community; on the other, that of their engagement with wider society. Young women's engagement with wider society has led them to learn to accept gender behaviour that does not conform to traditions within the Armenian community. For young Armenian women, the Russian (vernacular) culture is used as a vehicle of engagement with the 'global', as Russian youth is perceived to be more oriented to the global than Armenians.

The negotiation of public spaces is central to leisure time. Young Armenians and Adyghs encounter xenophobic attitudes in public spaces and these are moments when ethnic difference becomes important. Both young Armenians and Adyghs acknowledge and routinize difference, apparently accepting the situation as *'that's the way it is'*. Some position themselves by silently accepting incidents of everyday racism without openly reacting to them. In this way, they seem to be able to defuse them. Others, however, respond by actively emphasizing their ethnic belonging during everyday interactions. While such attitudes can be understood as a form of opposing the dominant political discourse (cf. Sewell 1996), it is argued in this book that, with regard to young men in particular, these attitudes are better understood as a performance of masculinity.

Besides incidents of everyday xenophobia, young Armenians and Adyghs also have to deal with racist attacks. In such instances, Caucasian identity - an inclusive identity, including all national minorities, regardless of cultural differences between them – is evoked. The appeal to 'Caucasian brotherhood' is a response to an external threat: Russian skinheads. Young Armenians and Adyghs know that skinheads do not distinguish between different ethnic peoples and, thus, they are able to employ a supra-ethnic (Caucasian) identity in response to this threat.

A final lived 'reality' uncovered in this research is that both Armenian and Adygh communities are characterized by a persistence of patriarchal gender roles that prescribe a subordinated role for women. It is through imagined traditional gender roles that particular male/female subjects are formed and embody the boundaries of group belonging. In both communities, womanhood is idealized as a repository of tradition and as 'keepers of the culture' (Billson 1995), which is a way of claiming moral distinctiveness for both communities. Discursive power resulting from a combination of parental authority, male dominance and community vigour together with established discursive meanings linked to female 'purity' and the significance of women for ethnic reproduction come to bear upon young women's identity performances.

With a gender order based on cultural traditions, Armenians as an ethnic minority are able to (re-)define their status in relation to the dominant group (Russians). This gender order also helps the Armenian community to create a strong sense of group identity and to maintain a link to their pan-Armenian identification. This patriarchal gender order, however, places restrictions on young Armenian women. Hence, young Armenian women develop different strategies and positions in accordance with communal expectations. While some young women manage to resist Armenian gender discourse by choosing a 'modern' position for themselves; others adopted a 'traditional' position in line with expectations of the Armenian discourse. Nevertheless, the degree of choice open to young women is limited to the extent that it largely depends on parents' socio-economic position and world outlook. Those women who come from wealthier backgrounds have more flexibility in choosing a 'modern' position for themselves; whereas young women from poorer backgrounds often position themselves in accordance with the Armenian community discourse.

Broadly speaking, young Armenian men and women display different 'ethnicized' gendered identities that conform to Armenian and Russian cultural norms. In this way, they draw on different cultural traditions. Their performance of gendered identities in different situations for different audiences enables them to overcome the cultural gap between what they are supposed to do and what they want to do. For young Armenian women, performances of gendered identities are different in so far as the majority chose to reaffirm at least some norms of the Armenian community, but at the same time oppose established norms. Discursive power arising from a coalescence of communal mores and social control, with the help of gossip and surveillance, comes to influence their gendered performances in certain situations. Their strategies for performing discursive constructions of how women are supposed to be are not always the same but vary in the degree to which they choose to resist and reaffirm what is expected from them.

In contrast to young Armenian women, young Adygh women chose to comply with Adygh cultural norms, since compliance gives them the advantage of a clearly defined group of belonging and the awareness of being a 'real' Adygh woman. This awareness is vital for them because of Adygh cultural norms, but also because being a minority in their 'own' republic ensures cultural belonging. Adygh society also has a historically-evolved, complex moral system of gender relations that has similar controlling effects, making it hard for young Adygh women or men to diverge from general norms in society. The issue of *Adyghage* (Adyghnness) has retained its eminence in contemporary Adygh society and is central to the preservation of Adygh ethnic culture and group belonging and is a category that defines Adygh ethnic identity.

To conclude this book, it is necessary to stress that the multi-sited ethnographic method of data collection and analysis employed in this research was especially valuable for revealing this strong connection between locality and youth cultural identities. This method of data collection and analysis added to the existing body of literature that stresses the desirability of a more open engagement with the dynamics of non-Western societies (Flynn *et al.* 2008). At the same time, such a research approach is essential for connecting the micro-level of the locally embodied fieldwork study of two ethnic minority groups in Southern Russia with the macro-level of globalizing processes. The latter in particular has a profound effect on the production of cultural identity and locates the studied phenomena in the broader historical context of post-socialism. This book has illustrated how the micro-politics of continuity and change are connected to broader globalizing processes that cut across a simple 'East-West' divide.

Appendices

Appendix 1: Distribution of interviews between the fieldwork sites

Fieldwork sites	Number of all interviews	Number of group Interviews	Number of interview participants
Krasnodar	20	5	20
Adygheisk	15	3	15

Appendix 2: Data on research participants

List of interview participants in the city of Krasnodar, Krasnodar krai

No.	Name of interview participant (pseudonym)	Age	Gender	Place of birth	Parents' place of origin
1.	Anahit	15 years	Female	Krasnodar	Krasnodar
2.	Ani	22 years	Female	Krasnodar	Krasnodar
3.	Anush	22 years	Female	Nagorno Karabakh	Baku, Azerbaijan

4.	Aram	16 years	Male	Krasnodar	Stepanakert, Nagorno Karabakh
5.	Armine	21 years	Female	Nagorno Karabakh	Nagorno Karabakh
6.	Ashot	16 years	Male	Martuni, Nagorno Karabakh	Martuni, Nagorno Karabakh
7.	Boghos	25 years	Male	Abkhazia	Abkhazia
8.	Gaiane	20 years	Female	Erevan, Armenia	Erevan, Armenia
9.	Khachig	18 years	Male	Krasnodar	Armenia
10.	Lala	20 years	Female	Baku, Azerbaijan	Baku, Azerbaijan
11.	Lusine	21 years	Female	Krasnodar	Tbilisi, Georgia
12.	Manana	21 years	Female	Krasnodar	Baku, Azerbaijan
13.	Mane	19 years	Female	Armenia	Baku, Azerbaijan
14.	Mariam	19 years	Female	Baku, Azerbaijan	Baku, Azerbaijan
15.	Narine	21 years	Female	Krasnodar	Baku, Azerbaijan
16.	Ruzanna	22 years	Female	Baku, Azerbaijan	Baku, Azerbaijan
17.	Sargis	22 years	Male	Armenia	Armenia
18.	Seda	23 years	Female	Armenia	Armenia
19.	Sona	17 years	Female	Krasnodar	Armenia
20.	Temine	19 years	Female	Baku, Azerbaijan	Baku, Azerbaijan

List of interview participants in Adygheisk, Republic of Adyghea

No.	Name of interview participant	Age	Gender
21	Alii	20 years	Male
22	Alii	24 years	Male
23	Artur	19 years	Male
24	Baizet	20 years	Male
25	Diana	19 years	Female
26	Emma	22 years	Female
27	Emma	22 years	Female
28	Fatima	18 years	Female
29	Madzhid	21 years	Male
30	Murat	19 years	Male
31	Oksana	22 years	Female
32	Pavel	23 years	Male
33	Renata	18 years	Female
34	Ruslan	21 years	Male
35	Zarema	19 years	Female

Appendix 3: An Interview with the head of the Dating Agency 'Aragil'

I: How did you get this idea to open up the first Armenian dating agency in Krasnodar krai?
A: I had some spare time and I asked myself, 'What can I do to help my people?' You probably agree that when living in a foreign country (*chuzhbina*) we face certain ongoing problems. One problem is the constantly changing genetic pool (*genofond*) as a result of mixed marriages. Besides this problem, behaviour and values have also changed, but not everyone can adapt to these changes. As a result, our boys and girls encounter a range of difficulties in building their families. Strictly speaking, all these factors were a reason for founding the Armenian dating agency '*Aragil*'.
I: How does the dating take place?
A: First of all, it's necessary to fill in a questionnaire, where you can describe yourself, like age, education, opinions about life, values expected in another person, your dreams, attitudes toward alcohol, smoking etc. It's also good to enclose a photo with the questionnaire. We've been working for a year now and we even had cases were parents brought photos of their children, filled in the questionnaire and asked us for help to find a suitable partner for their daughter or son.
I: How many people are included in your database? And how old are they?
A: Unfortunately, I can't give you an exact number, but I think we've approximately 70 to 80 people. As for the age, we've got a good mixture: from 16 years to 50 years of age, but most members are between 25 and 35 years old. The choice is big and so finding a life partner is not difficult!
I: Are Armenians the only ones to contact your dating agency?
A: No, not long ago we registered someone from Armenia and there's a guy from Novorossiisk, but also one from Sochi and Armavir. Our database also includes people from a mixed background, as in Russian-Armenian, who like to meet an Armenian. I can give you an

example. Not long ago, a 22 year old man approached us. He told us that his dad was Armenian, but had died 14 years ago and his mum was Russian. The young man wanted to learn Armenian language and, of course, wanted to find friends amongst Armenians.

I: Those people who register with you, do they hope to find a life partner or just a friend who shares the same interests?

A: Young people between 16 to 18 years, of course, don't want to get married. They just register to find friends. Those, who are older and are not married, divorced, widowed, hope to find their 'other half'.

I: Your dating agency was founded a year ago and you've probably already heard what people think about this Armenian dating agency?

A: Well, generally most people (narod) think it's a good idea and understand that there's a need for it. But there are those people who judge our activities. Luckily, there are only a few of them.

I: Could you tell me a bit more about last year's results?

A: Of course, I can. Thanks to our efforts and activities, we had three couples getting married. Another couple will get married in April. Most young people, however, are just getting to know each other at the moment.

Bibliography

Abelsky, P. (2007) 'A Balancing Act', *Russia Profile*, 1 August. Online. Available HTTP: <http://www.circassianworld.com/news/Abelsky_Adygeya.html> (accessed 14 September 2007).

Adelaja, T. (2010) 'Zero Sum Game', *Russia Profile*, 07 December. Online. Available HTTP: <http://russiaprofile.org/politics/a1291737441.html> (accessed 13 December 2010).

Aghanian, D. (2007) *The Armenian Diaspora: Cohesion and Fracture*, Lanham: University Press of America.

Alayarian, A. (2008) *Consequences of Denial: The Armenian Genocide*, London: Karnac Books.

Alexander, C. (1996) *The Art of Being Black: The Creation of Black British Youth Identities*, Oxford: Oxford University Press.

—— (2004) 'Imagining the Asian Gang: Ethnicity, Masculinity and Youth after "the Riots"', *Critical Social Policy* 24, 4: 526-49.

Ali, S. (2003) *Mixed-Race, Post-Race: Gender, New Ethnicities and Cultural Practices*, Oxford: Berg.

Ali, Y. (1992) 'Muslim Women and the Politics of Ethnicity and Culture in Northern England', in G. Sahgal & N. Yuval-Davis (eds) *Refusing Holy Orders: Women and Fundamentalism in Britain*, London: Virago Press.

Althusser, L. (2000 [1969]) 'Ideology Interpellates Individuals as Subjects', in P. Du Gay, J. Evans & P. Redman (eds) *Identity: A Reader*, London: Sage Publications.

Amin, A. (2004) 'Multi-Ethnicity and the Idea of Europe', *Theory, Culture & Society* 21, 2: 1-24.

Anderson, B. (1991 [1983]) *Imagined Communities: Reflections on the Origin and Spread of Nationalism*, London: Verso.

Ang, I. (2001) *On Not Speaking Chinese*, London: Routledge.

Anthias, F. (1992) 'Connecting "Race" and Ethnic Phenomena', *Sociology* 26, 3: 421-38.

—— (1998) 'Evaluating "Diaspora:" Beyond Ethnicity?', *Sociology* 32, 3: 557-80.

—— (2005) 'Rethinking Social Divisions: Some Notes', *Sociological Review* 30, 3: 505-35.

―――― (2006) 'Belongings in a Globalising and Unequal World: Rethinking Translocations', in N. Yuval-Davis, K. Kannabiran & U. M. Vieten (eds) *The Situated Politics of Belonging*, London: Sage Publications.

Anthias, F., & Yuval-Davis, N. (1992) 'Connecting Race and Gender', in F. Anthias & N. Yuval-Davis (eds) *Racialized Boundaries: Race, Nation, Gender, Colour and Class and the Anti-Racist Struggle*, London, New York: Routledge.

Appadurai, A. (1988) 'Putting Hiearchy in its Place', *Cultural Anthropology* 3, 1: 36-49.

―――― (1995) 'The Production of Locality', in R. Fardon (ed.), *Counterworks: Managing the Diversity of Knowledge*, London: Routledge.

―――― (2003) *Modernity at Large: Cultural Dimensions of Globalization*, London: University of Minnesota Press.

Appadurai, A., & Beckenridge, C. (1989) 'On Moving Targets', *Public Culture* 2: i-iv.

Appiah, K. A. (Spring 1997) 'Cosmopolitan Patriot', *Critical Inquiry* 23, 3: 617-39.

―――― (1998) 'Cosmopolitan Patriots', in P. Cheah & B. Robbins (eds), *Cosmopolitics: Thinking and Feeling beyond the Nation*, London: University of Minnesota Press.

―――― (2005) *The Ethics of Identity*, Princeton: Princeton University Press.

Archer, L. (2001) '"Muslim Brothers, Black Lads, Traditional Asians": British Muslim Young Men's Constructions of Race, Religion and Masculinity', *Feminism and Psychology* 11, 1: 79-105.

Arutiunian, I. V., & Drobizheva, L. M. (2000) 'Etnosotsiologiia: proidennoe i novye gorizonty', *Sotsiologicheskie issledovaniia* 4: 11-21.

Autalipov, A. (2009) 'Russia: Xenophobia on the Rise', *Johnson's Russia List*. 22 January 2009, Online. Available HTTP: <http://www.cdi.org/russia/johnson/2009-14-9.cfm> (accessed 10 April 2009).

Avakian, A. V. (2000) 'Surviving the Survivors of the Armenian Genocide: Daughters and Granddaughters', in B. Mergeurian & J. Renjilian-Burgy (eds) *Voices of Armenian Women*, Belmont, Massachusetts: AIWA Press.

Babich, I. (2004) 'Respublika Adygeia: islam i obshchestvo na rubezhe vekov', *Tsentralnaia Aziia i Kavkaz Zhurnal sotsial'no-politicheskikh issledovanii* 6,36: 64-73.

Back, L. (1993) 'Gendered Participation: Masculinity and Fieldwork in a South London Adolescent Community', in D. Bell, P. Caplan & W. J. Karim (eds) *Gendered Fields: Women, Men and Ethnography*, London: Routledge.

―――― (1996) *New Ethnicities and Urban Culture: Racisms and Multiculture in Young Lives*, London: UCL Press.

―――― (2007) *The Art of Listening*, Oxford: Berg.

Bakalian, A. (1993) *Armenian-Americans: From Being to Feeling Armenian*, News Brunswick, NJ: Transaction.

Bamberger, J. (2000) 'Daughters of Time: The American Legacy of the Armenian Genocide', in B. Mergeurian & J. Renjilian-Burgy (eds) *Voices of Armenian Women*, Belmont: AIWA Press.

Banton, M. (1987) *Racial Theories*, Cambridge: Cambridge University Press.

—— (2005) 'Historical and Contemporary Modes of Racialization', in K. Murji & J. Solomos (eds) *Racialization: Studies in Theory and Practice*, Oxford: Oxford University Press.

Beck, U. (2002) 'The Cosmopolitan Society and its Enemies', *Theory, Culture & Society* 19, 1-2: 17-44.

—— (2006) *Cosmopolitan Vision*, Cambridge: Polity Press.

Begletsov, M. (2004) 'Kto kogo ugnetaet?', *Kuban' segodnia*, 05 March, 1-2.

—— (2005) 'Migranty spasut ...Rossiiu?', *Kuban' segodnia*, 01 November, 1, 3.

Berkok, I. (1958) *Tarihte Kafkasya*, Istanbul: Istanbul Matbaasi.

Bhabha, H. K. (1990) 'The Third Space', in J. Rutherford (ed.) *Identity: Community, Culture, Difference*, London: Lawrence & Wishart.

Bhattacharjee, A. (1992) 'The Habit of Ex-Nomination: Nation, Woman, and the Indian Immigrant Bourgeoisie', *Public Culture* 5, 1: 19-44.

Bhavnani, R. (2001) *Rethinking Interventions to Combat Racism*, Stoke-on-Trent: Trentham Books.

Bigg, C. (2006) '*Russia: Kondopoga Violence Continues Unabated*', Radio Free Europe/Radio Liberty. Online. Available HTTP: <http://www.rferl.org/content/article/1071116.html> (accessed 3 February 2011).

Billson, J. M. (1995) *Keepers of the Culture: Women in a Changing World*, New York: Lexington.

Boeck, B. J. (1998) 'The Kuban' Cossack Revival (1989-1993): The Beginnings of a Cossack National Movement in the North Caucasus Region', *Nationalities Papers* 26, 4: 633-57.

Bourdieu, P. (1986) 'The Three Forms of Capital', in J. G. Richardson (ed.) *Handbook of Theory and Research for the Sociology of Education*, New York: Greenwood Press.

—— (1989) '*A Social Critique of the Judgement of Taste*', London: Routledge.

Bourdieu, P., & Passeron, J. C. (1977) *Reproduction in Education, Society and Culture*, London: Sage Publications.

Bournoutian, G. (1993) *A History of the Armenian People*, Costa Mesa, CA: Mazda Publishers.

Brah, A. (1996) *Cartographies of Diaspora: Contesting Identities*, London: Routledge.

Bromlei, I. V. (1973) *Etnos i etnografiia*, Moskva: Nauka.

Bromley, Y. V., & Kozlov, V. I. (1989) 'The Theory of Ethnos and Ethnic Processes in Soviet Social Sciences', *Comparative Studies in Society and History* 31, 3: 425-38.

Brown, L. M. (1998) 'Voice and Ventriloquation in Girls' Development', in K. Henwood, C. Griffin & A. Phoenix (eds) *Standpoints and Differences: Essays in the Practice of Feminist Psychology*, London: Sage Publications.

Brubaker, R. (1996) *Nationalism Reframed: Nationhood and the National Question in the New Europe*, Cambridge: Cambridge University Press.

Brubaker, R., & Cooper, F. (2000) 'Beyond "Identity"', *Theory and Society* 29: 1-47.

Burawoy, M., & Verdery, K. (1999) *Uncertain Transition: Ethnographies of Change in the Postsocialist World*, Oxford: Rowman & Littlefield Publishers.

Butler, J. (1993) *Bodies that Matter: On the Discursive Limits of 'Sex'*, London: Routledge.

―――― (1999 [1990]) *Gender Trouble: Feminism and the Subversion of Identity*, London: Routledge.

Caputo, V. (1995) 'Anthropology's Silent "Others": A Consideration of Some Conceptual and Methodological Issues of the Study of Youth and Children's Cultures', in V. Amit-Talai & H. Wulff (eds) *Youth Cultures: A Cross-Cultural Perspective*, London: Routledge.

Castells, M. (1997) *The Power of Identity*, Oxford: Blackwell.

Chernova, O. N. (1997) 'Psikhologicheskie aspekty rosta natsional'nogo samosoznaniia russkikh', *Etnicheskaia psikhologiia i obshchestvo*.

Chorbaijian, L. (2001) *The Making of Nagorno-Karabagh: From Secession to Republic*, Basingstoke: Palgrave.

Clifford, J. (1994) 'Diasporas', *Cultural Anthropology* 9, 3: 302-38.

―――― (1997a) *Routes: Travel and Translation in the Late Twentieth Century*, London: Havard University Press.

―――― (1997b) 'Spatial Practices: Fieldwork, Travel, and Disciplining Anthropology', in A. Gupta & J. Ferguson (eds) *Anthropological Locations: Boundaries and Grounds of a Field Science*, London: University of California Press.

Cohen, A. (1985) *The Symbolic Construction of Community*, New York: Tavistock.

Cohen, R. (1996) 'Diasporas and the Nation-State: from Victims to Challengers', *International Affairs* 72: 507-20.

—— (1997) *Global Diasporas: An Introduction*, London: UCL Press.

—— (September 2007) 'Creolization and Cultural Globalization: The Soft Sounds of Fugitive Power', *Globalizations* 4, 3: 369-84.

Connell, R. W. (1998 [1987]) *Gender and Power: Society, the Person and Sexual Politics*, Cambridge: Polity Press.

Connor, W. (1988) *Socialism's Dilemmas*, New York: Columbia University Press.

Dafflon, D. (2009) *Youth in Russia: The Portrait of a Generation in Transition*. Bienne: Swiss Academy for Development (SAD). Online. Avalaible HTTP: <http://www.sad.ch/images/stories/Publikationen/sad-youth-in-russia.pdf> (accessed 29 November 2009).

De Genova, N. P. (2002) 'Migrant "Illegality" and Deportability in Everyday Life', *Annual Review of Anthropology* 31: 419-47.

Delanty, G. (2006) 'The Cosmopolitan Imagination: Critical Cosmopolitanism and Social Theory', *The British Journal of Sociology* 57, 1: 26-47.

Demchenko, A., & Petrosian, A. (2002) 'Skiny letiat na iug', *Izvestiia*, 19 April, 2.

Der-Martirosian, C., Sabagh, G., & Bozorgmehr, M. (1993) 'Sub-Ethnicity: Armenians in Los Angeles', in H. I. Right & P. Bhachu (eds) *Immigration and Entrepreneurship: Culture, Capital and Ethnic Networks*, London: Transaction Publishers.

de Waal, T. (2003) *The Black Garden: Armenian and Azerbaijan through Peace and War*, New York: New York University Press.

'Dom sta narodov', *Krasnodarksie Izvestiia*, 11 March 2006, 4.

Drobizheva, L., & Gotte Moelier, R. (1996) *Ethnic Conflict in the Post-Soviet World: Case Studies and Analysis*, London: M. E. Sharpe.

Dubas, A. (2008) *The Menace of a 'Brown' Russia. Ethnically Motivated Xenophobia - Symptoms, Causes and Prospects for the Future*, Warsaw: Centre for Eastern Studies.

Duncan, P. S. J. (2005) 'Contemporary Russian Identity between East and West', *The Historical Journal* 48, 1: 277-94.

Dwyer, C. (1999) 'Negotiations of Femininity and Identity for Young British Muslim Women', in N. Laurie, C. Dwyer, S. L. Holloway & F. M. Smith (eds) *Geographies of New Femininities*, Harlow: Pearson Education.

—— (2000) 'Negotiating Diasporic Identities Young British South Asian Muslim Women', *Women's Studies International Forum* 23, 4: 475-86.

Edwards, R., Franklin, J., & Holland, J. (2003) *Families and Social Capital: Exploring the Issues, Families and Social Capital ESRC Research Group Working Paper No. 1.* London: London South Bank University.

Essed, P. (1991) *Understanding Everyday Racism: An Interdisciplinary Theory: An Interdisciplinary Study,* London: Sage Publications.

Evans, G., & Whitefield, S. (1993) 'Identifying the Bases of Party Competition in Eastern Europe', *British Journal of Political Science* 23, 4: 521-48.

Falzon, M. A. (July 2003) '"Bombay, Our Cultural Heart": Rethinking the Relation between Homeland and Diaspora', *Ethnic and Racial Studies* 26, 4: 662-83.

―――― (2005) *Cosmopolitan Connections: The Sindhi Diaspora, 1860-2000,* New Delhi: Oxford University Press.

―――― (2009) 'Ethnic Groups Unbound: A Case Study of the Social Organization of Cosmopolitanism', in M. Nowicka & M. Rovisco (eds) *Cosmopolitanism in Practice,* Farnham: Ashgate.

Flenley, P. (1996) 'From Soviet to Russian Identity: The Origins of contemporary Russian Nationalism and National Identity', in B. Jenkins & S. A. Sofos (eds) *Nation and Identity in Contemporary Europe,* London: Routledge.

Flynn, M., Kay, R., & Oldfield, J. (2008) *Trans-National Issues, Local Concerns and Meanings of Post-Socialism: Insights from Russia, Central Eastern Europe, and Beyond,* New York: University Press of America.

Galatsan, A. (2006) 'Meniaiu familiiu radi uluchsheniia kar'ery i karmy....', *Krasnodarskie izvestiia,* 14 January, 6-7.

George, R. (2007) 'Urban Girls' "Race" Friendship and School Choice: Changing Schools, Changing Friendships', *Race, Ethnicity and Education* 10, 2: 115-29.

Gidley, B. (2007) 'Youth Culture and Ethnicity: Emerging Youth Interculture in South London', in P. Hodkinson & W. Deicke (eds) *Youth Cultures: Scenes, Subcultures and Tribes,* London: Routledge.

Gilroy, P. (1987) '"There Ain't No Black in the Union Jack": The Cultural Politics of Race and Nation',* London: Routledge.

―――― (1993) *Small Acts: Thoughts on the Politics of Black Cultures,* London: Serpent's Tail.

Giragosian, R. (2002) *Community at Risk: The Armenians of Krasnodar,* Online. Available HTTP: <http://www.hairenik.com/armenianweekly/august_september_2002/society005.html> (accessed 13 July 2004).

Gluckman, M. (1963) 'Papers in Honor of Melville J. Herskovits: Gossip and Scandal', *Current Anthropology* 4, 3: 307-16.

Goffman, E. (1959) *The Presentation of Self in Everyday Life*, Harmondsworth: Penguin Books.

—— (1976) 'Gender Display', *Studies in Anthropology of Visual Communication* 3: 69-77.

Griffin, C. (1985) *Typical Girls? Young Women from School to the Job Market*, London: Routledge & Paul Kegan.

Griffiths, G. (1999) 'Other', in B. Ashcroft, G. Griffiths & H. Tiffin (eds) *Key Concepts in Postcolonial Studies*, London: Routledge.

Gudkov, L. D. (1995) 'Dinamika etnicheskikh stereotipov (sravnenie zamerov 1989-1994): ekonomicheskie i sotsialnye peremeny', *Monitoring obshchestvennye mneniia* 5: 14-6.

Gunter, A., & Watt, P. (2009) 'Grafting, Going to College and Working on Road: Youth Transitions and Cultures in an East London Neighbourhood', *Journal of Youth Studies*, 12, 5: 515-29.

Gupta, A., & Ferguson, J. (1992) 'Beyond "Culture": Space, Identity, and the Politics of Difference', *Cultural Anthropology* 7, 1: 6-23.

Gvozdetskaia, I. (2004) 'Tadzhiki na Kubani', *Kuban' segodnia*, 24 September, 4.

Hall, S. (1990) 'Cultural Identity and Diaspora', in J. Rutherford (ed.) *Identity, Community, Culture, Difference*, London: Lawrence and Wishart.

—— (1996a) 'Introduction: Who Needs Identity?', in S. Hall & P. Du Gay (eds) *Questions of Cultural Identity*, London: Sage Publications.

—— (1996b) 'New Ethnicities', in D. Morley & K. H. Chen (eds) *Stuart Hall: Critical Dialogues in Cultural Studies*, London: Routledge.

—— (1996c) 'Ethnicity: Identity and Difference', in G. Eley & R. Suny (eds) *Becoming National: A Reader*, Oxford: Oxford University Press.

Hannerz, U. (1990) 'Cosmopolitans and Locals in World Culture', in M. Featherstone (ed.) *Global Culture*, London: Sage Publications.

—— (1992) *Cultural Complexity*, New York: Columbia University.

Harris, C. (2004) *Control and Subversion: Gender Relations in Tajikistan*, London: Pluto Press.

Heleniak, T. (2003) 'The 2002 Census in Russia: Preliminary Results', *Eurasian Geography and Economics* 44, 6: 430-42.

—— (2008) 'An Overview of Migration in the Post-Soviet Space', in C. J. Buckley, B. A. Ruble & T. E. Hofman (eds) *Migration, Homeland and Belonging in Eurasia*, Baltimore: The Johns Hopkins University Press.

Hollands, R. (2003) 'Double Exposure: Exploring the Social and Political Relations of Ethnographic Youth Research', in A. Bennett, M. Cieslik & S. Miles (eds) *Researching Youth*, Basingstoke: Palgrave Macmillan.

Hopkins, P. (2007) '"Blue Squares," "Proper" Muslims and Transnational Networks: Narratives of National and Religious Identities amongst Young Muslim Men Living in Scottland', *Ethnicities* 7, 1: 61-81.

Hovannisian, R. (2007) *The Armenian Genocide: Cultural and Ethical Legacies*, New Brunswick: Transaction Publishers.

Human Rights Watch (2009) *'Are You Happy to Cheat us?' Exploitation of Migrant Construction Workers in Russia.* Online. Available HTTP: http://www.hrw.org/sites/default/files/reports/russia0209web_0.pdf> (accessed 18 February 2010).

Huysmans, J. (2000) 'The European Union and the Securitization of Migration', *Journal of Common Market Studies* 38, 5: 751-77.

Iskandarian, A. (1996) Chernofobiia, *Novoe Vremia* 32: 12-4.

Ishkanian, A. (2004) 'Armenians', in C. R. Ember & M. Ember (eds) *Encyclopedia of Sex and Gender: Men and Women in the World's Cultures*, London: Plenum Publishers.

Jaimoukha, A. (2001) *The Circassians: A Handbook*, Richmond: Curzon Press.

Jordan, S. A. (2002) 'Ethnographic Encounters: The Processes of Cultural Translation', *Language and Intercultural Communication* 2, 2: 96-110.

Karapetian, L. A. (2006). 'Severnyi Kavkaz/Kuban' v 1900-1910-e gody: armianskaia natsionalisticheskaia partiia "Dashnaktsutiun"', *Bulletin: Anthropology, Minorities, Mutliculturalism* 1, 7: 410-17.

Karpat, K. (1972) 'Ottoman Immigration Policies and Settlement in Palestine', in I. Abu-Lughod & B. Abu-Laban (eds) *Settler Regimes in Africa and the Arab World*, Wilmett, IL: Medina University Press International.

—— (1990) 'The *hijra* from Russia and the Balkans: The Process of Self-definition in the Late Ottoman State', in D. F. Eickelman & J. Piscatori (eds) *Muslim Travellers: Pilgrimage, Migration, and the Religious Imagination*, London: Routledge.

Katz, C. (1994) 'Playing the Field: Questions of Fieldwork in Geography', *Geographer* 46, 1: 67-72.

Kay, R., & Kostenko, M. (2008) 'Men in Crisis or in Critical Need for Support? Insights from Russia and the UK', in M. Flynn, R. Kay & J. Oldfield (eds) *Trans-National Issues, Local Concerns and Meanings of Post-Socialism: Insights from Russia, Central Eastern Europe, and Beyond*, New York: University Press of America.

Khachaturian, V. (2000) 'Stanovlenie armianskikh kolonii v Rossii',. *Diaspory* 1-2: 78-97.

Khadzhebiekov, R., & Poliakova, T. (1994) 'Etnopoliticheskaia situatsiia v Adygee. *Issledovaniia po prikladnoi i neotlozhnoi etnologii*', Online. Available HTTP: <http://old.iea.ras.ru/Russian/publications/applied/70.html> (accessed 5 November 2006).

Khanakhu, R. (2001) *Traditsionnaia kul'tura severnogo Kavkaza: vyzovy vremeni*, Rostov-na-Donu.

Kimmel, M. S. (2000) *The Gendered Society*, New York: Oxford University Press.

Klimenko, O., Bowers, S. R., & Solovyeva, L. (2009) 'North Caucasus Baseline Project: Adygea', Liberty University. Center for Security and Science. Online. Available HTTP: <http://digitalcommons.liberty.edu/cgi/viewcontent.cgi?article=1017&context=gov_fac_pubs> (accessed 30 August 2009).

Kolsto, P., & Blakkisrud, H. (May 2008) 'Living with Non-Recognition: State- and Nation-Building in South Caucasian Quasi-States', *Europe-Asia Studies* 60, 3: 483-09.

Koriakin, K. V. (2006) 'Problemy adaptatsii i integratsii armian-migrantov v Krasnodarskom krae', *Etnograficheskoe obozrenie* 1: 62-72.

Korobkov, A. V. (2008) 'Post-Soviet Migration: New Trends at the Beginning of the Twenty-First Century', in C. J. Buckley, B. A. Ruble & E. T. Hofman (eds) *Migration, Homeland and Belonging in Eurasia*, Washington D.C.: Woodrow Wilson Center Press.

Kozhevnikova, G., & Verkhovskii, A. (2009) *Radikalnyi russkii natsionalizm—struktury, idei, litsa*, Moskva: Sova Tsentr.

Krasnodar Human Rights Centre (2002) '*Monitoring proiavlenie natsionalizma, ksenofobii i neterpimost'*, Online. Avalaible HTTP: <http://www.hro.org/ngo/krasnodar/dnaci.html> (accessed 24 May 2004).

Krasnodarskii kraevoi komitet gosudarstvennoi statistiki (2005) *Natsional'nyi sostav i vladenie iazykami, grazhdanstvo. Itogi vserossiiskoi perepisi naseleniia 2002 goda po Krasnodarskomu Kraiu*, Tom 4, Krasnodar.

Kurkchiyan, M. (2005) 'The Karabagh Conflict: From Soviet Past to post-Soviet Uncertainty', in M. Kurkchiyan & E. Herzig (eds) *The Armenians: Past and Present in the Making of National Identity*, Abingdon: RoutledgeCurzon.

Kuromatchenko, A., & Shevchenko, D. (2006) 'Rossiia - eto my! Pervyi kazachii karaul', *Krasnodarskie Izvestiia* 14 June, 1 and 5.

Kuznetsov, I. (1995) *Odezhda armian Ponta. Semiotika material'noi kul'tury*, Moskva: Nauka.

―― (2000) 'Turki-khemshily ili islamizirovannye armiane? (Sluchai "neiasnoi" etnicheskoi identichnosti)', *Diaspory* 1-2: 226-58.

―― (2004) 'Severo-zapadnyi Kavkaz: chto proiskhodit s etnicheskimi men'shinstvami?', *Diaspory* 4: 59-84.

―― (2007a) 'Rossiiskaia Federatsiia: konstruirovanie identichnosti i sotsial'nye seti', in T. Trier & A. Khanzhin (eds) *Turki-Meskhetintsy: integratsiia, repatriatsiia, emigratsiia*, Sankt Peterburg: Aleteiia.

―― (2007b) 'Pervye Armiane na Kubani', *Khachkar*, p. 23.

―― (2008) *Pontiisko-Kavkazskie issledovaniia*, Krasnodar: Kubanskii gosudarstvennoi universitet.

Lacan, J. (2000 [1949]) 'The Mirror Stage', in P. du Gay, J. Evans & P. Redman (eds) *Identity: A Reader*, London: Sage Publications.

Laitin, D. D., & Suny, R. G. (1999) 'Armenia and Azerbaijan: Thinking a Way Out of Karabakh', *Middle East Policy* VII: 145-76.

Lamont, M., & Aksartova, S. (2002) 'Ordinary Cosmopolitanisms: Strategies for Bridging Racial Boundaries among Working-Class Men', *Theory, Culture & Society* 19, 4: 1-25.

Laruelle, M. (2010) 'The Ideological Shift on the Russian Radical Right', *Problems of Post-Communism* 57, 6: 19-31.

Laryš, M., & Mareš, M. (2011) 'Right-Wing Extremist Violence in the Russian Federation', *Europe-Asia Studies* 63, 1, 129-54.

Lees, S. (1993) *Sugar and Spice: Sexuality and Adolescent Girls*, Middlesex: Penguin Books.

Magomedov, A. K., & Kirichenko, M. M. (2004) 'Ot El'tsina k Putinu: kreml' i regional'naia Rossiia (na primere Ul'ianovskoi oblasti i Krasnodarskogo kraia', in K. Matsuzato (ed.) *Fenomen Vladimira Putina i rossiiskie regiony: pobeda neozhidannaia ili zakonomernaia?*, Moscow: Slavic-Eurasian Research.

Malashenko, A. (1999) *Neterpimost' v Rossii: starye i novye fobii*. Moskva: Moskovskii Tsentr Carnegie.

Malia, M. E. (1994) *The Soviet Tragedy: History of Socialism in Russia 1917-1991*, New York: Free Press.

Mandel, R. (2002) 'Seeding Civil Society', in C. M. Hann (ed.), *Postsocialism: Ideals, Ideologies and Practices in Eurasia*, London and New York: Routledge.

Mansoor, A., & Quillin, B. (2006) Migration and Remittances: Eastern Europe and the Former Soviet Union, *World Bank Publications*. Online. Available HTTP: <http://siteresources.worldbank.org/INTECA/Resources/257896-1167856389505/Migration_FullReport.pdf> (accessed 13 November 2010).

Manoogian, M. M., Walker, A. J., & Richards, L. N. (April 2007) 'Gender, Genocide, and Ethnicity: The Legacies of Older Armenian American Mothers', *Journal of Family Issues* 23, 4: 567-89.

Matveev, O. V., Rakachev, V. N., & Rakachev, D. N. (2003) *Etnicheskie migratsii Kubani: istoriia i sovremmennost'*, Krasnodar: Kubanskii gosudarstvennyi universitet.

McAuley, M. (1997) *Russia' Politics of Uncertainty*, Cambridge: Cambridge University Press.

Messner, M. A. (2001) 'Friendship, Intimacy, and Sexuality', in S. M. Whitehead & F. J. Barret (eds) *The Masculinities Reader*, Malden: Polity Press.

Mirza, H. S. (1992) *Young, Female and Black*, London: Routledge.

Molodovika, I. (2007) 'Transformation of Migration Patterns in Post-Soviet Space: Russian New Migration Policy of "Open Doors" and its Effect on European Migration Flows', *Review of Sociology* 13, 2: 57-76.

Mørck, Y. (2000) 'Hyphenated Dance: Contested Fields of Gender, Generation and Ethnicity', *Young, Nordic Journal of Youth Research* 8, 3: 2-16.

Muggleton, D. (2005) 'From Classlessness to Club-Culture - A Genealogy of Post-War British Youth Cultural Analysis', *Young, Nordic Journal of Youth Research* 13, 2: 205-19.

Mukomel, V. (October 2006). Immigration and Russian Migration Policy: Debating the Future. *Russian Analytical Digest*, 7. Online. Available HTTP: <http://home.datacomm.ch/l-info/RAD031006.pdf> (accessed 2 October 2010).

——— 'Trends and Conditions of Brain Drain and Brain Circulation within the Post-Soviet Area: Russia and CIS Countries', paper presented at the International Studies Association Annual Conference, Baltimore, October 2008.

Murphy, P. D. (1999) 'Doing Audience Ethnography: A Narrative Account of Establishing Ethnographic Identity and Locating Interpretive Communities in Fieldwork', *Qualitative Inquiry* 5, 4: 479-04.

Nassehi, A., & Richter, D. (1996) 'Die Form "Nation" und der Einschluss durch Anschluss: Überlegungen zur Fremdenfeindlichkeit in Deutschland',. *Sociologia Internationalis* 34, 2: 151-76.

Nava, M. (2007) *Visceral Cosmopolitanism: Gender, Culture and the Normalisation of Difference*, Oxford: Berg.

Nayak, A. (2003) '"Ivory Lives" - Economic Restructuring and the Making of Whiteness in a Post-Industrial Youth Community', *European Journal of Cultural Studies* 6, 3: 305-25.

—— (2004) *Race, Place and Globalization: Youth Culture in a Changing World*, Oxford: Berg.

—— (2006) 'Displaced Masculinities: Chavs, Youth and Class in the Post-Industrial City', *Sociology* 40: 813-31.

Nayak, A., & Kehily, M. J. (2008) *Gender, Youth and Culture: Young Masculinities and Femininities*, New York: Palgrave Macmillan.

'New Adygeya President Sworn In', *Radio Free Europe Liberty/ Radio Liberty*, 16 January 2007. Online. Available HTTP: <http://www.rferl.org/newsline/2007/01/01-rus/rus-160107.asp> (accessed 27 January 2007).

'New Laws on Migrants Take Effect', *Radio Free Europe/ Radio Liberty*, 16 January 2007. Online. Available HTTP: <http://www.rferl.org/newsline/2007/01/1-rus/rus-160107.asp> (accessed 27 January 2007).

Nilan, P., & Feixa, C. (2006) *Global Youth? Hybrid Identities, Plural Worlds*, Abingdon: Routledge.

Novokhatskii, S. (2004) 'Etnoterrorizm', *Kuban' segodnia*, 16 July, 14.

Nowicka, M., & Rovisco, M. (2009) *Cosmopolitanism in Practice*, Farnham: Ashgate.

O'Donnell, M., & Sharpe, S. (2000) *Uncertain Masculinities: Youth, Ethnicity and Class in Contemporary Britain*, London: Taylor & Francis.

Oakley, A. (1972) *Sex, Gender and Society*, London: Maurice Temple Smith.

Osipov, A. G. (1999a) *Rossiiskii opyt etnicheskoi diskriminatsii: Meskhetintsy v Krasnodarskom krae*, Moscow: Memorial.

—— (1999b) 'Diskriminatsiia po etnicheskomu priznaku protiv migrantov v Rossiiskoi Federatsii', *Bulletin: Anthropology, Minorities, Mutliculturalism*, 100-108.

—— (2004) 'Krasnodarskii krai kak vitrina Rossiiskoi natsional'noi politiki', *Diaspory* 4, 6-37.

Ossipow, A. (2003) 'Prüfung der Identität - Ethnische Intoleranz and Diskriminierung in Russland', in W. Gefter, V. Deile, L. Alexejewa, J. Dschibladse & S. Schiffer (eds) *Russland auf dem Weg zum Rechtsstaat? Antworten aus der Zivilgesellschaft*, Berlin: German Institute for Human Rights.

Oswald, I. (2000) *Die Nachfahren des 'homo sovieticus': Ethnische Orientierung nach dem Zerfall der Sowjetunion*, Berlin: Waxmann.

Pallotta-Chiarolli, M. (1989) 'From Coercion to Choice: Second-Generation Women Seeking a Personal Identity in the Italo-Australian Setting', *Journal of Intercultural Studies* 10, 1: 49-63.

Panchenko, N. (2003) 'Aleksandr Tkachev: My sami navedem poriadok v svoem dome', *Rossiiskaia gazeta*, 18 September, 1.

Panossian, R. (2002) 'The Past as Nation: Three Dimensions of Armenian Identity', *Geopolitics* 7, 2: 121-46.

Parekh, B. (2000a) *The Future of Multi-Ethnic Britain: Report of the Commission on the Future of Multi-Ethnic Britain*, London: Profile Books.

—— (2000b) *Rethinking Multiculturalism: Cultural Diversity and Political Theory*, Basingstoke, New York: Palgrave.

Parker, D., & Song, M. (2006) 'Ethnicity, Social Capital and the Internet: British Chinese Websites', *Ethnicities* 6, 2: 178-02.

Pavlova, I. (2004) 'Pervyi v Rossii deportatsionnyi punkt otkryt', *Kuban' segodnia*, 29 December, 1.

—— (2005) 'Krasnodar - edinaia sem'ia', *Kuban' segodnia*, 12 December, 27.

Payaslian, S. (2008). *The History of Armenia*. New York, Basingstoke: Palgrave Macmillan.

Peroomanian, R. (2000) 'The Role of Armenian Women in the Struggle to Maintain Ethnic Identity', in B. Mergeurian & J. Renjilian-Burgy (eds) *Voices of Armenian Women*, Belmont, Massachusetts: AIWA.

Petrosian, A. (2002a) 'Pofamil'naia zachistka: Gubernator Kubani provozglasil kampaniiu protiv etnicheskoi migratsii', *Izvestiia*, 20 March, 4.

—— (2002b) 'S Kubani depotiruiut nezakonnykh migrantov', *Izvestiia*, 28 March, 3.

Petrov, V. N., Rakachev, V. N., Rakacheva, I. V., & Chernyi, V. I. (2002) *Migranty v Krasnodarskom krae: problemy adaptatsii i formirovaniia tolerantnoi kul'tury*, Krasnodar: Kubanskii gosudarstvennyi universitet.

Pilkington, H. (1994) *Russia's Youth and Its Culture: A Nation's Constructor's and Constructed*, London: Routledge.

—— (1998) *Migration, Displacement and Identity in Post-Soviet Russia*, London: Routledge.

—— (2002) 'The Dark Side of the Moon? Global and Local Horizons', in H. Pilkington, E. Omel'chenko, M. Flynn, U. Bliudina & E. Starkova (eds) *Looking West? Cultural*

Globalization and Russian Youth Cultures, Pennsylvania: The Pennsylvania State University Press.

Pilkington, H., & Johnson, R. (2003) 'Peripheral Youth: Relations of Identity and Power in Global/ Local Context', *European Journal of Cultural Studies* 6, 3: 259-83.

Pilkington, H., Omel'chenko, E., Flynn, M., Bliudina, U., & Starkova, E. (2002) *Looking West: Cultural Globalization and Russian Youth Cultures*, Pennsylvania: The Pennsylvania State University.

Pilkington, H., Omel'chenko, E., & Garifzianova, A. (2010) *Russia's Skinheads: Exploring and Rethinking Subcultural Lives*, London: Routledge.

Pilkington, H., & Popov, A. (2008) 'Cultural Production and Transmission of Ethnic Tolerance and Prejudice: Introduction', *Anthropology of East Europe Review* 26: 7-21.

Pilkington, H., & Yemelianova, G. (2003) *Islam in Post-Soviet Russia: Public and Private Faces'*, London: Routledge Curzon.

Polyakova, T. (2002) 'Adygea Relies on Old Traditions to Build New Self-Governments', in V. Tishkov & E. Filippova (eds) *Local Governance and Minority Empowerment in the CIS*, Budapest: Open Society Institute.

Popov, A. (2002) 'Polozhenie etnicheskikh men'zhinstv i migratsionnye protsessy v Krasnodarskom krae', *Tsentralnaia Aziia i Kavkaz: Zhurnal sotsial'no-politicheskikh issledovanii* 1, 19: 194-204.

—— (2005) *Transnational Locals: The Cultural Production of Identity among Greeks in the Southern Russian Federation'*, unpublished thesis, University of Birmingham.

—— (2008) 'Ethnicity and Civil Society after Socialism: The Politics of Representation among Greek Communities in Southern Russia', in M. Flynn, R. Kay & J. Oldfield (eds) *Trans-National Issues, Local Concerns and Meanings of Post-Socialism: Insights from Russia, Central Eastern Europe, and Beyond*, Plymouth: University Press of America.

Popov, A., & Kuznetsov, I. (2008) 'Ethnic Discrimination and the Discourse of "Indigenization": The Regional Regime, "Indigenous Majority" and Ethnic Minorities in Krasnodar Krai in Russia, *Nationalities Papers* 36, 2: 223-52.

Pratt, M. L. (1992) *Imperial Eyes: Travel Writing and Transculturalism*, London: Routledge.

Press-sluzhba administratsii Krasnodarskogo kraia. 'Arestovany migranty – narkosbytchiki'. *Kuban' segodnia*, 3 February 2006, 4.

Purdenko, V. (2008) 'Vladimir: Karatayev: "The Union of Slavs of Adygea is Persecuted"'. *North Caucasus Newspaper*, 14 October, Online. Available HTTP: <http://en.sknews.ru/main/855-vladimir-karatayev-the-union-of-slavs.html> (accessed 30 August 2009).

Pusic, V. (1995) 'Uses of Nationalism and the Politics of Recognition', *Anthropological Journal of European Cultures* 4, 1: 43-61.

Putin, V. (2007) *Poslanie federal'nomu sobraniiu Rossiiskoi Federatsii, Prezident Rossii*, Online. Available HTTP: <http://archive.kremlin.ru/text/appears/2007/04/125339.shtml> (accessed 23 March 2011).

Qureshi, K. (2004) 'Respected and Respectable: The Centrality of "Performance" and "Audiences" in the (Re)production and Potential Revision of Gendered Ethnicities', *Journal of Audience and Reception Studies* 1, 2, Available HTTP: <http://www.participations.org/volume%201/issue%202/1_02_qureshi_article.htm> (accessed 15 June 2007).

—— (2006) Trans-boundary Spaces: Scottish Pakistanis and Trans-local/national Identities, *International Journal of Cultural Studies* 9, 2: 207-26.

Qureshi, K., & Moores, S. (1999) 'Identity Remix: Tradition and Translation in the Lives of Young Pakistani Scots', *European Journal of Cultural Studies* 2, 3: 311-30.

Rakachev, V. N., & Rakacheva, I. N. (2003) *Krasnodarskii krai: etnosotsialnye i etnodemograficheskie protsessy (vtoraia polovina 18-kh - nachalo 2000-kh gg)*, Krasnodar: Kubanskii gosudarstvennyi universitet.

Raskin, P. (2006) 'Rus' britoglavaia', *Russkii Newsweek*, 24 April - 14 May, 19-24.

Reynolds, T. (2007) 'Friendship Networks, Social Capital and Ethnic Identity: Researching the Perspectives of Caribbean Young People in Britain', *Journal of Youth Studies* 10,4: 383-98.

Richardson, J., & Lambert, J. (1985) *The Sociology of Race*, Ormskirk: Causway Press.

Richardson, T. (2006) 'Living Cosmopolitanism? Tolerance, Religion and Local Identity in Odessa', in C. Hann (ed.) *The Postsocialist Religious Question: Faith and Power in Central Asia and East-Central Europe*, Halle: Lit Verlag.

Robarts, A. (2008) 'The Russian State and Migration: A Theoretical and Practical Look at the Russian Federation's Migration Regime', in C. Buckley, B. A. Ruble & E. T. Hofman (eds) *Migration, Homeland and Belonging in Eurasia*, Washington, D.C.: Woodrow Wilson Center Press.

Roberts, K., & Pollock, G. (2009) 'New Class Divisions in the New Market Economies: Evidence from the Careers of Young Adults in post-Soviet Armenia, Azerbaijan and Georgia', *Journal of Youth Studies* 12, 5: 579-96.

Roberts, K., Pollock, G., Rustamova, S., Mammadova, Z., & Tholend, J. (2009) 'Young Adults' Family and Housing Life-Stage Transitions during post-Communist Transition in the South Caucasus', *Journal of Youth Studies* 12, 2: 151-66.

Roman, M. L. (2002) 'Making Caucasians Black: Moscow since the Fall of Communism and the Racialization of non-Russians', *Journal of Communist Studies and Transition Politics* 18, 2: 1-27.

Rubins, N. (1998) 'The Demise and Resurrection of the Propiska: Freedom of Movement in the Russian Federation', *Havard International Law Journal* 39: 545-66.

Russell, J. (2002) 'Mujahedeen, Mafia, Madmen: Russian Perceptions of Chechens during the Wars in Chechnya 1994-1996 and 1999-2001', *Journal of Communist Studies and Transition Politics* 18, 1: 73-96.

Russell, J. R. (2005) 'Early Armenian Civilization', in M. Kurkchiyan & E. Herzig (eds) *The Armenians: Past and Present in the Making of National Identity*, New York: Routledge Curzon.

Rutherford, J. (1990) 'A Place Called Home: Identity and the Cultural Politics of Difference', in J. Rutherford (ed.) *Identity: Community, Culture and Difference*, London: Lawrence & Wishart.

Ryzhova, S. (2005) 'Tolerance and Extremism: Russian Ethnicity in the Orthodox Discourse of the 1990s', in J. Johnson, M. Stepaniants & B. Forest (eds) *Religion and Identity in Modern Russia: The Revival of Orthodoxy and Islam*, Aldershot: Ashgate.

Sabirova, G. (2008) 'Both War and Peace in the "Country of the Soul": The Young People of Abkhazia on War', Tradition and Independence', *Anthropology of East Europe Review* 26, 1: 51-68.

Safran, W. (1991) 'Diasporas in Modern Societies: Myths of Homeland and Return', *Diaspora* 1, 1: 83-99.

Sahgal, G., & Yuval-Davis, N. (1992) *Refusing Holy Orders. Women and Fundamentalism in Britain*, London: Virago.

Said, E.W. (1983) *The World, the Text and the Critic*, Cambridge, Massachusetts: Havard University Press.

Salo, E. (2003) 'Negotiating Gender and Personhood in the New South Africa - Adolescent Women and Gangsters in Manenberg Township on the Cape Flats', *European Journal of Cultural Studies* 6, 3: 345-65.

Savva, M. V., & Savva, E. V. (2002) *Pressa, vlast' i etnicheskii konflikt (vzaimosviaz' na primere Krasnodarskogo kraia)*, Krasnodar: Kubanskii gosudarstvennyi universitet.

—— (2003) 'Vozdeistvie pechatnykh SMI na sostoianie mezhetnicheskikh otnoshenii (na primere Krasnodarskogo kraia)', *Bulletin: Anthropology, Minorities, Mutliculturalism* 4: 17-24.

Schorkowitz, D. (2008) *Postkommunismus und Verordneter Nationalismus'*, Frankfurt am Main: Internationaler Verlag der Wissenschaften.

Sewell, T. (1996) *Black Masculinities and Schooling: How Black Boys Survive Modern Schooling*, Stoke-on-Trent: Trentham Books Ltd.

Shahnazaryan, N. (2008) 'Hemshin, Homshetsi, or Hemshinli? Armenian Speaking Muslim People of the Black Sea Region', *PONARS Eurasia Policy Memo No. 53*. Online. Available HTTP: <http://ceres.georgetown.edu/esp/ponarsmemos/page/63415.html> (accessed 23 August 2009).

Shakhnazarian, N. (2005) 'Gendernye problemy armian Nagorno Karabakha (sovremmennyi period)', Stepeni kandidata istoricheskikh nauk, Kubanskii gosudarstvennyi universitet.

—— (2011) *V tesnyx obiatiiax traditsii: voina i patriarkhat*, Sankt Peterburg: Izdatel'stvo Aleteia.

Shami, S. (1998) 'Circassian Encounters: The Self as Other and the Production of the Homeland in the North Caucasus', *Development and Change* 29: 617-46.

Shanin, T. (1989) 'Ethnicity in the Soviet Union: Analytical Perceptions and Political Strategies', *Comparative Studies in Society and History* 31, 3: 409-24.

Shargunov, I. (2002) 'Khail' vmeste', *Novaia gazeta*, 23 September, 3.

Shildrick, T., Blackman, S., & MacDonald, R. (2009) 'Young People, Class and Place', *Journal of Youth Studies* 12, 5: 457-65.

Shlapentokh, V. (2010) '"Kondopoga" - Ethnic/Social Tension in Putin's Russia', *European Review* 18, 2: 177-06.

Shogenova, F. A. (2004) 'Nravstvennaia kul'tura v traditsionnom bytu adygov', Stepeni kandidata istoricheskikh nauk, Kabardino-Balkarskii institut gumanitarnykh issledovanii pravitel'stva KBR i KBNTS RAN.

Shukla, S. (1997) 'Building Diaspora and Nation: The 1991 "Cultural Festival of India"', *Cultural Studies* 2, 2: 296-15.

Sikevich, S. V. (1996) *Natsionalnoe samosoznanie russkikh*, Moskva: Otkrytoe obshchestvo.

—— (1999) *Neterpimost' v Rossii*, Moskva: Otkrytoe obshchestvo.

Silverstone, R. (2006) *Media and Morality: On the Rise of the Mediapolis*, London: Polity.

Simonian, M. S. (2003) 'Armianskaia diaspora severo-zapadnogo Kavkaza: formirovanie, kul'turno-konfessional'nyi oblik, vzaimootnosheniia s vlast'iu, obshchestvennymi i religioznymi ob'edineniiami', Stepeni kandidata istoricheskikh nauk, Krasnodarskii gosudarstvennyi universitet kul'tury i iskusstv.

Simonsen, S. G. (2005) 'Between Minority Rights and Civil Liberties: Russia's Discourse Over "Nationality" Registration and the Internal Passport', *Nationalities Papers* 33, 2: 211-29.

Sinyavsky, A. (1990) 'Russian Nationalism', *The Massachusetts Review*, 475-94.

Skeggs, B. (1997) *Formations of Class and Gender*, London: Sage Publications.

Skelton, T., & Valentine, G. (1998) *Cool Places: Geographies of Youth Cultures*, London: Routledge.

Skrbis, Z., Kendall, G., & Woodward, I. (2004) 'Locating Cosmopolitanism: Between Humanist Ideal and Grounded Social Category', *Theory, Culture & Society* 21, 6: 115-36.

Slezkine, Y. (1994) 'The USSR as a Communal Apartment, or How a Socialist State Promoted Ethnic Particularism', *Slavic Review* 53, 2: 414-52.

―――― (1996) 'The USSR as a Communal Appartment, or How a Socialist State Promoted Ethnic Particularism', in G. Eley & R. Suny (eds) *Becoming National: A Reader*, Oxford: Oxford University Press.

Smirnov, A. (2006) 'Trouble on the Horizon? Ethnic Unrest in Adygea', The Jamestown Foundation. Online. Available HTTP: <http://www.jamestown.org/docs/Smirnov-14Sep06.pdf> (accessed 29 January 2007).

Smith, A. D. (1981) *The Ethnic Revival*, Cambridge: Cambridge University Press.

―――― (1995) *Nations and Nationalism in a Global Era*, Cambridge: Polity Press.

Sokolov-Mitrich, D. (2002) 'Internatsional, kotoryi lopnul: "Izvestiia" rassleduiut kubanskii sindrom', *Izvestiia*, 23 April, 1.

―――― (2007) 'Legko li byt' russkim v Adygee i adygom – v Rossii', *Izvestiia*, 20 March, 5.

Sokolovski, S. V. (not dated) *Structures of Russian Political Discourse on Nationality Problems: Anthropological Perspectives*, OP No 272. Online. Available HTTP: <http://wwics.si.edu/topics/pubs/ACF28A.pdf> (accessed 31 January 2005).

Somers, M., & Gibson, G. D. (1994) 'Reclaiming the Epistemological "Other": Narrative and the Social Constitution of Identity', in C. Calhoun (ed.) *Social Theory and the Politics of Identity*, Oxford: Blackwell Publishers.

Soysal, Y. N. (2000) 'Citizenship and Identity: Living in Diaspora in post-war Europe?', *Ethnic and Racial Studies* 23, 1: 1-15.

Spülbeck, S. (1996) 'Anti-Semitism and Fear of the Public Sphere in a Post-Totalitarian Society: East Germany', in C. Hann & E. Dunn (eds) *Civil Society: Challenging Western Models*, London: Routledge.

Stammler-Grossman, A. (2009) 'Who is Indigenous? Construction of "Indigenousness" in Russian Legislation', *International Community Law Review* 11: 69-102.

Stepanenko, T. G. (1997) 'Etnicheskaia identichnost' v situatsii sotsial'noi nestabil'nosti', *Etnicheskaia psikhologiia i obshchestvo*.

Stiglitz, J. (1994) *Whither Socialism*, Cambridge: MIT Press.

Stivens, M. (2008) 'Gender, Rights and Cosmopolitanisms', in P. Werbner (ed.) *Anthropology and the New Cosmopolitanism*, Oxford: Berg.

Suny, R. (1993). *The Revenge of the Past: Nationalism, Revolution, and the Collapse of the Soviet Union*. Stanford: Stanford University Press.

—— (2005) 'Soviet Armenia, 1921-1991', in M. Kurkchiyan & E. Herzig (eds) *The Armenians: Past and Present in the Making of National Identity*, New York: Routledge Curzon.

Szporluk, R. (1990) 'The Imperial Legacy and the Soviet Nationalities Problem', in L. Hajda & M. Beissinger (eds) *The Nationalities Factor in Soviet Politics and Society*, Oxford: Westview Press.

Talai, V. A. (1986) 'Social Boundaries Within and Between Ethnic Groups: Armenians in London', *Man* 21, 2: 251-70.

Talai, V. A. (1989) *Armenians in London: The Management of Social Boundaries*, Manchester: Manchester University Press.

Taylor, Y., & Addison, M. (2009) '(Re)constituting the Past, (Re)branding the Present and (Re)imagining the Future: Women's Spatial Negotiation of Gender and Class', *Journal of Youth Studies* 12, 5: 563-78.

Tebbutt, M. (1995) *Women's Talk? A Social History of 'Gossip' in Working-class Neighbourhoods, 1880-1960*, Aldershot, Brookfield: Scholar Press.

Ter-Sarkisiants, A. (1995) 'Etnokul'turnyi oblik armian severnogo Kavkaz: istoriia i sovremmennost'', in A. Faktorovich, T. Gorbulich & I. Kuznetsov (eds) *Armiane severnogo Kavkaza*. Krasnodar: Kubanskii gosudarstvennyi universitet.

—— (1998) *Armiane: istoriia i etnokul'turnye traditsii*, Moskva: Vostochnaia literatura RAN.

Therborn, G. (2004) *Between Sex and Power: Family in the World, 1900-2000*, London: Routledge.

Tishkov, V. A. (1997) *Ethnicity, Nationalism and Conflict and after the Soviet Union*, London: Sage Publications.

Tolman, D. L., & Higgins, T. E. (1996) 'How Being a Good Girl Can Be Bad for Girls', in N. Bauer Maglin & D. Perry (eds) *Women, Sex & Power in the Nineties*, News Brunswick, N.J.: Rutgers University Press.

Totten, S. (2005) 'Does History Matter? Ask the Armenians', *Social Education* 69: 328-31.

Tsygankov, V. (2003) 'Gubernator Tkachev pokhvalil armian i grekov. No vyrazil nedovol-st'vo agrarnym lobbi v Gosdume', *Nezavisimaia gazeta*, 28 March, 4.

Vakulin, G. (2004) 'V edinoi sem'e kazach'ei', *Kuban' segodnia*, 14 September, 2.

Verdery, K. (1993) 'Ethnic Relations, Economies of Shortage, and the Transition in Eastern Europe', in C. Hann (ed.) *Socialism: Ideals, Ideologies, and Local Practice*, London: Routledge.

Verkhovsky, A. (2009) 'Future Prospects of Contemporary Russian Nationalism', in M. Laruelle (ed.) *Russian Nationalism and the National Reassertion of Russia*, Oxford: Routledge.

Vertovec, S. (1997) 'Three Meanings of "Diaspora", Exemplified Among South Asian Religions', *Diaspora* 6, 3: 277-300.

von Voss, H. (2007) *Potraits of Hope: Armenians in the Contemporary World*, New York: Berhahn Books.

Voronina, N. (2006) 'Outlook on Migration Policy Reform in Russia: Contemporary Challenges and Political Paradoxes', in R. R. Rios (ed.) *Planning and Managing Labour Migration*, Vienna: International Organization for Migration. Online. Available HTTP: <http://publications.iom.int/bookstore/index.php?main_page=product_info&cPath=4 1_7&products_id=122> (accessed 8 May 2009).

Voznaya, A. (2006) *The North Caucasus Knot: Adygeya's and Ingushetia's Struggle for Autonomy*. Online. Available HTTP: <http://www.balkananalysis.com/2006/08/08/the-north-caucasus-knot-adygeyas-and-ingushetias-struggle-for-autonomy> (accessed 30 November 2006).

Walby, S. (1990) *Theorizing Patriarchy*, Oxford: Blackwell.

Walker, C. (2007) 'Navigating a "Zombie" System: Youth Transitions from Vocational Education in Post-Soviet Russia', *International Journal of Lifelong Education* 26, 5: 513-31.

—— (2009) 'From "Inheritance" to Individualization: Disembedding Working-Class Youth Transitions in post-Soviet Russia', *Journal of Youth Studies* 12, 5: 531-45.

—— (2010). *Learning to Labour in Post-Soviet Russia: Vocational Youth in Transition*, London: Routledge.

Ware, R. B., & Kisriev, E. (2001) 'Ethnic Parity and Democratic Pluralism in Dagestan: A Consociational Approach', *Europe-Asia Studies* 53, 1: 105-31.

Weitz, E. D. (2002) 'Racial Politics without the Concept of Race: Reevaluating Soviet Ethnic and National Purges', *Slavic Review* 61, 1: 1-29.

Werbner, P. (1999) 'Global Pathways. Working Class Cosmopolitans and the Creation of Transnational Ethnic Worlds', *Social Anthropology* 7, 1: 17-35.

Werbner, P. (2008) *Anthropology and the New Cosmopolitanism*, Oxford: Berg.

West, C., & Zimmerman, D. H. (1987) 'Doing Gender', *Gender & Society* 1, 2: 125-51.

Wolczuk, K., & Yemelianova, G. (2008) 'When the West Meets the East: Exploring Ethnic Diversity in Eastern Europe', *Nationalities Papers* 36, 2: 177-95.

Wood, J. (1984) 'Groping towards Sexism: Boys' Sex Talk', in A. McRobbie & M. Nava (eds) *Gender and Generation*, Basingstoke: Macmillan Education.

Wulff, H. (1995) 'Inter-racial Friendship: Consuming Youth Styles, Ethnicity and Teenage Femininity in South London', in V. Amit-Talai & H. Wulff (eds) *Youth Cultures: A Cross-Cultural Perspective*, London: Routlegde.

Yemelianova, G. M. (2001) 'Sufism and Politics in the North Caucasus', *Nationalities Papers* 29, 4: 661-88.

—— (2005) 'Kinship, Ethnicity and Religion in post-Communist Societies', *Ethnicities* 5, 1: 51-82.

—— (2007) 'The Rise of Islam in Muslim Eurasia: Internal Determinants and Potential Consequences', *China and Eurasia Quarterly* 5, 2: 73-91.

Yoon, K. (2003) 'Retraditionalizing the Mobile', *European Journal of Cultural Studies* 6, 3: 327-43.

Young, R. (1996) *Colonial Desire: Hybridity in Theory, Culture and Race*, London: Routledge.

Zdravomyslova, E., & Temkina, A. (2001) Krizis maskulinnosti v pozdnesovetskom diskurse, in S. Ushakina (ed.) *Sbornik po issledovaniiam maskulinnosti v Rossii*, Moskva: Nauka.

—— (2007) *Seksual'nost' and gender v post(sovetskikh) obshchestvakh*. Sankt-Peterburg: Aleteia.

Zekiyan, B. L. (2005) 'Christianity to Modernity', in M. Kurkchiyan & E. Herzig (eds) *The Armenians: Past and Present in the Making of National Identity*, New York: Routledge Curzon.

Zhukava, N. (2006) 'The Russian Federation: New Immigration Pole in Eurasia', paper presented at the Florence School on Euro-Mediterranean Migration and Development, European University Institute. Online. Available HTTP: <http://www.eui.eu/RSCAS/Research/SchoolOnEuro-MedMigration/2006pdfs/Paper%20Zhukava.pdf> (accessed 17 July 2009).

Ziemer, U. (2011) 'Minority Youth, Everyday Racism and Public Spaces in Contemporary Russia', *European Journal of Cultural Studies* 14, 2: 229-42.

—— (2010) 'Tackling Tensions and Ambivalences: Armenian Girls' Diasporic Identities in Russia', *Nationalities Papers* 38, 5: 689-03.

—— (2010) 'Belonging and Longing: Armenian Youth and Diasporic Long-Distance Nationalism in Contemporary Russia', *Studies in Ethnicity and Nationalism* 10, 2: 290-03.

—— (2009) 'Narratives of Translocation, Dislocation and Location: Armenian Youth Cultural Identities in Southern Russia', *Europe-Asia Studies* 61, 3: 409-33.

SOVIET AND POST-SOVIET POLITICS AND SOCIETY

Edited by Dr. Andreas Umland

ISSN 1614-3515

1   *Андреас Умланд (ред.)*
    Воплощение Европейской
    конвенции по правам человека в
    России
    Философские, юридические и
    эмпирические исследования
    ISBN 3-89821-387-0

2   *Christian Wipperfürth*
    Russland – ein vertrauenswürdiger
    Partner?
    Grundlagen, Hintergründe und Praxis
    gegenwärtiger russischer Außenpolitik
    Mit einem Vorwort von Heinz Timmermann
    ISBN 3-89821-401-X

3   *Manja Hussner*
    Die Übernahme internationalen Rechts
    in die russische und deutsche
    Rechtsordnung
    Eine vergleichende Analyse zur
    Völkerrechtsfreundlichkeit der Verfassungen
    der Russländischen Föderation und der
    Bundesrepublik Deutschland
    Mit einem Vorwort von Rainer Arnold
    ISBN 3-89821-438-9

4   *Matthew Tejada*
    Bulgaria's Democratic Consolidation
    and the Kozloduy Nuclear Power Plant
    (KNPP)
    The Unattainability of Closure
    With a foreword by Richard J. Crampton
    ISBN 3-89821-439-7

5   *Марк Григорьевич Меерович*
    Квадратные метры, определяющие
    сознание
    Государственная жилищная политика в
    СССР. 1921 – 1941 гг
    ISBN 3-89821-474-5

6   *Andrei P. Tsygankov, Pavel
    A. Tsygankov (Eds.)*
    New Directions in Russian
    International Studies
    ISBN 3-89821-422-2

7   *Марк Григорьевич Меерович*
    Как власть народ к труду приучала
    Жилище в СССР – средство управления
    людьми. 1917 – 1941 гг.
    С предисловием Елены Осокиной
    ISBN 3-89821-495-8

8   *David J. Galbreath*
    Nation-Building and Minority Politics
    in Post-Socialist States
    Interests, Influence and Identities in Estonia
    and Latvia
    With a foreword by David J. Smith
    ISBN 3-89821-467-2

9   *Алексей Юрьевич Безугольный*
    Народы Кавказа в Вооруженных
    силах СССР в годы Великой
    Отечественной войны 1941-1945 гг.
    С предисловием Николая Бугая
    ISBN 3-89821-475-3

10 *Вячеслав Лихачев и Владимир
    Прибыловский (ред.)*
    Русское Национальное Единство,
    1990-2000. В 2-х томах
    ISBN 3-89821-523-7

11 *Николай Бугай (ред.)*
    Народы стран Балтии в условиях
    сталинизма (1940-е – 1950-е годы)
    Документированная история
    ISBN 3-89821-525-3

12 *Ingmar Bredies (Hrsg.)*
    Zur Anatomie der Orange Revolution
    in der Ukraine
    Wechsel des Elitenregimes oder Triumph des
    Parlamentarismus?
    ISBN 3-89821-524-5

13 *Anastasia V. Mitrofanova*
    The Politicization of Russian
    Orthodoxy
    Actors and Ideas
    With a foreword by William C. Gay
    ISBN 3-89821-481-8

14 Nathan D. Larson
    Alexander Solzhenitsyn and the
    Russo-Jewish Question
    ISBN 3-89821-483-4

15 Guido Houben
    Kulturpolitik und Ethnizität
    Staatliche Kunstförderung im Russland der
    neunziger Jahre
    Mit einem Vorwort von Gert Weisskirchen
    ISBN 3-89821-542-3

16 Leonid Luks
    Der russische „Sonderweg"?
    Aufsätze zur neuesten Geschichte Russlands
    im europäischen Kontext
    ISBN 3-89821-496-6

17 Евгений Мороз
    История «Мёртвой воды» – от
    страшной сказки к большой
    политике
    Политическое неоязычество в
    постсоветской России
    ISBN 3-89821-551-2

18 Александр Верховский и Галина
    Кожевникова (ред.)
    Этническая и религиозная
    интолерантность в российских СМИ
    Результаты мониторинга 2001-2004 гг.
    ISBN 3-89821-569-5

19 Christian Ganzer
    Sowjetisches Erbe und ukrainische
    Nation
    Das Museum der Geschichte des Zaporoger
    Kosakentums auf der Insel Chortycja
    Mit einem Vorwort von Frank Golczewski
    ISBN 3-89821-504-0

20 Эльза-Баир Гучинова
    Помнить нельзя забыть
    Антропология депортационной травмы
    калмыков
    С предисловием Кэролайн Хамфри
    ISBN 3-89821-506-7

21 Юлия Лидерман
    Мотивы «проверки» и «испытания»
    в постсоветской культуре
    Советское прошлое в российском
    кинематографе 1990-х годов
    С предисловием Евгения Марголита
    ISBN 3-89821-511-3

22 Tanya Lokshina, Ray Thomas, Mary
    Mayer (Eds.)
    The Imposition of a Fake Political
    Settlement in the Northern Caucasus
    The 2003 Chechen Presidential Election
    ISBN 3-89821-436-2

23 Timothy McCajor Hall, Rosie Read
    (Eds.)
    Changes in the Heart of Europe
    Recent Ethnographies of Czechs, Slovaks,
    Roma, and Sorbs
    With an afterword by Zdeněk Salzmann
    ISBN 3-89821-606-3

24 Christian Autengruber
    Die politischen Parteien in Bulgarien
    und Rumänien
    Eine vergleichende Analyse seit Beginn der
    90er Jahre
    Mit einem Vorwort von Dorothée de Nève
    ISBN 3-89821-476-1

25 Annette Freyberg-Inan with Radu
    Cristescu
    The Ghosts in Our Classrooms, or:
    John Dewey Meets Ceauşescu
    The Promise and the Failures of Civic
    Education in Romania
    ISBN 3-89821-416-8

26 John B. Dunlop
    The 2002 Dubrovka and 2004 Beslan
    Hostage Crises
    A Critique of Russian Counter-Terrorism
    With a foreword by Donald N. Jensen
    ISBN 3-89821-608-X

27 Peter Koller
    Das touristische Potenzial von
    Kam''janec'-Podil's'kyj
    Eine fremdenverkehrsgeographische
    Untersuchung der Zukunftsperspektiven und
    Maßnahmenplanung zur
    Destinationsentwicklung des „ukrainischen
    Rothenburg"
    Mit einem Vorwort von Kristiane Klemm
    ISBN 3-89821-640-3

28 Françoise Daucé, Elisabeth Sieca-
    Kozlowski (Eds.)
    Dedovshchina in the Post-Soviet
    Military
    Hazing of Russian Army Conscripts in a
    Comparative Perspective
    With a foreword by Dale Herspring
    ISBN 3-89821-616-0

29 *Florian Strasser*
    Zivilgesellschaftliche Einflüsse auf die
    Orange Revolution
    Die gewaltlose Massenbewegung und die
    ukrainische Wahlkrise 2004
    Mit einem Vorwort von Egbert Jahn
    ISBN 3-89821-648-9

30 *Rebecca S. Katz*
    The Georgian Regime Crisis of 2003-
    2004
    A Case Study in Post-Soviet Media
    Representation of Politics, Crime and
    Corruption
    ISBN 3-89821-413-3

31 *Vladimir Kantor*
    Willkür oder Freiheit
    Beiträge zur russischen Geschichtsphilosophie
    Ediert von Dagmar Herrmann sowie mit
    einem Vorwort versehen von Leonid Luks
    ISBN 3-89821-589-X

32 *Laura A. Victoir*
    The Russian Land Estate Today
    A Case Study of Cultural Politics in Post-
    Soviet Russia
    With a foreword by Priscilla Roosevelt
    ISBN 3-89821-426-5

33 *Ivan Katchanovski*
    Cleft Countries
    Regional Political Divisions and Cultures in
    Post-Soviet Ukraine and Moldova
    With a foreword by Francis Fukuyama
    ISBN 3-89821-558-X

34 *Florian Mühlfried*
    Postsowjetische Feiern
    Das Georgische Bankett im Wandel
    Mit einem Vorwort von Kevin Tuite
    ISBN 3-89821-601-2

35 *Roger Griffin, Werner Loh, Andreas
    Umland (Eds.)*
    Fascism Past and Present, West and
    East
    An International Debate on Concepts and
    Cases in the Comparative Study of the
    Extreme Right
    With an afterword by Walter Laqueur
    ISBN 3-89821-674-8

36 *Sebastian Schlegel*
    Der „Weiße Archipel"
    Sowjetische Atomstädte 1945-1991
    Mit einem Geleitwort von Thomas Bohn
    ISBN 3-89821-679-9

37 *Vyacheslav Likhachev*
    Political Anti-Semitism in Post-Soviet
    Russia
    Actors and Ideas in 1991-2003
    Edited and translated from Russian by Eugene
    Veklerov
    ISBN 3-89821-529-6

38 *Josette Baer (Ed.)*
    Preparing Liberty in Central Europe
    Political Texts from the Spring of Nations
    1848 to the Spring of Prague 1968
    With a foreword by Zdeněk V. David
    ISBN 3-89821-546-6

39 *Михаил Лукьянов*
    Российский консерватизм и
    реформа, 1907-1914
    С предисловием Марка Д. Стейнберга
    ISBN 3-89821-503-2

40 *Nicola Melloni*
    Market Without Economy
    The 1998 Russian Financial Crisis
    With a foreword by Eiji Furukawa
    ISBN 3-89821-407-9

41 *Dmitrij Chmelnizki*
    Die Architektur Stalins
    Bd. 1: Studien zu Ideologie und Stil
    Bd. 2: Bilddokumentation
    Mit einem Vorwort von Bruno Flierl
    ISBN 3-89821-515-6

42 *Katja Yafimava*
    Post-Soviet Russian-Belarussian
    Relationships
    The Role of Gas Transit Pipelines
    With a foreword by Jonathan P. Stern
    ISBN 3-89821-655-1

43 *Boris Chavkin*
    Verflechtungen der deutschen und
    russischen Zeitgeschichte
    Aufsätze und Archivfunde zu den
    Beziehungen Deutschlands und der
    Sowjetunion von 1917 bis 1991
    Ediert von Markus Edlinger sowie mit einem
    Vorwort versehen von Leonid Luks
    ISBN 3-89821-756-6

44 *Anastasija Grynenko in Zusammenarbeit mit Claudia Dathe*
Die Terminologie des Gerichtswesens der Ukraine und Deutschlands im Vergleich
Eine übersetzungswissenschaftliche Analyse juristischer Fachbegriffe im Deutschen, Ukrainischen und Russischen
Mit einem Vorwort von Ulrich Hartmann
ISBN 3-89821-691-8

45 *Anton Burkov*
The Impact of the European Convention on Human Rights on Russian Law
Legislation and Application in 1996-2006
With a foreword by Françoise Hampson
ISBN 978-3-89821-639-5

46 *Stina Torjesen, Indra Overland (Eds.)*
International Election Observers in Post-Soviet Azerbaijan
Geopolitical Pawns or Agents of Change?
ISBN 978-3-89821-743-9

47 *Taras Kuzio*
Ukraine – Crimea – Russia
Triangle of Conflict
ISBN 978-3-89821-761-3

48 *Claudia Šabić*
"Ich erinnere mich nicht, aber L'viv!"
Zur Funktion kultureller Faktoren für die Institutionalisierung und Entwicklung einer ukrainischen Region
Mit einem Vorwort von Melanie Tatur
ISBN 978-3-89821-752-1

49 *Marlies Bilz*
Tatarstan in der Transformation
Nationaler Diskurs und Politische Praxis 1988-1994
Mit einem Vorwort von Frank Golczewski
ISBN 978-3-89821-722-4

50 *Марлен Ларюэль (ред.)*
Современные интерпретации русского национализма
ISBN 978-3-89821-795-8

51 *Sonja Schüler*
Die ethnische Dimension der Armut
Roma im postsozialistischen Rumänien
Mit einem Vorwort von Anton Sterbling
ISBN 978-3-89821-776-7

52 *Галина Кожевникова*
Радикальный национализм в России и противодействие ему
Сборник докладов Центра «Сова» за 2004-2007 гг.
С предисловием Александра Верховского
ISBN 978-3-89821-721-7

53 *Галина Кожевникова и Владимир Прибыловский*
Российская власть в биографиях I
Высшие должностные лица РФ в 2004 г.
ISBN 978-3-89821-796-5

54 *Галина Кожевникова и Владимир Прибыловский*
Российская власть в биографиях II
Члены Правительства РФ в 2004 г.
ISBN 978-3-89821-797-2

55 *Галина Кожевникова и Владимир Прибыловский*
Российская власть в биографиях III
Руководители федеральных служб и агентств РФ в 2004 г.
ISBN 978-3-89821-798-9

56 *Ileana Petroniu*
Privatisierung in Transformationsökonomien
Determinanten der Restrukturierungs-Bereitschaft am Beispiel Polens, Rumäniens und der Ukraine
Mit einem Vorwort von Rainer W. Schäfer
ISBN 978-3-89821-790-3

57 *Christian Wipperfürth*
Russland und seine GUS-Nachbarn
Hintergründe, aktuelle Entwicklungen und Konflikte in einer ressourcenreichen Region
ISBN 978-3-89821-801-6

58 *Togzhan Kassenova*
From Antagonism to Partnership
The Uneasy Path of the U.S.-Russian Cooperative Threat Reduction
With a foreword by Christoph Bluth
ISBN 978-3-89821-707-1

59 *Alexander Höllwerth*
Das sakrale eurasische Imperium des Aleksandr Dugin
Eine Diskursanalyse zum postsowjetischen russischen Rechtsextremismus
Mit einem Vorwort von Dirk Uffelmann
ISBN 978-3-89821-813-9

60 Олег Рябов
    «Россия-Матушка»
    Национализм, гендер и война в России XX века
    С предисловием Елены Гощило
    ISBN 978-3-89821-487-2

61 Ivan Maistrenko
    Borot'bism
    A Chapter in the History of the Ukrainian Revolution
    With a new introduction by Chris Ford
    Translated by George S. N. Luckyj with the assistance of Ivan L. Rudnytsky
    ISBN 978-3-89821-697-5

62 Maryna Romanets
    Anamorphosic Texts and Reconfigured Visions
    Improvised Traditions in Contemporary Ukrainian and Irish Literature
    ISBN 978-3-89821-576-3

63 Paul D'Anieri and Taras Kuzio (Eds.)
    Aspects of the Orange Revolution I
    Democratization and Elections in Post-Communist Ukraine
    ISBN 978-3-89821-698-2

64 Bohdan Harasymiw in collaboration with Oleh S. Ilnytzkyj (Eds.)
    Aspects of the Orange Revolution II
    Information and Manipulation Strategies in the 2004 Ukrainian Presidential Elections
    ISBN 978-3-89821-699-9

65 Ingmar Bredies, Andreas Umland and Valentin Yakushik (Eds.)
    Aspects of the Orange Revolution III
    The Context and Dynamics of the 2004 Ukrainian Presidential Elections
    ISBN 978-3-89821-803-0

66 Ingmar Bredies, Andreas Umland and Valentin Yakushik (Eds.)
    Aspects of the Orange Revolution IV
    Foreign Assistance and Civic Action in the 2004 Ukrainian Presidential Elections
    ISBN 978-3-89821-808-5

67 Ingmar Bredies, Andreas Umland and Valentin Yakushik (Eds.)
    Aspects of the Orange Revolution V
    Institutional Observation Reports on the 2004 Ukrainian Presidential Elections
    ISBN 978-3-89821-809-2

68 Taras Kuzio (Ed.)
    Aspects of the Orange Revolution VI
    Post-Communist Democratic Revolutions in Comparative Perspective
    ISBN 978-3-89821-820-7

69 Tim Bohse
    Autoritarismus statt Selbstverwaltung
    Die Transformation der kommunalen Politik in der Stadt Kaliningrad 1990-2005
    Mit einem Geleitwort von Stefan Troebst
    ISBN 978-3-89821-782-8

70 David Rupp
    Die Rußländische Föderation und die russischsprachige Minderheit in Lettland
    Eine Fallstudie zur Anwaltspolitik Moskaus gegenüber den russophonen Minderheiten im „Nahen Ausland" von 1991 bis 2002
    Mit einem Vorwort von Helmut Wagner
    ISBN 978-3-89821-778-1

71 Taras Kuzio
    Theoretical and Comparative Perspectives on Nationalism
    New Directions in Cross-Cultural and Post-Communist Studies
    With a foreword by Paul Robert Magocsi
    ISBN 978-3-89821-815-3

72 Christine Teichmann
    Die Hochschultransformation im heutigen Osteuropa
    Kontinuität und Wandel bei der Entwicklung des postkommunistischen Universitätswesens
    Mit einem Vorwort von Oskar Anweiler
    ISBN 978-3-89821-842-9

73 Julia Kusznir
    Der politische Einfluss von Wirtschaftseliten in russischen Regionen
    Eine Analyse am Beispiel der Erdöl- und Erdgasindustrie, 1992-2005
    Mit einem Vorwort von Wolfgang Eichwede
    ISBN 978-3-89821-821-4

74 Alena Vysotskaya
    Russland, Belarus und die EU-Osterweiterung
    Zur Minderheitenfrage und zum Problem der Freizügigkeit des Personenverkehrs
    Mit einem Vorwort von Katlijn Malfliet
    ISBN 978-3-89821-822-1

75   Heiko Pleines (Hrsg.)
      Corporate Governance in post-
      sozialistischen Volkswirtschaften
      ISBN 978-3-89821-766-8

76   Stefan Ihrig
      Wer sind die Moldawier?
      Rumänismus versus Moldowanismus in
      Historiographie und Schulbüchern der
      Republik Moldova, 1991-2006
      Mit einem Vorwort von Holm Sundhaussen
      ISBN 978-3-89821-466-7

77   Galina Kozhevnikova in collaboration
      with Alexander Verkhovsky and
      Eugene Veklerov
      Ultra-Nationalism and Hate Crimes in
      Contemporary Russia
      The 2004-2006 Annual Reports of Moscow's
      SOVA Center
      With a foreword by Stephen D. Shenfield
      ISBN 978-3-89821-868-9

78   Florian Küchler
      The Role of the European Union in
      Moldova's Transnistria Conflict
      With a foreword by Christopher Hill
      ISBN 978-3-89821-850-4

79   Bernd Rechel
      The Long Way Back to Europe
      Minority Protection in Bulgaria
      With a foreword by Richard Crampton
      ISBN 978-3-89821-863-4

80   Peter W. Rodgers
      Nation, Region and History in Post-
      Communist Transitions
      Identity Politics in Ukraine, 1991-2006
      With a foreword by Vera Tolz
      ISBN 978-3-89821-903-7

81   Stephanie Solywoda
      The Life and Work of
      Semen L. Frank
      A Study of Russian Religious Philosophy
      With a foreword by Philip Walters
      ISBN 978-3-89821-457-5

82   Vera Sokolova
      Cultural Politics of Ethnicity
      Discourses on Roma in Communist
      Czechoslovakia
      ISBN 978-3-89821-864-1

83   Natalya Shevchik Ketenci
      Kazakhstani Enterprises in Transition
      The Role of Historical Regional Development
      in Kazakhstan's Post-Soviet Economic
      Transformation
      ISBN 978-3-89821-831-3

84   Martin Malek, Anna Schor-
      Tschudnowskaja (Hrsg.)
      Europa im Tschetschenienkrieg
      Zwischen politischer Ohnmacht und
      Gleichgültigkeit
      Mit einem Vorwort von Lipchan Basajewa
      ISBN 978-3-89821-676-0

85   Stefan Meister
      Das postsowjetische Universitätswesen
      zwischen nationalem und
      internationalem Wandel
      Die Entwicklung der regionalen Hochschule
      in Russland als Gradmesser der
      Systemtransformation
      Mit einem Vorwort von Joan DeBardeleben
      ISBN 978-3-89821-891-7

86   Konstantin Sheiko in collaboration
      with Stephen Brown
      Nationalist Imaginings of the
      Russian Past
      Anatolii Fomenko and the Rise of Alternative
      History in Post-Communist Russia
      With a foreword by Donald Ostrowski
      ISBN 978-3-89821-915-0

87   Sabine Jenni
      Wie stark ist das „Einige Russland"?
      Zur Parteibindung der Eliten und zum
      Wahlerfolg der Machtpartei
      im Dezember 2007
      Mit einem Vorwort von Klaus Armingeon
      ISBN 978-3-89821-961-7

88   Thomas Borén
      Meeting-Places of Transformation
      Urban Identity, Spatial Representations and
      Local Politics in Post-Soviet St Petersburg
      ISBN 978-3-89821-739-2

89   Aygul Ashirova
      Stalinismus und Stalin-Kult in
      Zentralasien
      Turkmenistan 1924-1953
      Mit einem Vorwort von Leonid Luks
      ISBN 978-3-89821-987-7

90 Leonid Luks
    Freiheit oder imperiale Größe?
    Essays zu einem russischen Dilemma
    ISBN 978-3-8382-0011-8

91 Christopher Gilley
    The 'Change of Signposts' in the
    Ukrainian Emigration
    A Contribution to the History of
    Sovietophilism in the 1920s
    With a foreword by Frank Golczewski
    ISBN 978-3-89821-965-5

92 Philipp Casula, Jeronim Perovic
    (Eds.)
    Identities and Politics
    During the Putin Presidency
    The Discursive Foundations of Russia's
    Stability
    With a foreword by Heiko Haumann
    ISBN 978-3-8382-0015-6

93 Marcel Viëtor
    Europa und die Frage
    nach seinen Grenzen im Osten
    Zur Konstruktion ‚europäischer Identität' in
    Geschichte und Gegenwart
    Mit einem Vorwort von Albrecht Lehmann
    ISBN 978-3-8382-0045-3

94 Ben Hellman, Andrei Rogachevskii
    Filming the Unfilmable
    Casper Wrede's 'One Day in the Life
    of Ivan Denisovich'
    ISBN 978-3-8382-0044-6

95 Eva Fuchslocher
    Vaterland, Sprache, Glaube
    Orthodoxie und Nationenbildung
    am Beispiel Georgiens
    Mit einem Vorwort von Christina von Braun
    ISBN 978-3-89821-884-9

96 Vladimir Kantor
    Das Westlertum und der Weg
    Russlands
    Zur Entwicklung der russischen Literatur und
    Philosophie
    Ediert von Dagmar Herrmann
    Mit einem Beitrag von Nikolaus Lobkowicz
    ISBN 978-3-8382-0102-3

97 Kamran Musayev
    Die postsowjetische Transformation
    im Baltikum und Südkaukasus
    Eine vergleichende Untersuchung der
    politischen Entwicklung Lettlands und
    Aserbaidschans 1985-2009
    Mit einem Vorwort von Leonid Luks
    Ediert von Sandro Henschel
    ISBN 978-3-8382-0103-0

98 Tatiana Zhurzhenko
    Borderlands into Bordered Lands
    Geopolitics of Identity in Post-Soviet Ukraine
    With a foreword by Dieter Segert
    ISBN 978-3-8382-0042-2

99 Кирилл Галушко, Лидия Смола
    (ред.)
    Пределы падения – варианты
    украинского будущего
    Аналитико-прогностические исследования
    ISBN 978-3-8382-0148-1

100 Michael Minkenberg (ed.)
    Historical Legacies and the Radical
    Right in Post-Cold War Central and
    Eastern Europe
    With an afterword by Sabrina P. Ramet
    ISBN 978-3-8382-0124-5

101 David-Emil Wickström
    "Okna otkroi!" – "Open the
    Windows!"
    Transcultural Flows and Identity Politics in
    the St. Petersburg Popular Music Scene
    With a foreword by Yngvar B. Steinholt
    ISBN 978-3-8382-0100-9

102 Eva Zabka
    Eine neue „Zeit der Wirren"?
    Der spät- und postsowjetische Systemwandel
    1985-2000 im Spiegel russischer
    gesellschaftspolitischer Diskurse
    Mit einem Vorwort von Margareta Mommsen
    ISBN 978-3-8382-0161-0

103 Ulrike Ziemer
    Ethnic Belonging, Gender, and
    Cultural Practices
    Youth Identitites in Contemporary Russia
    With a foreword by Anoop Nayak
    ISBN 978-3-8382-0152-8

Series Subscription

Please enter my subscription to the series *Soviet and Post-Soviet Politics and Society*, ISSN 1614-3515, as follows:

❏ complete series   OR   ❏ English-language titles
                                                         ❏ German-language titles
                                                         ❏ Russian-language titles

starting with
❏ volume # 1
❏ volume # ___
     ❏ please also include the following volumes: #___, ___, ___, ___, ___, ___, ___
❏ the next volume being published
     ❏ please also include the following volumes: #___, ___, ___, ___, ___, ___, ___

❏ 1 copy per volume   OR   ❏ ___ copies per volume

Subscription within Germany:

You will receive every volume at 1st publication at the regular bookseller's price – incl. s & h and VAT.

Payment:
❏ Please bill me for every volume.
❏ Lastschriftverfahren: Ich/wir ermächtige(n) Sie hiermit widerruflich, den Rechnungsbetrag je Band von meinem/unserem folgendem Konto einzuziehen.

Kontoinhaber: _____ Kreditinstitut: _____
Kontonummer. _____ Bankleitzahl: _____

International Subscription:

Payment (incl. s & h and VAT) in advance for
❏ 10 volumes/copies (€ 319.80)   ❏ 20 volumes/copies (€ 599.80)
❏ 40 volumes/copies (€ 1,099.80)
Please send my books to:

NAME_____ DEPARTMENT_____
ADDRESS_____
POST/ZIP CODE_____ COUNTRY_____
TELEPHONE_____ EMAIL_____

date/signature_____

A hint for librarians in the former Soviet Union: Your academic library might be eligible to receive free-of-cost scholarly literature from Germany via the German Research Foundation. For Russian-language information on this program, see
http://www.dfg.de/forschungsfoerderung/formulare/download/12_54.pdf.

Please fax to: **0511 / 262 2201 (+49 511 262 2201)**
or mail to: *ibidem*-Verlag, Julius-Leber-Weg 11, D-30457 Hannover, Germany
or send an e-mail: ibidem@ibidem-verlag.de

ibidem-Verlag

Melchiorstr. 15

D-70439 Stuttgart

info@ibidem-verlag.de

www.ibidem-verlag.de
www.ibidem.eu
www.edition-noema.de
www.autorenbetreuung.de